# MULTIPLY AND REPLENISH

## MORMON ESSAYS ON SEX AND FAMILY

# MULTIPLY AND REPLENISH

## MORMON ESSAYS ON SEX AND FAMILY

Edited by
*Brent Corcoran*

Signature Books Salt Lake City 1994

*For*
*Miles Alan Merrell*

COVER ILLUSTRATION: *THE FOURTH ARTICLE OF FAITH* BY MICHAEL CLANE GRAVES, 1976, ACRYLIC ON CANVAS

COVER DESIGN: JULIE EASTON

Printed on acid free paper.


Composed and printed in the United States of America.

98 97 96 95 94 6 5 4 3 2 1

*Library of Congress Cataloging-in-Publication Data*
Multiply and replenish : Mormon essays on sex and family / edited by Brent D. Corcoran.
p. cm.
Includes bibliographical references.
ISBN 1-56085-050-7
1. Sex—Religious aspects—Mormon Church. 2. Sex—Religious aspects—Church of Jesus Christ of Latter-day Saints 3. Marriage—Religious aspects—Mormon church 4. Marriage—Religious aspects—Church of Jesus Christ of Latter-day Saints 5. Mormon church—Doctrines. 6. Church of Jesus Christ of Latter-day Saints—Doctrines. 7. Sexual ethics. 8. Family—Religious life.
I. Corcoran, Brent D.
BX8643.S49M85 1994
261.8'343—dc20 94-14855
CIP

# CONTENTS


Editors' Introduction vii

1. Between Heaven and Earth: Mormon Theology of the Family in Comparative Perspective
*Lawrence Foster* 1

2. Changing Perspectives on Sexuality and Marriage
*Klaus J. Hansen* 19

3. "They Shall Be One Flesh": Sexuality and Contemporary Mormonism
*Romel W. Mackelprang* 47

4. The Persistence of Chastity: Built-in Resistance in Mormon Culture to Secular Trends
*Harold T. Christensen* 67

5. Exhortations for Chastity: A Content Analysis of Church Literature
*Marvin Rytting* 85

6. Fidelity, Polygamy, and Celestial Marriage
*Eugene England* 103

7. "The Abominable and Detestable Crime Against Nature": A Brief History of Homosexuality and Mormonism, 1840-1980
*Rocky O'Donovan* 123

8. Gender and Spirit
*Jeffrey E. Keller* 171

9. Ethical Issues in Reproductive Medicine: A Mormon Perspective
*Lester E. Bush* 183

10. Single Cursedness: An Overview of LDS Authorities' Statements about Unmarried People
*Marybeth Raynes* and *Erin Parsons* 217

11. A Lone Man in the Garden
*Delmont R. Oswald* 231

12. In Defense of Mormon Erotica
*Levi S. Peterson* 239

13. The Demography of Utah Mormons
*Tim Heaton* 249

Epilogue: Mormon Ideas of Home
*Stephen L Richards* 263

Contributors 271

# EDITOR'S INTRODUCTION

For members of the Church of Jesus Christ of Latter-day Saints, God's injunction to Adam and Eve to multiply and replenish the earth (Gen. 1:28) provides the answer to life's existential question. God created human beings to reproduce, and in so doing to glorify himself. This is our purpose.

The following collection seeks to document the Latter-day Saint experience with family, reproduction, and sexuality. In reality, a single compilation of such essays can only begin to explore the universal implications of family life in Mormonism, for the Mormon family is of eternal proportion. The cosmos is structured along family lines, with a heavenly father and mother, God and God's wife, and their human children—literally their spirit offspring—who are all brothers and sisters. Mormons must be married to attain the highest degree of exaltation in the next life. Some feel that their future reward is related to the number of children they produce in this life.

In the first two essays, Lawrence Foster and Klaus J. Hansen explore the historical importance of the Mormon family. They argue that Mormonism began as a reaction to the disintegration of social institutions, especially the family, on the nineteenth-century American frontier. Church founder Joseph Smith sought to establish a bulwark against epidemic "latter-day" wickedness and to provide the faithful few with a refuge to prepare for Jesus Christ's second advent and millennial reign. Plural marriage functioned to establish boundaries between the faithful and faithless, and to ensure that the faithful would persist in being so.

Hansen documents changes in Mormon theology from the nineteenth- to the twentieth-century LDS church. He believes that Mormons have always been sexually conservative. But while in the nineteenth century they were not significantly preoccupied with sexual vice, by the twentieth century they had internalized general American sexual mores and become more concerned with this particular area of human behavior. This evangelizing trend, according to Hansen, occurred because with the 1890 Manifesto ostensibly banning plural marriage, polygamy was no longer available to supply its peculiarizing function. In essence, twentieth-century Mormons "began to adapt to the forces of modernization by internalizing their sexual mores." Mormons were compelled to "out-Victorian" the Victorians. Foster warns in turn that the twentieth-century "sentimentalized ideal of family life which Latter-day Saints have chosen to emphasize in their proselytizing efforts" may descend into idolatry when "overriding importance is given to any human institution" at the expense of others.

The disruption between nineteenth- and twentieth-century Mormon family values holds a center place in the scholarly discussion of Mormon family life. As other essayists point out, this disruption is the result of more than just the abandonment of polygamy.

Lester Bush, for example, explores the Mormon encounter with medical science, especially reproductive medicine and birth control. Early Mormons were antagonistic toward Western medical doctors. But the twentieth-century church came to embrace medical science. The church historically taught that the body must be treated as sacred, as a temple. The essential cause of illness was the fall of Adam, a supernatural event which led to a break with the divine presence. Some early LDS leaders taught that the sins of the parents were passed on to their offspring in the form of a weakened physical constitution.

These sacral medical beliefs can be contrasted with the dominant attitude toward health and the body in modern industrial societies where illness is attributed to a physical defect or foreign intrusion into the organism. Physicians exclude from scrutiny events that take place away from the person.

When Mormons began to embrace Western medicine, they faced two competing systems for understanding the human body. Questions arose: Are sexual desires part of the fate of carnal man, something to be controlled, or related to hormones, or the psychology of instinct? Are bodies of divine creation or animal? Medical science desacralized sex, and Mormons have been confronted by issues of reproductive control technologies, sexual orientation, and the flexibility of family structure and gender roles.

Mormonism's uneasy accommodation to profane conceptualizations of reproductive and family issues is evidenced by the persistence of conservative sexual behavior and values. Studies by Marvin Rytting, Tim B. Heaton, and Harold T. Christensen have documented this persistence into the last decade. Christensen notes the reaction by Mormon officials to the perception that Latter-day Saints have been influenced by secular philosophies. Rytting demonstrates a corresponding intensification of sermonizing by church leaders on sexual and family issues. Heaton's work shows constancy among Mormons to maintain large families.

In current affairs, Mormons have sometimes joined political hands with Christian fundamentalists in pursuing a conservative family agenda against lesbians and gay men, including same-sex marriages and spousal benefits. They have also ventured into political campaigns against abortion rights and dissemination of sexual and birth control education, as well as public sex education generally.

The church's modern mission is defined as a struggle against the secularization of family life and sexual experience. In 1993 LDS leader Boyd K. Packer specifically singled out homosexuals and feminists as part of a triumvirate of arch-enemies to the church's mission (the third was intellectuals). The church has asked professionals to prepare scholarly responses to secularizing trends, to become a kind of Mormon "Jesuitical" order to defend itself against the forces of secular humanism. Romel W. Mackelprang and Rocky O'Donovan in part chronicle the endeavors of some of these Mormon Jesuits.

Unofficially, other scholars are also endeavoring to explore the modern contradictions and struggles within Mormon family life and sexual experience. As physicians, Lester Bush and Jeffrey Keller examine the implications of medicine on theology. Marybeth Raynes, Erin Parsons, and Delmont Oswald address the unmarried Mormon's place in the church's social life and theology. Rocky O'Donovan's account of gay and lesbian experience—perhaps the most radical perspective in this book—is a critique of Mormon homosociality and homophobia. Levi Peterson, a member of the growing LDS *literati*, tackles the perennial problem of art versus pornography.

Eugene England's thought-provoking essay reflects the discomfort many feel for the historical contradictions of Mormon family theology. England admits the problems of a nineteenth-century polygamous heritage, seeking to create a modern theological context for monogamous heterosexual marriage with a reproductive emphasis.

One area that is underrepresented in this compilation is Mormon women's perspectives on family life and sexuality. To date Mormon feminist scholarship has tended to focus almost exclusively on the historical relationship of women to the church's patriarchal hierarchy and male priesthood structure. Therefore, I see as redundant republication of work readily accessible in such recent compilations as *Sisters in Spirit: Mormon Women in Historical and Cultural Perspective*, edited by Maureen Ursenbach and Lavina Fielding Anderson, and *Women and Authority: Re-emerging Mormon Feminism*, edited by Maxine Hanks.

As an epilogue to the present compilation I have selected a sermon given on national radio by Mormon apostle Stephen L Richards. Richards spoke in the 1930s, but his discussion sounds as though it were delivered today. Richards was administrator of the church's missionary program, and he seems to have originated the central place the family plays in today's Mormon society. He decried the abandonment of "old-fashioned American family values" and thought that apartment-living families did constitute "good homes." Richards's sermon could have as easily been given during the LDS church's semi-annual world general conference.

Richards's address is also interesting for its historical position on the crest between nineteenth-century and twentieth-century Mormon family life. In 1933 the governing First Presidency was compelled to issue an official statement again denouncing polygamy because of fundamentalist Mormon resurgence.

Reading Richards's sermon in the context of the essays it follows, one may conclude that for all the church's responses to modern challenges, little has really changed. Indeed, change is inconceivable within the eternal family.

I have endeavored to include essays with a variety of points of view. In one case, that of O'Donovan's previously unpublished gay history, I felt that the author represented a fairly widely-accepted point of view among gay Mormons. A recently published collection, *Peculiar People: Mormons and Same-Sex Orientation,* provides an opportunity for lesbian and gay Mormons to share experiences. But its moderate ideological stance does not necessarily represent the perspective of many lesbians and gays who share a Mormon "heritage." Taken as a whole *Multiply and Replenish* provides insight into the wide (perhaps wider than many readers will have expected to exist) range of perspectives on the experiences and problems of the Mormon family. Perhaps, within an institution with rigid roles, it would be expected to encounter such diversity as individuals seek to interpret these forms within the context of their own experiences.

Appreciation is extended to the following authors and publications for permission to reproduce, sometimes in a different format, the essays appearing here: to *Dialogue: A Journal of Mormon Thought* for essays by Lester E. Bush, Eugene England, Klaus J. Hansen, Romel W. Mackelprang, Delmont Oswald, Levi S. Peterson, and Marybeth Raynes and Erin Parsons; to *Sunstone* magazine for essays by Harold T. Christensen, Lawrence Foster, Jeffrey E. Keller, and Marvin Rytting; and to Signature Books for the essay by Tim B. Heaton. The essay by Rocky O'Donovan is published here for the first time.

# 1.

# Between Heaven and Earth: Mormon Theology of the Family in Comparative Perspective

*Lawrence Foster*

> I have looked upon the community of Latter-day Saints in a vision and beheld them organized as one great family of heaven, each person performing his several duties in his line of industry, working for the good of the whole more than for individual aggrandizement: and in this I have beheld the most beautiful order that the mind of man can contemplate, and the grandest results for the upbuilding of the kingdom of God and the spread of righteousness upon the earth. . . . Why can we not so live in this world? –Brigham Young[1]

BRIGHAM YOUNG'S SERMON OF 12 JANUARY 1868 UNDERSCORES THE importance of the concept of the family in the Church of Jesus Christ of Latter-day Saints. Although the family has been an important topic of theological concern in nearly all religions, few groups have placed such extraordinary emphasis on the family as have the Mormons. Like many other groups, the Latter-day Saints have seen the family as the basic building block of social order, as well as the model for larger institutions such as church and government. Yet Mormonism has gone farther than have most other religious movements in seeing the family not merely as the basis of social order in this life, but also as the foundation for all growth and development in the afterlife as well. In a very fundamental sense, Mormonism is not simply concerned *with* the family; it is *about* the family. The church is conceived as the family writ large, with both the strengths and weaknesses that such an emphasis entails.[2]

To understand the development of Mormon theological approaches to the family, one must first understand the basic concerns of the Latter-day Saint religious movement as a whole. Western New York state, where Joseph Smith grew up and founded the Mormon church in 1830, was an area that was experiencing rapid economic growth, unstable social conditions, and sharply conflicting religious movements during the antebellum period. Much as California today serves as both a source and magnet for all manner of religious and social causes, western New York in the early nineteenth century was repeatedly "burned over" by the fires of religious revivalism and by crusades to transform society. Joseph Smith, a poor and uneducated but precocious and sensitive young man, was deeply disturbed by the cacophony of ideas and causes that surrounded him. How was he or anyone else to know what was really true? he asked. Eventually Smith reached the conclusion that all existing religions were wrong and that God had specially called him to set up a new religious and social synthesis—both for himself and for others. Through what he described as the "translation" of a set of golden plates and a series of "revelations" from God, he began to create a set of beliefs and a religious organization that he conceived as a restoration of early Christianity and a synthesis of all previously valid human truth. The new faith, he believed, ultimately would usher in a millennium of earthly peace and harmony—the kingdom of heaven on earth.[3]

If Smith was concerned about the religious disorder in the "burned over district," he must also have been disturbed by the disruption of family life, marriage, and sex roles in the area. Western New York was a hotbed of competing sexual attitudes and experiments, ranging from the celibacy of the Shakers to the promiscuous sexual activities that came to be known by the pejorative catch-all term, "spiritual wifery."[4] Joseph Smith was an active and inquisitive young man who was coming of age himself. It is thus surely no accident that concern for a restoration of proper family ties was implicit in the commission Smith said had been given him in his vision of 21 September 1823—when, according to his account, the angel Moroni told him that he would eventually bring forth the Book of Mormon. It was said then that Elijah would restore to Joseph Smith the priesthood powers of the true church before the Second Coming. "And he shall plant in the hearts of children the promises made to the fathers, and the hearts of the children shall turn to their fathers. If it were not so, the whole earth would be utterly wasted at his coming" (D&C 2:2-3). The Book of Mormon itself similarly included discussions of the "fornication and lasciviousness and every kind of sin" that were running rampant in its time (Jacob 2:31, 35). Such excesses, and the family disharmony with which they were associated, were denounced in no uncertain terms, although no detailed blueprints for overcoming such problems were offered.

It was one thing to be disturbed by the family disorder in western New York during the antebellum years, and quite another to do something about it. In attempting to develop principles upon which order could be reestablished in family relations as well as in religious life, Smith could draw on many sources. One of the most important of these undoubtedly came from his New England heritage. In many respects Mormonism was, as Emerson described it, "an afterclap of Puritanism"[5]—both in its approach to religion and to the family. The Puritans who emigrated to Massachusetts were attempting to overcome the religious and social disorder they had experienced in England by creating a cohesive new "Bible Commonwealth" in which the good of the community would take precedence over individual self-interest. The family for them served as a model for other social institutions, with its hierarchical relations between husband and wife, parents and children fitting into a larger hierarchy of relationships extending up to God. Puritans strongly opposed fornication and adultery, as well as other less common sexual transgressions. Yet given their Calvinistic belief in the innate depravity of human nature, Puritans anticipated that lapses from ideal standards would occur.

They therefore took careful and realistic steps to restrain such behavior as much as possible. On the other hand, and contrary to the popular stereotype, Puritans were certainly not sexual prudes. They held very positive attitudes toward sexual expression within marriage, which they considered part of the natural blessings and expectations of God. Although Puritan society faced many challenges, during the seventeenth century it was characterized by stability, hierarchy, and a strong emphasis on achieving consensus.[6]

The descendants of the Puritans with whom Joseph Smith came in contact during the nineteenth century had changed in many ways, both theologically and socially, from their forebears. Beginning in the late seventeenth century, the intensity of Puritan religious commitment had begun to wane (this was true in other groups as well) and by the time of the American Revolution, church membership in the American colonies as a whole had dropped to less than 10 percent, the lowest level in American history. In addition, by the aftermath of the American Revolution the rate of premarital pregnancies in America had climbed from earlier relatively low figures to over 25 percent of the first born children, suggesting a breakdown of previous forms of social control.[7]

Following the Revolution, religious groups concerned about the weakness of the churches in America began a concerted evangelical campaign against religious "infidelity." New revivalistic techniques—including dramatic preaching styles, mass meetings, and exhortations to total commitment—were pioneered to bring in new members and money. The Calvinistic emphasis on human depravity and helplessness gave way increasingly to a more optimistic Arminian view which stressed the active role that individuals could play in achieving their own salvation.[8]

With regard to family ideals and practices, the evangelical counterthrust also had a profound impact. Although initially concerned with specifically religious issues, many revivalists eventually began to apply religious principles to pressing social problems as well. Using arguments similar to those of the revivalists, temperance crusaders denounced the drinking of alcohol as a sin and stressed the devastating effects of drink on family life. Criticizing the widespread experimentation and uncertainty in family and sexual matters in the 1830s and 1840s, ministers and secular reformers alike by the 1850s were advocating more restrictive attitudes toward sexual relations, even within marriage. This developing Victorian ethos, with its "cult of true womanhood," stress on domesticity, and sentimentalized view of the family, placed enormous, even cosmic emphasis on the importance of "the home." The home for many became a retreat from the unbridled competition of the rapidly developing capitalistic society outside, a way of preserving cooperative values in the face of excessive individualism. Writers such as Horace Bushnell in his *Christian Nurture,* Catherine Beecher in her *Treatise on Domestic Economy,* and innumerable others, all in their various ways stressed that the home and the nuclear family could play an essential part in holding society together in an age of increasing fragmentation.[9] Sermons and hymns further emphasized such themes using explicitly religious metaphors.

Out of this social milieu, and in reaction to it, evolved Mormonism, as well as several other restorationist groups that looked toward the literal establishment of the kingdom of heaven on earth. Some of these groups were dissatisfied with the narrowness of the antebellum emphasis on the nuclear family and instituted religious practices which, they insisted, did not reject the family ideal, but raised it to a higher level. The Shakers, who practiced celibacy, and the Oneida Perfectionists, who engaged in complex marriage, both felt that an expanded family would prove superior to the more constricted nuclear family union.

Interpreting the New Testament passage that "in the resurrection they neither marry nor are given in marriage" to mean that the afterlife was celibate, the Shakers attempted to realize what they took to be that heavenly model on earth.[10] By the 1830s they had established some sixty semi-monastic communities or "families" stretching from Maine to Indiana, governed under an hierarchical and oligarchic family-style paternalism.[11] Within each communal family, individual Shakers referred to each other as "brother" and "sister," and especially beloved adult members were addressed as "father" and "mother." Family imagery is particularly pronounced in Shaker hymns, which speak, over and over again, of the love of their foundress Mother Ann Lee for her loyal children and of her children's love for Mother and for each other. Even more than the revivalistic songs of the larger society, Shaker hymns convey a sense of childlike simplicity, delight, and yearning for unity. Only the sexual and individualistic attachments of normal family life were eliminated so that total loyalty could be devoted to their community and to God.[12]

The Oneida Perfectionists, who established their chief community in central New York state in the late 1840s with a system of complex marriage or group marriage, dealt even more skillfully and explicitly than did the Shakers with the problem of how ideal family relations were to be realized. John Humphrey Noyes, the founder of the Oneida Community, described it over and over again as an "enlarged family," and he vehemently rejected the claim that he was breaking the family apart. Rather, he declared that he was securing for all individuals in the community the benefits of a larger group. Noyes argued, in contrast to the Shakers, that while monogamous marriage would not exist in the afterlife, sex would. The Saints would all love each other equally, and this would include expression of sexual love between men and women. At Oneida, therefore, where an attempt was made to realize this heavenly pattern on earth, "each was married to all" in a complex marriage. In the words of the community hymn, they "all [had] one home and one family relation." The entire community lived under one roof in a large, sprawling "Mansion House"; they joined in the daily religious-and-business meetings at which Noyes often delivered his didactic "Home Talks"; and they participated in the full range of communal work, rather as though they were living under a feudal manorial system. Like the Shakers, their elimination of the exclusive sexual, emotional, and economic attachments of the nuclear family allowed them to develop a more inclusive loyalty to the community and to God.[13]

How did Mormon attitudes toward the family compare with these other restorationist groups and with the ideals developing in Victorian America? In the 1830s, as Klaus Hansen has suggested in his provocative analysis in *Mormonism and the American Experience,* the Latter-day Saints initially seem to have looked back primarily toward earlier more "traditional" approaches to the family such as those of the Puritans.[14] On the one hand, Joseph Smith, like the Puritans, rejected celibacy. In his revelation to the Shakers in March 1831, Smith sharply criticized them, both because of their celibacy and because they were founded by a woman.[15] On the other hand, early Mormons appear, like the Puritans, to have accepted the idea of sex within marriage as a good thing, a part of the natural blessings and expectations of God. While records of their attitudes on this point are scarce, there is little evidence that they accepted the nascent Victorian notions that even within marriage sexual relations should be strictly limited. Finally, like the Puritans, the early church was strict in punishing lapses against conventional sexual morality, including excommunicating unrepentant offenders, yet they viewed such sins as only one among a number of sins rather than as a uniquely dangerous threat to "purity" as the Victorians would later. In short, Mormons of the 1830s gave little public indication that their family and sexual ideals differed significantly from those of their Puritan forebears.

The chief factors that would lead Mormons of the next decade towards a new family theology and unorthodox family practices grew out of their combination of intense biblicism and their millennial commitment to establishing the kingdom of heaven on earth. Like the early Puritans, early Mormons looked back toward Old Testament Hebrew models for many of their family ideals and considered themselves in some sense literally a "New Israel," replicating earlier Hebrew tribal practices. Like many of his nineteenth-century contemporaries as well, Joseph Smith immersed himself in the Bible and conceived of the whole of human history within the context established by biblical record. Yet Smith and the early Mormons went beyond conventional biblicism, either of the Puritans or of their own day. The Book of Mormon, for example, purported to be a continuation of scripture, and Smith claimed continuing revelations, asserting that the direct influx of the divine into human history had not ceased with New Testament days. As he reflected on the lives of the Hebrew patriarchs whom he greatly admired, Smith could hardly have helped but wonder why the Lord apparently sanctioned their taking of plural wives. If the millennial dispensation was to be a "restoration of all things," a synthesis of all previously valid human truth, might it not also include a restoration of polygamous marriage? These and other family-related concerns had remained in the background during most of the 1830s as the Latter-day Saints attempted to establish their religious faith on a firm foundation. But during the early 1840s in Nauvoo, Illinois, family and kinship concerns came to the fore as the Mormons increasingly devoted themselves to the effort to establish their political kingdom of God, an autonomous, self-sufficient organization with which they expected to govern the world during the Millennium.[16]

The period between 1839 and 1844 which the Latter-day Saints spent in Nauvoo, Illinois, under Joseph Smith's leadership proved to be pivotal in their history in almost every respect, including the development of a new family theology. Nauvoo saw the climax of an earlier phase of Mormon development and set the pattern of new doctrinal, social, and political approaches that would be further developed and tested in Utah. From one perspective, Nauvoo was a typical Jacksonian boom town, representative of the raw potentiality, enthusiasm, crassness, and tensions that characterized the era. Yet at a more fundamental level, the Mormons in Nauvoo were attacking and attempting to overcome the rampant, exploitative individualism that surrounded them. They were seeking a total solution, more akin to medieval ideals in which religious and social life were inextricably intertwined and the good of the community took precedence over individual self-interest. Mundane secular life would be re-sacralized and integrated into a new organic unity which in turn had its place and meaning in the cosmic order.

During this period Smith moved vigorously to present new doctrines that had long been germinating in his mind, doctrines designed to reestablish social cohesion not only on earth, but also throughout all eternity.[17] Basic to these new doctrines was an elaboration of church authority through ceremonies viewed as indissolubly linking the living and the dead. Smith claimed the keys of St. Peter, with the power to bind and to loose, on earth and in heaven. This was the basis for the doctrine of baptism for the dead, which was designed to allow dead relatives to accept the Mormon gospel in the afterlife. The material and spiritual worlds were described as a continuum. God was seen in anthropomorphic terms—once a man, he had progressed to godhood, as man could too.

The most important of these new doctrines were special sealing ceremonies designed to give permanence to earthly marriage after death. In contrast to Shaker or Oneida Perfectionist doctrine, Mormon modern revelation declared that while no marriages would be *performed* in heaven, marriage and the social cohesion provided by family and kinship ties would be the basis for all growth and progression in the afterlife.[18] Earthly marriage itself was an ephemeral state; unless marriages were properly sealed by the Mormon priesthood on earth, in the light of eternity, they would not continue. Those who were not married for eternity would be the lowest class in the afterlife—solitary "ministering angels," a sort of perpetual servant class unable to progress further. Sealings for eternity, on the other hand, made possible progression toward godhood, as men became great patriarchs who ruled over an ever-increasing posterity and moved on to settle whole worlds. There was a sense of the awesome power of sexuality and procreation in human development.

Most controversial, Smith revealed that polygamous marriage was a particularly exalted form of eternal or celestial marriage. If marriage with one wife, sealed under the authority of the Priesthood, could bring ultimate godhood for men, then having more than one wife merely accelerated the process, in line with God's promise to Abraham that his seed eventually would be as numerous as the stars in the sky or the sands on the seashore. Furthermore, polygamy made possible the reuniting of all family members around patriarchal leaders in the afterlife. Even if a man had lost a wife and remarried, those wives would be his again after he died. Though giving few details of exactly how polygamy was to be practiced, the revelation on plural and celestial marriage repeatedly stressed that any unauthorized liaisons established outside church law were heinously sinful and required drastic measures for atonement. Once again. total loyalty to the church was put forward as the supreme principle.[19]

These Nauvoo doctrines represented a sharp departure from normative Judaic and Christian belief. Yet Latter-day Saint concepts such as the close linkage of matter and spirit, an anthropomorphic god with a plurality of other originally human gods progressing toward the achievement of similar divinity, baptism for the dead, and, above all, an afterlife in which the relationships of this life could continue in some literal sense, had much potential appeal in the nineteenth century. What were the reasons for that appeal? How well did these doctrines "meet the needs of the human family?"[20]

In examining and evaluating the effects of these doctrines about continuing family ties, it is important to keep in mind the distinction between a basic principle, which may be viewed by believers as eternal, and the specific and often highly variable ways in which that principle may be realized in practice. The underlying goal in Nauvoo was to achieve cohesion by strengthening and extending kinship ties and loyalties, but the precise *ways* in which such increased cohesion could be achieved varied greatly. For example, both Joseph Smith and Brigham Young (as well as the RLDS and Strangite Mormons) attempted at different times to set up the Order of Enoch or United Order, yet in each case they backed off from such efforts when they failed to strengthen the group as had been hoped. Similarly, during the exodus to Utah Brigham Young attempted to introduce a form of the law of adoption in which all Mormon men would ultimately be sealed to the leaders of the church and each other, thereby indissolubly linking all members together in an enlarged family. In practice, however, the adoptionary system contributed to jealously and tension rather than unity and so it was largely abandoned by the late 1840s.[21]

Keeping in mind this distinction between principle and practice, let us look at the strengths and weaknesses of the Mormon emphasis on the importance of the family. In the nineteenth century, when the Mormons were heavily persecuted, moved frequently, and could not rely fully on normal legal channels for redress of grievances, family and kinship ties could provide an essential source of strength and cohesion. The tribal sense of being a chosen people, a New Israel, produced a feeling of special pride and commitment. The belief that valued earthly relationships could be eternal was a comfort in the face of long absences of missionary husbands, as well as the struggles, sickness, and death that were experienced by so many Mormons.

Plural marriage, both in theory and in practice, could further extend such loyalties. As only one example, by his death at age 88, the Mormon patriarch Benjamin F. Johnson was related by blood or marriage to over 800 people.[22] Furthermore, marriage, plural or otherwise, provided experience in cooperative action and subordination of individual desires to larger group goals which could carry over into the cooperative Mormon effort to achieve rapid settlement and development of the intermountain West. As Leonard Arrington has observed, initially "only a high degree of religious devotion and discipline, superb organization and planning, made survival possible."[23] Mormon family experiences and commitment to a family model played an essential role in this larger settlement effort.

Yet there were problems with the Mormon family system,

especially with polygamy. Although the Latter-day Saints, like the Shakers and Oneida Perfectionists, found that their divergence from conventional monogamous belief and practice could be useful as a means of developing group cohesion and sifting out the fainthearted, in the long run all three groups found that their unorthodox family systems contributed to severe internal and external tensions.[24] As the largest and most aggressive of the three movements, the Latter-day Saints were seen as a serious threat to accepted family patterns and were the most heavily persecuted by the external society. In addition, although the evidence has not yet been fully explored, there also appears to have been a strong undercurrent of unhappiness with plural marriage among church members. A combination of external pressure and internal tensions ultimately combined to result in the issuance of the Manifesto of 1890, which ostensibly withdrew public sanction for any further plural marriages in the United States.[25] During subsequent years, especially following the so-called "Second Manifesto" of 1904 which led to the excommunication of recalcitrant polygamists, Mormonism began a major transformation that would ultimately bring it closer to mainstream American values and practices.

Today there are several paradoxes in the Mormon concept and practice of family life that continue to create tensions for the devout. The fact that plural marriage is still viewed as an eternally valid principle while strictly discouraged in practice causes intellectual confusion and uncertainty for some Latter-day Saints.[26] More far-reaching and less apparent to average church members is the important shift that appears to have taken place in Mormon family life and sexual attitudes, changes which began in the late nineteenth century but which have increasingly accelerated since World War II with the rapid influx of new converts, many of whom hold beliefs divergent from earlier Mormonism. Nineteenth-century Mormonism under leaders such as Joseph Smith and Brigham Young was heavily influenced by pragmatic Puritan notions of the conduct of family and sexual relationships and critical of the hyper-sentimentality of Victorianism. Brigham Young's support of the functional Bloomer-style Deseret Costume, his criticism of sentimentalized Victorian novels as trash, and his forthrightness in dealing bluntly and directly in public with family and sexual issues that polite Victorian society thought should be kept strictly private, if discussed at all, were characteristic of the approaches of many other early church leaders. With the encouragement of the church, nineteenth-century Mormon women developed their powerful Relief Society, voted earlier than women in any other state or territory in the United States, established a distinguished woman-managed, -edited, and -written newspaper of their own, the *Women's Exponent*, and exercised a remarkable degree of real power, influence, and independence. There was no hesitation in dealing fully and frankly with a host of important issues that affected women and family life.

By contrast, today popular church literature and exhortations appear, if anything, to be more Victorian than the Victorians. Almost everywhere, from the visitor's center display lauding family home evening to the exhortations in the *Church News* section of the *Deseret News,* the family ideal held up for Mormons conveys the gush and cloying sentimentality of a Hallmark gift card. The images that are suggested for emulation tend to be those of pasteboard saints, supermen and superwomen whose blemishes as well as humanity are blotted out. While high standards and ideals are certainly desirable, unrealistic views of what constitutes perfection and the extent to which it may be achieved can produce severe problems. Some highly committed Saints come to feel great inadequacy in the face of impossible standards that they feel they somehow *ought* to be able to achieve. Others eventually become inactive altogether or develop a deep-seated cynicism about a faith which otherwise might offer them much. Ironically, more realistic and less propagandistic portrayals of the tensions and challenges of daily life and how Saints have tried to meet them might well be more "faith promoting" in the long run than the church's public relations literature which tries to give the impression that all is unrelieved sweetness and light if only one has sufficient faith. There are a few examples of more candid and appealing styles of writing, such as the superb biography of President Spencer W. Kimball, but realistic and appealing models of what family life can and should be are rare.[27]

In short, the intense Mormon emphasis on family life and kinship ties has both strengths and weaknesses. During the nineteenth century, such an emphasis could provide a powerful source of cohesion for the church, helping to call forth almost herculean efforts at building up the "kingdom of God" in an arid and initially hostile environment. More recently, however, even Mormonism itself and some of its other fundamental doctrines appear at times to be overshadowed by the preoccupation with a sentimentalized ideal of family life which Latter-day Saints have chosen to emphasize in their proselytizing efforts to the world.

Whenever overriding importance is given to any human institution, whether family, state, or even church, there is always the danger of idolatry, of worshiping that institution and losing sight of God who stands above and beyond all human institutions and whose mystery is ultimately beyond direct human comprehension. Edmund Morgan's classic study, *The Puritan Family,* concludes with a cautionary chapter on "Puritan Tribalism" which suggests some insights that may apply to the Latter-day Saints as well. Morgan begins the chapter by noting that: "the family metaphor seems to have dominated Puritan thought so completely as to suggest that the Puritans' religious experience in some way duplicated their domestic experience." Indeed the Puritans almost had a tendency to "domesticate the Almighty." "Puritans of course thought of their God as the one God of the universe, but they made him so much their own, in the guise of making themselves his, that eventually and at times he took on the character of a tribal deity." Morgan observes that as the seventeenth century progressed, the New England Puritans began to lose sight of the original "errand into the wilderness" that had brought them to the New World to set up "a city upon a hill." Instead, they increasingly turned inward and developed "a defensive tribal attitude." Morgan concludes: "The Puritans had, in fact, committed the very sin that they had so often admonished themselves to avoid: they had allowed their children to usurp a higher place than God in their affections. . . . When theology became the handmaid of genealogy, Puritanism no longer deserved its name."[28]

Do Morgan's observations about New England Puritan attitudes have anything to say to Mormons today? Certainly the comparison is not exact: lack of evangelical zeal, for example, is definitely not a problem in either of the main branches of the Mormon movement at present. But in more subtle ways, Morgan's analysis causes us to reflect on disturbing tendencies within Mormonism toward idolatry and insularity. The Mormon church, more than many other religious movements, has made God literally theirs. Often it has been all too easy in Mormonism to assume that the specific, limited, earthly *practices* of the Saints, developing originally because of pragmatic earthly reasons, were really divinely ordained and immutable rather than being subject to progressive change due to continuing revelation or insight. With regard to the family, for example, it seems possible that by focusing on specific and limited present-day family patterns as though they were fixed and eternal truths, Mormons may in fact sometimes lose sight of the larger concept of the family and its importance that underlies their faith. Particularly as the Church of Jesus Christ of Latter-day Saints reaches outward across the world in an attempt to become a truly universal church rather than an intermountain American sect, a progressive openness to truth wherever it may be found will be essential. Principles may be eternal, but their application must always remain flexible and open to new insight.

*NOTES*

1. *Journal of Discourses*, 26 vols. (Liverpool: F. W. Richards and others, 1854-86), 12:153.

2. The importance of the family in the Church of Jesus Christ of Latter-day Saints has been frequently discussed. For some valuable Mormon analyses, see Leonard J. Arrington and Davis Bitton, *The Mormon Experience: A History of the Latter-day Saints* (New York: Alfred A. Knopf, 1979); Rex Eugene Cooper, *Promises Made to the Fathers: Mormon Covenant Organization* (Salt Lake City: University of Utah Press, 1990); and Herbert Ray Larsen, "'Familism' in Mormon Social Structure," Ph.D. diss., University of Utah, 1954. For non-Mormon perspectives, Thomas F. O'Dea, *The Mormons* (Chicago: University of Chicago Press, 1957), is still the most insightful starting point. See also Melvyn Hammarberg, "An Ethnographic Perspective on Mormon Marriage and Family," unpublished paper presented at the annual meeting of the Society for the Scientific Study of Religion, Chicago, 1971. A detailed analysis of early Mormon family concerns is found in Lawrence Foster, *Religion and Sexuality: Three American Communal Experiments of the Nineteenth Century* (New York: Oxford University Press, 1981), esp. 123-225. Portions of that study are used here by permission of Oxford University Press.

3. See volume 1 of Joseph Smith's *History of the Church of Jesus Christ of Latter-day Saints*, ed. Brigham H. Roberts, 6 vols. (Salt Lake City: Deseret Book Co., 1951). Among important secondary accounts, see Arrington and

Bitton, *The Mormon Experience,* 1-43; O'Dea, *The Mormons,* 2-40; Mario S. DePillis, "The Quest for Religious Authority and the Rise of Mormonism," *Dialogue: A Journal of Mormon Thought* 1 (Mar. 1966): 68-88; Marvin S. Hill, "The Shaping of the Mormon Mind in New York," *Brigham Young University Studies* 9 (Spring 1969): 351-372; Jan Shipps, "The Prophet Puzzle: Suggestions Leading Toward a More Comprehensive Interpretation of Joseph Smith," *Journal of Mormon History* 1 (1974): 4-20; and Lawrence Foster, "First Visions: Personal Reflections on Joseph Smith's Religious Experience," *Sunstone* 8 (Sept.-Oct. 1983): 39-43.

4. Whitney Cross, *The Burned-Over District: The Social and Intellectual History of Enthusiastic Religion in Western New York* (Ithaca, NY: Cornell University Press, 1950).

5. Quoted in William Mulder and A. Russel Mortensen, *Among the Mormons: Historic Accounts by Contemporary Observers* (Lincoln: University of Nebraska Press, 1973), 384.

6. For an introduction to Puritan family life, see Edmund S. Morgan, *The Puritan Family: Religion and Domestic Relations in Seventeenth-Century New England* (New York: Harper and Row, 1966). A classic analysis of Puritan sexual attitudes is Edmund S. Morgan, "The Puritans and Sex," *New England Quarterly* 15 (Dec. 1942): 591-607. Among the many accounts of the role of Puritan women, a useful starting point is Laurel Thatcher Ulrich, *Good Wives: Image and Reality in the Lives of Women in Northern New England, 1650-1750* (New York: Alfred A. Knopf, 1982).

7. Daniel Scott Smith and Michael S. Hundus, "Premarital Pregnancy in America, 1640-1971: An Overview and Interpretation," *Journal of Interdisciplinary History* 5 (Spring 1975): 538.

8. For an introduction to these issues, see Sidney E. Mead, *The Lively Experiment: The Shaping of Christianity in America* (New York: Harper & Row, 1963); Bernard A. Weisberger, *They Gathered at the River: The Story of the Great Revivalists and Their Impact on Religion in America* (Chicago: Quadrangle, 1966); and Cross, *Burned-Over District.*

9. An entree into these topics is provided in Barbara Welter, "The Cult of True Womanhood, 1820-1860," *American Quarterly* 18 (Summer 1966): 151-174; Kathryn Kish Sklar, *Catharine Beecher: A Study in Domesticity* (New Haven: Yale University Press, 1973); and Ronald G. Walters, ed., *Primers for Prudery: Sexual Advice to Victorian America* (Englewood Cliffs, NJ: Prentice-Hall, 1974).

10. The three variants of the biblical story are found in Matthew 22:15-22, Mark 12: 18-27, and Luke 20:27-40. The Shaker interpretation runs throughout almost all of their writings as an underlying theme. For an early account, see *Testimonies of the Life, Character, Revelations, and Doctrines of Our Ever Blessed Mother Ann Lee and the Elders With Her* (Hancock, MA: J. Talcott and J. Deming, Junrs., 1816), 17.

11. There were eighteen Shaker community sites at the high point of the group's expansion, but many of those sites contained three or four semi-autonomous Shaker communities.

12. For one of the more accessible documentary sources, see Edward Deming Andrews, *The Gift to Be Simple: Songs, Dances, and Rituals of the American Shakers* (New York: Dover, 1962). Some analytical treatments include Marjorie Proctor-Smith, *Women in Shaker Community and Worship: A Feminist Analysis of the Uses of Religious Symbolism* (Lewiston, MA: Edwin Mellen, 1985); and Sally M. Promey, *Spiritual Spectacles: Vision and Image in Mid-Nineteenth-Century Shakerism* (Bloomington: University of Indiana Press, 1993).

13. See John Humphrey Noyes, *History of American Socialisms* (Philadelphia: J. B. Lippincott, 1870), 623-40. The most readily accessible source for the Oneida Community hymn is Charles Nordhoff's *The Communistic Societies of the United States* (New York: Harper and Brothers, 1875), 299-300.

14. See the chapter, "Changing Perspectives on Sexuality and Marriage," in Klaus J. Hansen, *Mormonism and the American Experience* (Chicago: University of Chicago Press, 1981), 147-78 (reprinted in this compilation).

15. The revelation is printed in *History of the Church*, 1:167-69 and in D&C 49. For a detailed account of the Shaker reaction to the revelation and Mormon proselytizing of their community at North Union, near Cleveland, Ohio, see Robert F. W. Meader, "The Shakers and Mormons," *Shaker Quarterly* 2 (Fall 1962): 83-96.

16. See Foster, *Religion and Sexuality*, 128-39. A path-breaking early analysis of Mormon political and cultural autonomy is Klaus J. Hansen, *Quest for Empire: The Political Kingdom of God and the Council of Fifty in Mormon History* (East Lansing: Michigan State University Press, 1967).

17. Five revelations—and four statements now accepted as revelation by the Utah church—were given between 19 January 1841 and 12 July 1843. These are now printed as sections 124 through 132 of the Utah version of the D&C.

18. For a comparison of the Shaker, Oneida Perfectionist, and Mormon interpretations of these New Testament passages, see Foster, *Religion and Sexuality*, 15-18.

19. The revelation on plural and celestial marriage was originally printed in the *Deseret News* Extra for 14 September 1852, and reprinted as a supplement to volume 15 of the *Millennial Star* in 1853. It currently appears as section 132 of the Utah Mormon version of the D&C. Although the Reorganized Church of Jesus Christ of Latter Day Saints has questioned whether Joseph Smith delivered the revelation, that linkage was conclusively established by Charles A. Shook, *The True Origins of Mormon Polygamy* (Cincinnati: Standard Publishing Company, 1914).

20. Supplement to volume 15 of the *Millennial Star*, page 63.

21. For the best analysis of Mormon communitarianism, see Leonard J. Arrington, Feramorz Y. Fox, and Dean L. May, *Building the City of God: Community and Cooperation Among the Mormons*, 2d ed. (Urbana: University of Illinois Press, 1992). The early form of the law of adoption is analyzed in Gordon Irving, "The Law of Adoption: One Phase of the Mormon Concept of Salvation, 1830-1900," *Brigham Young University Studies* 14 (Spring 1974): 291-314.

22. Benjamin F. Johnson, *My Life's Review* (Independence, MO: Zion's Printing and Publishing Company, 1947), 94.

23. Leonard J. Arrington, *Great Basin Kingdom: An Economic History of the Latter-day Saints, 1830-1900* (Cambridge, MA: Harvard University Press, 1958), 38.

24. A comparative treatment of these difficulties is in Foster, *Religion and Sexuality*, 243-45.

25. For an overview of the persecution, see Gustive O. Larson, *The "Americanization" of Utah for Statehood* (San Marino, CA: Huntington Library, 1971).

26. Increasing scholarly attention is being devoted to these tensions and how they developed. An overall assessment is Thomas G. Alexander, *Mormonism in Transition: A History of the Latter-day Saints, 1890-1930* (Urbana: University of Illinois Press, 1986). For insight into the strains of life in polygamy after the Manifesto of 1890, see B. Carmon Hardy, *Solemn Covenant: The Mormon Polygamous Passage* (Urbana: University of Illinois Press, 1992); D. Michael Quinn, "LDS Church Authority and New Plural Marriages, 1890-1904," *Dialogue: A Journal of Mormon Thought* 18 (Spring 1985): 9-105; and Kenneth Cannon II, "Beyond the Manifesto: Polygamous Cohabitation Among LDS General Authorities After 1890," *Utah Historical Quarterly* 46 (Winter 1978): 24-36.

27. See Edward L. Kimball and Andrew E. Kimball, Jr., *Spencer W. Kimball* (Salt Lake City: Bookcraft, 1977). An overview analysis of changes in the role of women and the family is in "From Activism to Domesticity: Mormon Women in the Nineteenth and Twentieth Centuries," in Lawrence Foster, *Women, Family, and Utopia: Communal Experiments of the Shakers, the Oneida Community, and the Mormons* (Syracuse: Syracuse University Press, 1991), 202-19. Also see Marilyn Warenski, *Patriarchs and Politics: The Plight of the Mormon Woman* (New York: McGraw-Hill, 1978); Sonia Johnson, *From Housewife to Heretic* (New York: Doubleday, 1981); Maureen Ursenbach Beecher and Lavina Fielding Anderson, eds., *Sisters in Spirit: Mormon Women in Historical and Cultural Perspective* (Urbana: University of Illinois Press, 1987); and Maxine Hanks, ed., *Women and Authority: Re-emerging Mormon Feminism* (Salt Lake City: Signature Books, 1992).

28. Morgan, *The Puritan Family*, 161-86.

# 2.
# Changing Perspectives on Sexuality and Marriage

*Klaus J. Hansen*

Mormonism is destined to thoroughly revolutionize the world with regard to the intercourse of the sexes. —Orson Pratt

MORMONISM HAS EXPERIENCED A SOCIAL AND INTELLECTUAL TRANSFORmation of such magnitude that a resurrected Joseph Smith, returning to earth today, might well wonder if this was indeed the same church he founded, given the disappearance of the political kingdom, of communal cooperation, and of plural marriage. These are the most obvious examples. Although the demise of all three institutions must be attributed to external as well as internal pressures, the interplay of these factors in the dynamics of change is particularly revealing in the case of sexuality and marriage, providing some glimpses into just how Mormonism was transformed from a nineteenth-century religious movement that encompassed all facets of human existence to its contemporary status as one of numerous denominations in the spectrum of American pluralism.

## I

Early Mormon attitudes regarding sex and marriage were derived from their New England heritage. In colonial America sexual attitudes and behavior were firmly rooted in a biblically-oriented Calvinism or Anglicanism and in a social order reflecting the values of these religions. Fornication and adultery, as well as other, less common sexual transgressions were regarded not only as heinous sins but as crimes to be punished. For later generations "puritanism" became a synonym for sexual repression. As Edmund Morgan's revisionist study pointed out long ago, however, the Puritans were far from being the sexual prudes that a hostile literature made them out to be. They regarded sex in marriage not only as a means of procreation but also as a natural expression of love between husband and wife. Celibacy in healthy persons was regarded as unnatural and against the will of God, as, of course, was sexual transgression. In either case, one was willfully rejecting the laws of God.[1]

However severely they condemned sin, the Puritans realized that living as they did in a fallen world, even they could not be absolutely certain about the state of their souls. Virtue could be achieved only at the cost of eternal vigilance. First and foremost, it was the responsibility of the family to monitor the behavior of its members. But the community likewise saw to the enforcement of morals, a task made easy by a relative lack of privacy. If these institutions failed, the law held immorality in check. When sin, nevertheless, did strike, the Saints rarely panicked. Realizing that there, but for the grace of God, went they, Puritans had a relatively relaxed attitude toward transgressors, no doubt encouraged by a stable social order in which rather infrequent premarital pregnancies and illegitimate births suggest a close correlation between prescription and behavior.

From about 1675 on, however, we can observe an increasing divergence between belief and conduct. By 1790, the premarital pregnancy record in America exceeded 25 percent of firstborn children, suggesting a dissolution of the social and intellectual underpinnings of traditional society. As the social controls of the community slackened, sexual mores slackened also. From this time on, however, the statistics begin a steady downward trend that reaches a low point of less than 10 percent by 1860.[2]

Interpreted without a context, such data might suggest that nineteenth-century Americans had reestablished the stable social order of a traditional society. The social and intellectual climate of the period, however, points to a different conclusion. By the 1820s and 1830s, the decades of the birth of Mormonism, American culture had moved a long way down the road from the relatively stable social order of colonial America to the increasingly atomistic society of capitalistic individualism; from the traditional Calvinism that saw God as the center of the universe to an Arminianized evangelism that saw man as the center; and from a society in which behavior was largely controlled by the norms of the community to a society in which moral standards were internalized. Teetotalism and sexual restraint became two of the most important means of expressing this modern attitude. Once again, as in colonial society, prescription and behavior coincided, but for very different reasons.[3]

As social control gave way to self-control, Americans developed a perfectionism that would brook no compromise with sin. In colonial society, sex in marriage was regarded as intrinsically wholesome. In the nineteenth century, an army of sexual reformers began to extol the virtues of sexual continence bordering on celibacy, even in marriage. If we can believe the rising chorus of anti-sexual rhetoric, severe doubt was cast on God's wisdom or at least propriety for having made human propagation a function that was so indelicate. Relatively perfunctory in their attacks on public vice, these reformers raised their crusade to a pitch of near-hysteria as they inveighed against the supposedly ubiquitous sexual excesses practiced within the privacy of the marriage bed or, even worse, by the individual alone.[4]

In the opinion of one historian, such attitudes "may have had a therapeutic value when [they] took hold in the 1830s, giving men and women an explanation and a set of cures for the frightening world they found themselves in." Another explanation for this seemingly puzzling shift in attitudes may be found in the individualistic, anti-institutional ethos of the period, which placed the burden of reform on the individual rather than on society. If the world was less than perfect, it was the fault of the individual. As a result, private sins assumed an unprecedented, monumental significance. Charles Rosenberg's assertion that masturbation was widely regarded as the "master vice" of the period finds a plausible explanation in the social and intellectual climate of antebellum America.[5]

Sexual attitudes thus had undergone a profound transformation.

To colonial Americans the idea that one particular form of sexual transgression was a "master vice" would have been incomprehensible. As vigorously as they disapproved of departures from the sexual norms, such lapses were merely sins among many other sins. For many nineteenth-century reformers, however, sin had virtually become synonymous with sex.

## II

These were the kinds of sexual attitudes emerging as Mormonism made its debut in America. Such values, however, were not congenial to early Saints, who scarcely fit into the pluralistic cultural pattern emerging in the antebellum period. Joseph Smith's millennial kingdom was intended as an alternative to the presumed deficiencies of American society rather than as an instrument for its reform. Mormonism, at least in its early phase, attempted to restore a society that reflected traditional values. Eventually, Smith envisioned a radical reordering of the family and of relations between the sexes, innovations scarcely foreshadowed in the Book of Mormon, which in its sexual ethos shared many of the values of colonial society. Though Puritans would have regarded Smith's idea of modern revelation as heretical, they would have been comfortable with the kind of Book of Mormon theology that asserted that the Fall "was the cause of all mankind becoming carnal, sensual, devillish" (Mosiah 16:3).

To the early Mormons this passage appears to have been a fact of life rather than a source of anxiety. There is little evidence suggesting that the Saints—at least prior to the death of Joseph Smith—shared the sexual concerns of their modern American contemporaries. As in traditional society, adultery, fornication, and other less common sexual transgressions were condemned, and unrepentant sinners excommunicated. But an examination of early church trials suggests that sexual offenses were but one cause among many for excommunication. Although demographic evidence for this early period is scant, it is likely that the sexual conduct of the Saints was on the whole exemplary by the standards of the period, though little was said about sex in diaries, journals, and letters.[6]

To modern, psychologically-oriented scholars, this silence may itself speak volumes. Yet it should be remembered that it was the age in which sexually-obsessed reformers articulated their concerns *ad nauseam.* If sexuality had been one of the Mormons' chief concerns, it is unlikely that they would have remained silent on that issue, especially since the new religion was very much a religion of the word. Aspiring Saints prepared for a manifestation of the spirit through a rational process of study.

Mormonism was an ideology preparing a new social and religious order and was not particularly evangelical or revivalistic. Converted Saints, to be sure, would manifest through their conduct that they had been "born again," but what set Mormons apart from the world was their ideological identification with the kingdom of God. Many gentiles lived lives of moral rectitude. But what they lacked, in the opinion of the Saints, was the true and everlasting gospel. Those who accepted Mormonism followed its moral regulations gladly. Yet these were not the central concern of their lives. The message of the Mormon restoration, priesthood authority, and gifts of the Spirit were central.

It appears that during the antebellum period, conceptions of sexuality were tied to changing perceptions and conditions of class. Middle-class sexual morality became a necessary adjunct to the profile of producers and managers. In an upwardly mobile society, this ethos was imitated by all who had middle-class aspirations. This kind of "Victorianism" also served to provide a sense of identity, to set the middle class off from both the lower classes and the aristocracy, who were either unable or unwilling to live by bourgeois moral precepts.[7] In spite of increasing stratification, class boundaries in America were clearly less defined than in Europe. Charles Rosenberg has argued persuasively that "a good many Americans must . . . have been all the more anxious in their internalization of those aspects of life-style which seemed to embody and assure class status."[8]

Sociologist Joseph Gusfield's study of the "bourgeoisification" of antebellum American cultural values provides striking support for this argument. For the overwhelming majority of those involved in the temperance movement, for example, abstinence became a symbol for the internalization of moral values and behavior. Because "there would be no compromise with Evil in any of its forms," sexual conduct would be of equal concern to upwardly mobile Americans.[9] The Saints, however, felt that they had escaped the psychological, social, and economic pressures of class. Although in their new world, temperance and sexual restraint were part of the social order, neither served as a means for social transformation.

Joseph Smith's dietary rules as revealed in the Word of Wisdom illustrate this clearly. Viewed superficially, these directives appear to be a typical expression of the temper of the times. Yet the very wording of the revelation is alien to the emerging spirit of "necessary moral action": "To be sent greeting; not by commandment or constraint, but by revelation and the word of Wisdom." Among Mormons the use of alcohol was governed by the same kind of sanctions that made moderate drinking in colonial America socially and morally acceptable. Smith remained a moderate drinker all his life, and it is perhaps safe to suggest that until his death the Word of Wisdom was honored almost as much in breach as in observance—a further indication that Mormon social norms, in many ways, resembled those of the seventeenth century more than those of the nineteenth (D&C 89).[10]

There is, of course, a point at which the analogy between drinking and sex breaks down. Neither Mormons nor Puritans would have agreed with Benjamin Franklin's moderate use of "venery" if it occurred outside of marriage. When applied to fornication or adultery, the concept of moderation, in the opinion of Mormons, ceased to have meaning. Rather, it can be said, Mormons, like Puritans, had a positive attitude toward sex in marriage and did not share the hysterical attitude of the reformers regarding masturbation. Lest I be misunderstood, I am not suggesting that the Saints condoned the "secret vice." All I am saying is that, having removed themselves from the presumed corruptions of the gentiles, they had no reason to invent a "master vice" in order to cope with the pressures of modernization. Mormons, for example, exhibited little if any anxiety over gender roles. Charles Rosenberg has shown that masturbation was connected to such anxieties and was, at the time, regarded as an "ultimate confession of male inadequacy." Masturbation was also regarded as socially isolating, thus conflicting with the male role demands for social and economic achievement. The social and economic communitarianism of Mormonism made such arguments irrelevant.[11]

An autobiographical statement by Joseph Smith suggests an

implicit lack of concern over issues that agitated moral reformers of the day. We cannot, of course, know what transgressions the prophet conjured in his readers' minds as he confessed, "I was left to all kinds of temptations; and, mingling with all kinds of society, I frequently fell into many foolish errors, and displayed the weakness of youth and the corruption of human nature, which I am sorry to say led me into diverse temptations, to the gratification of many appetites offensive in the sight of God." But given the preconceptions of the day, it is hard to believe that his detractors would have gone out of their way to read trivial foibles into the passage. The sentence, surely, has a potential for offending the squeamish. Certainly, those editors who much later changed "corruption" to "foibles," and struck out the phrase, "to the gratification of many appetites," must have been sensitive to the uses that could be made of this passage. By that time (1902), as we shall see, Mormons had adopted the "modern," nineteenth-century attitudes of their erstwhile antagonists. Quite possibly, the young Smith was not only more ingenuous but also more "traditional" in his response to his imperfections.[12]

Having thus far stressed the traditional aspects of Mormon culture and Mormon sexuality, I hasten to add that even in its early phase Mormonism contained many of the germs of its later evolution into a "modern" religion. Emerson's statements that Mormonism was "an after-clap of Puritanism," while containing a great deal of insight, was clearly an oversimplification. Even the Book of Mormon contains too many Arminian heresies to make the comparison stick, and Smith's later pronouncement that "men will be punished for their own sins, and not for Adam's transgression" was fully compatible with the beliefs of one form of liberal Protestantism. Still, having extricated themselves from the pressures of modernization, Mormons, unlike their gentile contemporaries, were not compelled to push for a frantic internalization of mores–sexual or otherwise.

With the benefit of hindsight, it is clear that many of Joseph Smith's unorthodox ideas were already contained in the Book of Mormon. By 1833, with the publication of the prophet's early revelations in the Book of Commandments, the novel side of Mormonism became more apparent. Continual altercations with gentiles prevented the full realization of many of these ideas. It was not until the early 1840s, when Smith believed he had placed the kingdom of God on a firmer footing in Nauvoo, that he was able to press for his innovative religious, political, and social ideas.

## III

Plural marriage was the most dramatic of these. Because of the extreme complexity of the origins of Mormon polygamy, all I can do here is summarize the most important points. On 12 July 1843, Joseph Smith secretly dictated a revelation pertaining to the doctrine of celestial marriage—the new and everlasting covenant—that sanctioned the principle of plural marriage. Part of the justification, in the revelation, was restorationist. In times past the Lord had given concubines and wives to Abraham, Isaac, and Jacob, as well as to David, Solomon, and Moses. In the latter days God was revealing the principles upon which these ancient patriarchs were justified, together with a stern injunction that "all those who have this law revealed unto them must obey the same . . . and if ye abide not that covenant, then ye are damned; for no one can reject this covenant and be permitted to enter into my glory." The major purpose of plural marriage was "to multiply and replenish the earth, according to my commandment, and to fulfil the promise which was given by my Father before the foundation of the world, and for their exaltation in the eternal worlds, that they may bear the souls of men; for herein is the work of my Father continued, that he may be glorified."[13]

Although it was only in the 1840s that Smith began to teach polygamy to his most trusted followers, and to practice it himself, there is strong evidence suggesting that some of the ideas may have originated as early as 1831 when he was engaged in retranslating the Old Testament. An unpublished revelation to a group of missionaries who had been sent to native Americans in Missouri in 1831 indicated that at a future date they would be permitted to take Indian women as plural wives, though none did.[14] In 1835 the church made the first of a number of pronouncements denying charges of polygamy at a time when rumors were spreading that Smith had taken up with Fanny Alger, a seventeen-year-old orphan. One Mormon faction, the Reorganized Church of Jesus Christ of Latter Day Saints, once used these denials as evidence that Smith never taught or practiced plural marriage, claiming it was instituted by Brigham Young. That Smith inaugurated plural marriage in theory and practice is irrefutable.[15]

In Nauvoo, Smith initiated some of his close and trusted associates into the new and everlasting covenant. Brigham Young later claimed that "it was the first time in my life that I desired the grave, and I could hardly get over it for a long time." Smith himself claimed that he took the fateful step only after God had repeatedly commanded him to do so. According to Eliza R. Snow, one of the most renowned of his plural wives, the prophet hesitated to carry out the fateful commandment "until an angel of God stood by him with a drawn sword, and told him that, unless he moved forward and established plural marriage, his priesthood would be taken from him and he should be destroyed."[16] Realizing the explosive potential of polygamy, Smith publicly denied and condemned the practice until his death. As a matter of fact, the Book of Mormon contained a passage denouncing polygamy, though with the significant escape clause that "if I will . . . raise seed unto me, I will command my people" (Jacob 2:30).

Privately, Smith made it clear that plural marriage was an important part of the social order of the kingdom of God. It may be more than coincidental that the revelation concerning the new and everlasting covenant was given more than a year after an important revelation that had launched the political organization of the kingdom. Because most states had bigamy laws, plural marriage could be practiced legally only in a separate political kingdom. It is for this reason that Brigham Young prudently deferred the public announcement of polygamy until he had established a quasi-independent kingdom of God in the Rocky Mountains.

Polygamy, perhaps more than most other principles of Mormonism, could identify the Saints as a peculiar people who had removed themselves from the mainstream of American culture. It could serve as a rallying point and a symbol of identification for a people who in spite of many idiosyncratic qualities of their faith shared many of the basic cultural characteristics of their fellow Americans. Perhaps even more importantly, polygamy irrevocably tied its practitioners to Mormonism. For polygamists it was virtually impossible to defect from the kingdom. Many opponents of Mormonism realized this only too well and conducted the anti-polygamy crusade of the 1880s not only on moral grounds but more importantly as a means of destroying the kingdom.

To all but devout Mormons and anti-polygamy crusaders the origin of polygamy presents a perplexing and intriguing historical problem. The Saints, of course, simply accepted it as a commandment of God, given for the reasons stated in Smith's revelations. The anti-Mormons had an equally simple explanation: A lecherous leader had to devise a system that would allow them to exercise their sexual appetites freely. A more sophisticated version of this "lecher school" is Fawn Brodie's, which argues that although Smith loved his wife Emma dearly, "monogamy seemed to him an intolerably circumscribed way of life." At the same time, "there was too much of the Puritan in him" to allow him to be content with clandestine affairs. Therefore, in order to calm his own conscience, "he could not rest until he had redefined the nature of sin and erected a stupendous theological edifice to support his new theories on marriage."[17]

As Brodie has shown, those last few years in Nauvoo prior to Smith's assassination were extremely turbulent. Like many public figures, he had a charismatic personality attractive to both men and women. This resulted in some very strong male friendships—and in the case of John C. Bennett in the exploitation of the prophet by someone who projected a great deal of personal magnetism of his own. It is clear that Smith exhibited no overt homosexual tendencies. But he had a magnetic attraction for women. At the same time, his own marriage appeared to be less than fulfilling. As leader of the church, he was the one who absorbed all the attention and adulation of followers. A woman's role, in the nineteenth century especially, was very much that of helpmate, and in the case of Emma under conditions more trying than those experienced by most women of the time. The itinerant years of persecution had taken their toll on Emma. She had borne Joseph nine children, of whom only four lived to maturity. If an 1843 description of Emma as "very plain in her personal appearance" can be trusted, these same years had enhanced the physical attractiveness of the prophet, who was a year younger than his wife.

In the culture of Victorian America, even more so than in our own times, there prevailed a sexual double standard regarding age. Joseph, at thirty-eight, was a man in the prime of life; Emma, at thirty-nine, was on the threshold of becoming an old woman. The double standard was even more pronounced regarding differences in sexuality. According to Sarah Grimke, woman was innately superior to man because "the sexual passion in man is ten times stronger than in woman."[18] Indeed, according to polite middle-class opinion, a "lady" had no sexual passion whatsoever. Mormons did not accept such middle-class notions. But it is also true that culturally Emma did not fit comfortably into Mormonism and aspired to middle-class respectability.[19]

One of the first non-Mormons to take issue with the crusaders against polygamy was George Bernard Shaw, who argued that Smith's puritanical followers would have quickly deserted him if they had suspected him of lecherous proclivities. Unfamiliar with the demographic realities of western America, Shaw thought that the major purpose of polygamy was to provide husbands for a surplus of women and ensure the rapid population of the Mormon frontier. Grateful for support from such an unexpected quarter, some Mormons convinced themselves that Shaw was right. The theory provided a kind of sociological respectability for plural marriage after its demise and found some currency in textbooks at a time when the frontier thesis was in vogue. The fact, of course, is that even in Mormon Utah women were in short supply. As a matter of fact, in some communities there was considerable competition between younger and older men for nubile women. Furthermore, as Stanley Ivins had demonstrated, plural marriage had an adverse effect on the birth rate. Fertility of women in polygamous marriages was lower than that of women in monogamous marriages—possibly because polygamous husbands tended to be older and hence less virile or often absent.[20]

Historians argue that polygamy can be understood only in the broader context of antebellum American culture. Lawrence Foster has presented the most ambitious and plausible explanation for the origins of plural marriage thus far.[21] He argues that Mormon polygamy was but one of numerous attempts in antebellum America to establish alternative family systems by millennial religious groups. He regards the Mormon introduction of polygamy "as part of a larger effort to reestablish social cohesion and kinship ties in a socially and intellectually disordered environment," or at least one that Mormons perceived as such. (After all, a large group of Americans was quite satisfied with the absence of institutional restraints.)

The kind of people who became Mormons or Shakers or Oneida Perfectionists found themselves thoroughly at sea in the world. As they saw it, old rules no longer applied and new rules had not yet been clearly defined (and in any case were not to their liking). In such an age it is therefore not surprising to find social and cultural minorities choosing to believe that social reality was arbitrary and developing alternative visions. In the words of Foster, "Smith was attempting to demolish an old way of life and to build a new social order from the ground up."[22] The conditions of the new and everlasting covenant illustrate this point forcefully: "All covenants, contracts, obligations, oaths, vows, performances, connections, associations, or expectations, that are not made and entered into and sealed by the Holy Spirit of promise . . . are of no efficacy, virtue, or force in and after the resurrection from the dead; for all contracts that are not made unto this end have an end when men are dead." These covenants have to be entered into in this life under the authority of someone "on whom this power and the keys of this priesthood are conferred." Contracts conducted under the auspices of eternity were clearly superior to those concluded only for time–like those of the gentile world (D&C 132:7).

Mormons regarded baptisms of other churches as invalid. In the early days of millennial enthusiasm in Ohio and Missouri, some Saints, erroneously to be sure, believed that traditional property arrangements were likewise superseded and began to help themselves to the belongings of their gentile neighbors. The concept of a political kingdom of God evolved to the point where it was regarded as the only legitimate governmental authority under heaven. It is as if the Mormons had reinvented Locke, who had remarked that "in the beginning, all the world was America." But Mormons also learned that America was no longer a *tabula rasa*–that the slate would have to be wiped clean before a new beginning could be made.

The nuclear, monogamous family was fast becoming the cornerstone of American social order as other, traditional institutions declined. The modern family had a seemingly paradoxical function. On the one hand, it served as a haven and retreat from the pressures of a heartless and competitive world. On the other hand, it created and nourished–aided by evangelical religion–the identities of self-motivated individuals who competed successfully in the modern world of trade, commerce, and manufacture. Thus, by striking at the American family, Mormonism was attacking not only the social but also the economic and even psychological foundations of antebellum America.[23]

Joseph Smith was extremely sensitive to the shift in the locus of authority that had led to the decline of the status of fathers. He insisted that the patriarchal order in the home be restored "if social chaos is to be avoided." "Multitudes of families are now in confusion and wretchedly governed. This is a great evil."[24] A contemporary observer of these conditions and an intimate of Joseph Smith, John D. Lee, reported on the prophet's views in Nauvoo: "At about the same time the doctrine of sealing for an eternal state was introduced, and the Saints were given to understand that their marriage relations with each other were not valid. That those who had solemnized the rites of matrimony had no authority of God to do so. . . . That they were married to each other only by their own covenants, and if their marriage relations had not been productive of blessings and peace, and they felt it oppressive to remain together, they were at liberty to make their own choice, as much as if they had not been married. That it was a sin for people to live together, and raise or beget children, in alienation from each other. That there should exist an affinity between each other, not a lustful one, as that can never cement that love and affection that should exist between a man and his wife."[25] With the restoration of the true priesthood this alienation could be reversed, and men and women could find eternal happiness in the new and everlasting covenant.

Mormons were not the only ones who perceived a sense of isolation and alienation in antebellum America. Tocqueville, who had an uncannily accurate perception of the temper of the times, remarked: "The woof of time is every instant broken, and the track of generations effaced. Those who went before are soon forgotten; of those who will come after, no one has any idea . . . Thus not only does democracy make every man forget his ancestors, but it hides his descendants and separates his contemporaries from him; it throws him back forever upon himself alone and threatens in the end to confine him entirely within the solitude of his own heart."[26] The

Mormon prophet taught "that the earth will be smitten with a curse unless there is a welding link of some kind or other between the fathers and the children" (D&C 128:18). This link was marriage under the new and everlasting covenant. To be binding "for time and eternity," such marriages had to be "sealed" by proper priesthood authority in temples dedicated for this purpose. Monogamous marriages performed in this manner were just as eternally binding as polygamous unions. Polygamous marriages, of course, have officially been discontinued since the so-called Manifesto of 1890. Nevertheless, Joseph Smith made it unmistakably clear that the highest degree of glory in the celestial kingdom, the attainment of Godhood, was reserved for those who had entered into polygamous relationships. It was polygamy that presented the most direct and visible challenge to the American social order. It was polygamy that more than any other Mormon institution came to symbolize the new heaven and new earth.

It is not surprising then that the promulgation of such ideas would lead to tension and conflict, not only between Mormons and the world, but also among the Saints themselves. By the time of Smith's martyrdom, theological and social innovations had accelerated at such a pace that they threatened to spin out of control. Social cohesion in Nauvoo was clearly loosening. The prophet's experimentation with "celestial marriage," if continued in the ad hoc fashion of those secretive liaisons of that last year prior to his death, had a potential for sexual anarchy. Certainly, the impact even on his most trusted followers was nothing less than traumatic. In fact, the prophet himself seems to have had second thoughts as he launched social and sexual practices in direct conflict with the Judaeo-Christian ethic and the established mores of American society. According to one of his followers, Smith had to be assured by revelation that he had not committed adultery. To detractors, particularly those in the church who were beginning to look askance at his vigorous round of experimentation and innovation, the revelation could be justification for transgression.[27]

## IV

After the death of Joseph Smith Mormonism continued to totter in precarious balance and began to split into numerous sects. Although Brigham Young professed to continue in the tradition of his predecessor, more conservative policies imply a recognition of the centrifugal forces that were pulling Mormonism apart during the Nauvoo years. If polygamy in Utah, publicly announced in 1852, was a major aberration from the social mores of Protestant America, its public, institutionalized, carefully-regulated practice involved social controls far beyond those recorded in the days of Joseph Smith. At the same time, its external controls contrasted sharply with the internal controls and self-repression that were the essential features of "modern" morality.[28]

In Utah Mormons developed a greater degree of self-consciousness about sexual matters. An increasing defensiveness in Mormon publications seems directly related to the announcement of polygamy in 1852. Anticipating or responding to charges of sexual profligacy, the Saints began to compare their supposedly superior sexual morality to a sexually corrupt Babylon. Because gentiles stressed that polygamy provided a convenient means of sexual gratification for men, the Saints now emphasized more strongly than before the idea that the primary if not the only purpose of marriage, monogamous or polygamous, was to have offspring. Sexual relations, said Heber C. Kimball, were not "to gratify the lusts of the flesh, but to raise up children." One of sociologist James Hulett's informants reported that "his father was sexually interested in his wives only for the purposes of procreation, and the Principle could not be lived in any other way."[29]

When M. R. Werner, a biographer of Brigham Young, coined the phrase "puritan polygamy," he probably was not far off the mark. It was an impression consistent with the observations of Richard Burton, the famous English traveller and linguist, who visited the city of the Saints in 1861. Burton reported that "All sensuality in the married state is strictly forbidden beyond the requisite for ensuring progeny—the practice, in fact, of Adam, and Abraham." He quoted one of his informants, Belinda Pratt, as saying that according to the Old Testament, during prescribed periods of gestation and lactation, sexual relations were prohibited: "should her husband come to her bed under such circumstances, he would commit a gross sin both against the laws of nature and the wise provisions of God's law, as revealed in His word; in short, he would commit an abomination."[30]

In Kimball's opinion, any man violating the divine laws of sexual conduct had no right to procreation: "if I am not a good man, I have no just right in this Church to a wife or wives, or to the power to propagate my species. What, then should be done with me? Make a eunuch of me, and stop my propagation." His hyperbolic solution, however, appears to have been intended for the life after death, in keeping with Parley P. Pratt's statement that "If they choose in this world to follow the wicked lusts and pleasures of the moment, . . . then . . . death closes the scene, and eternity finds them poor wanderers and outcasts from the commonwealth of the celestial family, and strangers to the covenant of promise."[31]

Thus the principle of deferred compensation found its way into the sexual economics of the kingdom of God, "this being the world of preparation and that the world of enjoyment," as Pratt put it. Under the "law of forfeiture," in the next life wives of men who had proved themselves "wholly unfit to sustain the sacred relationship of a husband . . . will most assuredly be given to the comparatively few men who keep themselves pure, and fulfil the laws made known to them from heaven." If there was an excess of righteous women over men eligible for the highest degree of glory, simple justice mandated polygamy in heaven to assure that all eligible women attained the exaltation they deserved. The polygamous husband was thus able all the more to increase his kingdom.[32]

For those who were able to control their sexual impulses, the rewards were awesome. According to an article in the *Millennial Star,* "the fountains of life are the source of His glory, dominion, and power. They are the germ of an infinitude of good if used only for pure and righteous purposes, and of unlimited evil if perverted and corrupted. Either way the consequences resulting are incalculable, and can only be measured by the mind that can grasp eternities of existence." Those who had the vision to live their lives in conformity with such insights and entered into the eternal covenant of plural marriage, said Brigham Young, would "hold control over the elements, and have power by their word to command the creation and redemption of worlds or to extinguish such by their breath, and disorganize worlds, hurling them back into their chaotic state. This is what you and I are created for." What, by comparison, were the sinful pleasures of this world?[33]

This awesome conception of the power of sex was supported by a positive philosophy of sex that gentiles found nothing less than blasphemous. In the opinion of Mormons, the traditional Christian world view was essentially hostile to human sexuality, supported as it was by a metaphysical dualism that elevated the soul above the body, mind above matter, spirit above flesh. Seen from this perspective, sex was at best a necessary evil to ensure the continuation of the human race. But because in Mormon theology the dichotomy between mind and matter has been eliminated, because, as Joseph Smith said, "all spirit is matter," and "nothing exists which is not material," sex in theory did not represent the corruption of the flesh against the sublimity of the spirit.

This spirit-matter continuum is complemented by a rejection of the traditional Christian view of men and women as contingent beings dependent on the existence of God. In the view of Joseph Smith, we are coeternal with God—"necessary beings"—and like God without beginning and end. In a certain sense, sexuality is a part of our eternal nature, even if its manifestation in mortality differs from that in other forms of existence. Orson Pratt asked rhetorically, "Will that principle of love which exists now, and which has existed from the beginning, exist after the resurrection?" His answer was in the affirmative.[34]

One of the most important consequences of this premise, and one that distinguished Mormonism radically from other Christian religions, is that sexuality is not a result of sin. This could hardly have been otherwise, since at least some Mormon leaders believe that the human spirits in the preexistence were begotten "upon the same principle that we reproduce one another." Consistent with such beliefs, Mormons rejected the notion of original sin.[35]

Pushing this literal-mindedness to its extreme, Mormons argue that divine sexuality is but an elevated form of human sexuality. Mary's conception of Jesus was interpreted as meaning that though she had not been touched by mortal man, God had literally begotten his son as we are by our fathers. For some Mormon authorities, it followed further that Jesus too was required to fulfil the law "to multiply and replenish the earth." In the opinion of Apostle Orson

Hyde, Jesus begat children, and in so doing "only did that which he had seen his Father do." It followed that both God and Jesus were married.[36]

It remained for a woman, Eliza R. Snow, plural wife of Joseph Smith and later Brigham Young, to pursue this idea to its logical conclusion in perhaps the most popular and certainly the most Mormon of all hymns, "O, My Father"[37]: "In the Heavens, are parents single?/ No! The thought makes reason stare!/ Truth is reason, truth eternal/ Tells me I've a mother there."

The next step might well have been the worship of this heavenly mother along with God the Father. For a number of compelling reasons, however, this did not happen. Most Mormons were Protestants before conversion. However much they saw Mormonism as a repudiation of the sectarianism of the Protestant tradition, they were emotionally unprepared for a practice that might have reminded them too much of "popery." For most Protestants, Maryolatry was a distasteful excess of Catholicism, and worship of a Mormon heavenly mother might have been too reminiscent of that practice.

A more important reason was that Mormon leadership was a male prerogative. The Mormon priesthood was for males only. They were under greater obligation than women to do right, and under greater condemnation if they sinned. "Whatever may be the character, conduct, or wishes of woman, the Lord expects man to do right, independent of her influence." According to Mormon theology, it was Eve who was led astray by the serpent. Adam, on the other hand, was not deceived, but acted in full knowledge of what he was doing, making a rational choice between two conflicting divine commandments. In emulation of Adam, man—not woman—was to be "a great centralizing power which will draw congenial spirits under his control." Therefore, "the man should stand at the head of and be the controlling power in his family, and they should yield the most implicit obedience to his counsels." It was the male who held responsibility for the salvation of his family, "and if he leads them astray, he will have to answer for it in their stead."[38]

Woman's role was clearly more circumscribed. Since her sexuality was regarded as passive, she lacked the broad sphere enjoyed by man for the exercise of free agency. Although she was "one of the choicest gifts of God to man," the Lord intended that she "should be obedient to the man. He made her the weakest of the two, and implanted in her nature a disposition to cleave to man, and a desire to please him and be obedient to his wishes." It is "under the guidance of a noble lord striving to magnify his manhood, [that] she becomes all that God and nature designed her to be." Such ideas, still current among contemporary Mormons, are a major reason for their strong opposition to the Equal Rights Amendment and feminism.[39]

In the opinion of one nineteenth-century observer, however, Mormons in those days did not place their women on a pedestal. According to Richard Burton, the Mormon woman was "not petted and spoiled as in the Eastern States; the inevitable revolution, indeed, has rather placed her below par, where, however, I believe her to be happier than when set upon an uncomfortable and unnatural eminence."[40] This situation, however, may have been more a result of necessity than of ideology. In the Mormon frontier environment, social realities worked against the male ideal envisioned by many a Mormon patriarch. For if Mormon women had meekly submitted to the male bias of their presumed superiors, it is doubtful that the group led by Brigham Young would have become the largest and most successful of the numerous movements claiming to be the heirs of Joseph Smith. As Leonard Arrington has observed, the survival of Mormon society in the Great Basin hinged largely on the courageous and self-reliant family leadership of those innumerable pioneer women whose husbands were forever abroad, on foreign missions, or who could devote only a limited amount of time to each family because of their polygamous obligations.[41] Significantly, it is only after Mormonism succumbed to the forces of modernization that we begin to encounter among the Saints what Christopher Lasch has called "that pious cant about the sanctity of motherhood, the sanctity of home and hearth, which was the real mark of women's degradation" in the nineteenth century. Women in territorial Utah had more in common in many ways with their sisters in colonial America than with their nineteenth-century American contemporaries.[42] Male roles likewise were determined at least as much by the social and economic realities of subsistence agriculture as by the ideology of priesthood supremacy. It was not until the twentieth century that Mormon women were raised onto that same pedestal from which their nineteenth-century antagonists had barely escaped.

V

This transformation in sex roles was part of a larger process of the "embourgeoisement" of Mormon culture after the Civil War–a period during which the Saints began to adapt to the forces of modernization by internalizing their sexual mores. By its very nature this process cannot be imposed by ecclesiastical fiat, but is by and large a spontaneous response to cultural change to which the institution must adapt itself if it wishes to survive. The plausibility of this theory is supported by the work of anthropologist Mark Leone, in whose opinion modern Mormonism developed a high degree of "adaptability" in its value system, which derived to a large extent from the sensitivity of its members to the cultural environment, as well as the ability of the Saints to influence the world around them: "Under the guise of strict literalism exists a diffuseness, individual inventiveness, and variability through time that contradicts usual views of the Mormon belief system." What Leone has done is to apply sociologist Robert Bellah's concept of "modern religion" to Mormonism; both have an ability to absorb and generate change.[43] Certainly without this adaptability it is doubtful that Mormonism would have been able to survive the elimination of those social, economic, and political institutions that were virtually synonymous with its cultural identity in the nineteenth century. These institutions rested on a theology that made Mormonism a "religion of the word," one that had a strong ideological orientation, stressing belief as much as behavior. As late as 1867 this emphasis is illustrated in the Godbeite heresy, which represented a more "modern" view by refusing to acknowledge the prophet's right to dictate to them "in all things temporal and spiritual." In an excommunication trial, "the High Council affirmed that this was contrary to church doctrine," and that the defendants "might as well ask whether [they] could honestly differ from the Almighty."[44]

The social and intellectual transformation that occurred is perhaps best illustrated by church president Joseph F. Smith in 1903 during the controversy over the seating of Mormon apostle Reed Smoot in the U.S. Senate. Smith said: "Our people are given the largest possible latitude for their convictions and if a man rejects a message that I may give him *but is still moral* and believes in the main principles of the gospel and desires to continue his membership in the church, he is permitted to remain and he is not unchurched" (my emphasis). By this time, Mormonism was well on its way to adopting the kind of self-revising value system that Bellah describes in *Beyond Belief* and that Leone sees as the key to modern Mormonism.[45]

Among American Protestant churches this transformation had largely occurred in the antebellum period. Under the impact of a pluralistic denominationalism, churches emphasized conduct more than belief, thus serving as effective tools of modernization. Tocqueville acutely observed: "Go into the churches, you will hear morality preached, of dogma not a word."[46] Mormonism now went the route of its erstwhile antagonists. Between 1880 and 1920, Mormonism experienced a profound cultural transformation reminiscent of the shift from Puritan to Yankee, of the shift from belief to behavior, of the shift from the total system in which religion encompassed all facets of life and the social order to one in which religion became "self-revising" to adapt itself to social, economic, and political change.

Internalized moral norms became an essential compass in this restless new world. As among the modernizing Protestants of antebellum America, abstinence from alcohol and sexual restraint became more important signifiers of faith than belief. It is no accident that in this period we perceive an intensified Mormon campaign for observance of the Word of Wisdom and an increase in excommunications due to sexual transgression (even though excommunications in general declined in this period). As among antebellum Protestants, sin was increasingly equated with sex, if not according to official doctrine, certainly according to the manner in which church authorities enforced compliance with sexual norms, thus shaping a quasi-official attitude. An early indicator of this changing climate of opinion was the expurgation of Joseph Smith's autobiography.[47]

In pioneer Utah numerous community sanctions had been applied to enforce sexual morality. As in colonial society, the community informally enforced its moral values. This was facilitated by a relative lack of privacy reinforced by settlement patterns. Like the New England village, the Mormon village consisted of houses that clustered in close proximity. Few families could afford separate rooms for each of their members.[48] At the same time, in a society that was primarily agrarian sexual pressures were somewhat minimized because most young people married early. Brigham Young encouraged young men to marry at the age of eighteen. Richard Burton reports that "girls rarely remain single past sixteen."[49] Thus the need for strict sexual control of adolescents was diminished.

As society became more urbanized and industrialized, early marriage became socially less desirable, or even possible. As marriages were postponed to a later age, sexual pressures understandably increased, thus necessitating greater sexual control. The need for greater control, however, coincided with the dissolution of traditional institutions. Given the premium Mormons continued to place on sexual purity, internalization of sexual mores was a necessary and inevitable response to social change. Leonard Arrington suggested that in this period the Word of Wisdom became a symbol of identification.[50] Sexual morality may well have become an even more profound symbol of identity. Again we are reminded that sex served an analogous function among upwardly mobile, antebellum, middle-class Americans.

This social transformation had its early beginnings at about the same time that Mormonism experienced an internal backlash against polygamy. Having been branded as sexual outcasts, the Saints may well have felt they had to "out-Victorian" the Victorians to become respectable members of American society. Quite possibly, Mormons went through a response analogous to the one Charles Rosenberg observed among aspiring members of the lower orders of Victorian England and America through "repression of sexuality."[51] Nevertheless, if the polygamy backlash contributed to the embourgeoisement of Mormon culture, a more profound and important reason, I believe, was the internalization of modern behavior patterns. In fact, the development of the modern Mormon personality may have contributed as much to the ultimate demise of polygamy as did the crusade of the gentiles.

By the 1870s polygamy was passively resisted by many devout Saints who quietly practiced monogamy. At the same time, this "relic of barbarism," as the Republican party platform branded polygamy, was more actively opposed by a growing number of Mormons who were beginning to embrace the social, economic, and political values of modern America. I believe it is possible to argue that when the Saints, by the turn of the twentieth century, gave up the political kingdom of God, communitarianism, and plural marriage, they did so as much from an internal response to modernization as from external pressure. It is not improbable that had it not been for the anti-polygamy crusade, this relic of barbarism, unlike its twin slavery, might have died with a whimper rather than a bang.

In any case the demise of polygamy signified the beginning of the end for Mormonism as a total institution. By the 1880s the modern market economy was invading Utah with a rush. Because its leaders had kept the government of the political kingdom secret, they were able to hang on to it a bit longer. But with the death of plural marriage the political kingdom seems to have died on the vine. The signs of the times were clearly irreversible. By the end of World War I most Saints had become as modern as their erstwhile antagonists.

## VI

In recent years the American sexual drama has opened to another scene. Some commentators have called its ethos postmodern, characterized by norms that are becoming increasingly tolerant of pre- and extramarital sex, abortion, and nonjudgmental attitudes toward masturbation and homosexuality. Twentieth-century American society has clearly moved away from sexual self-control and self-repression—those inner-directed norms of nineteenth-century individualism—toward "sexual liberation." Mormons understandably see such norms as a threat to their own values and are discovering that internalization of morals leading to self-control is increasingly difficult to achieve. Considerable evidence points to an emerging tendency of Mormons to return to externally sanctioned mechanisms of social control. In recent times these have resulted not only in stricter surveillance of sexual morality and observance of the Word of Wisdom, especially among adolescents, but also in stricter standards of grooming and dress, for example, at Brigham Young University. For better or for worse, it is these symbols of behavior that are increasingly determining who and what a Mormon is. Modern Mormons have clearly joined "a nation of behavers."[52]

Yet it may come as a shock to modern Americans that these same Mormons still profess to believe in the principle of plural marriage. As a matter of fact the entire Mormon belief system is still very much intact. Supporting Marty's thesis, Jan Shipps has demonstrated that anti-Mormon crusaders were offended not so much by Mormon beliefs but by their sociopolitical behavior. After the Saints wholeheartedly embraced political pluralism, economic individualism, and the monogamous nuclear family they were permitted to believe as they chose. A telling illustration of this attitude is the remark of a prominent participant in the Smoot hearings that he preferred "a polygamist that didn't polyg [Smoot] to a monogamist that didn't monog."[53]

This raises an interesting question about the possible reintroduction of polygamy among Mormons. It is not inconceivable that a postmodern American society may extend its liberalized attitude toward sexual behavior to the principle of plural marriage, or even same-sex marriage, and that at some future date the United States Supreme Court may overturn *Reynolds* v. *United States* just as the Warren Court overturned *Plessy* v. *Ferguson.* Should that happen, what would the response of Mormons be? My crystal ball, admittedly, is cloudy. Nevertheless, I can hardly believe that the Saints would be overjoyed at such a decision. No doubt they will be able to avoid the unpleasant prospect of reintroducing polygamy, for example, should they be faced with such a choice. That, however, does not make such a situation any less ironic.

### *NOTES*

1. "The Puritans and Sex," *New England Quarterly* 15 (1942): 591-607; *The Puritan Family: Religion and Domestic Relations in Seventeenth-Century New England* (rev. ed.: New York, 1966), 29-64; John Demos, *A Little Commonwealth: Family Life in Plymouth Colony* (New York, 1970); Michael Vernon Wells, "Sex and the Law in Colonial New England," Ph.D. diss., Ohio State University, 1974.

2. Daniel Scott Smith and Michael S. Hindus, "Premarital Pregnancy in America, 1640-1971: An Overview and Interpretation," *Journal of Interdisciplinary History* 5 (Spring 1975), 538.

3. Three important works dealing with this transformation from differing perspectives are Ronald D. Walters, *American Reformers, 1815-1860* (New York, 1978); Richard D. Brown, *Modernization: The Transformation of American Life, 1600-1865* (New York, 1976); and Joseph R. Gusfield, *Symbolic Crusade: Status Politics and the American Temperance Movement* (Urbana, IL, 1966).

4. See Ronald G. Walters, ed., *Primers for Prudery: Sexual Advice to Victorian America* (Englewood Cliffs, NJ, 1974).

5. Stephen W. Nissenbaum, "Sex, Reform, and Social Change," quoted in Walters, *Primers for Prudery*, 17; "Sexuality, Class and Role in Nineteenth-Century America," *American Quarterly* 25 (May 1973): 136.

6. Based on an examination of 84 trials prior to the death of Joseph Smith, in Joseph Smith, Jr., et al., *History of the Church of Jesus Christ of Latter-day Saints*, ed. B. H. Roberts, 6 vols. (Salt Lake City, 1948). Sexual transgression is an issue in only three cases. Out of twenty-seven "disfellowship" cases (a member may not partake of the sacrament and exercise his priesthood) only two involved sexual irregularities.

7. Steven Marcus, *The Other Victorians: A Study of Sexuality and Pornography in Mid-Nineteenth-Century England* (New York, 1966); Ronald Walters, "Sexuality and Reform in Nineteenth-Century America," paper presented at Seminar in American Civilization, Columbia University, 19 Sept. 1974.

8. "Sexuality, Class and Role," 143.

9. Gusfield, *Symbolic Crusade*, 46-57.

10. Leonard J. Arrington, "An Economic Interpretation of the 'Word of Wisdom'," *Brigham Young University Studies* 1 (Winter 1959): 40-41. Significantly, references to violations of the Word of Wisdom were eliminated from the edition of the *History of the Church* published in 1902.

11. "Sexuality, Class and Role," 145; H. Tristram Engelhardt, Jr., "The Disease of Masturbation: Values and the Concept of Disease," *Bulletin of the History of Medicine* 48 (Summer 1974): 234-48.

12. Quoted in Davis Bitton, "B. H. Roberts as Historian," *Dialogue: A Journal of Mormon Thought* 3 (Winter 1968): 31-32.

13. *Deseret News Extra*, 14 Sept. 1852. Added to the D&C as sec. 132 in 1876.

14. Ezra Booth to *Ohio Star*, 8 Dec. 1831, quoted in Jerald Tanner and Sandra Tanner, *Mormonism Like Watergate?* (Salt Lake City, 1974), 9.

15. See especially Foster, "Between Two Worlds"; also Danel Bachman, "A Study of the Mormon Practice of Plural Marriage before the Death of Joseph Smith," M.A. thesis, Indiana-Purdue University, 1975; a useful survey of the scholarly literature is Davis Bitton, "Mormon Polygamy: A Review Article," *Journal of Mormon History* 4 (1977): 101-108.

16. Quoted in William Alexander Linn, *The Story of the Mormons* (New York, 1902), 280; *Biography of Lorenzo Snow* (Salt Lake City, 1884), 70.

17. Fawn Brodie, *No Man Knows My History: The Life of Joseph Smith the Mormon Prophet*, 2d ed. (New York, 1971), 297.

18. Quoted in Ronald G. Walters, "The Erotic South," *American Quarterly* 25 (May 1973): 196.

19. I find support for this assertion in my reading of Valeen Tippetts

Avery and Linda King Newell, *Mormon Enigma: Emma Hale Smith* (Garden City, NY: Doubleday, 1984).

20. "The Future of Political Science in America," quoted in "George Bernard Shaw Speaks," *Improvement Era* 40 (July 1937): 413.

21. Foster, "Between Two Worlds," 189-403.

22. Ibid., 226.

23. See William E. Bridges, "Family Patterns and Social Values in America, 1825-1875," *American Quarterly* 17 (Spring 1965): 311; Kirk Jeffrey, Jr., "The Family as Utopian Retreat from the City: The Nineteenth-Century Contribution," *Soundings: An Interdisciplinary Journal* 55 (1972): 21-41; Ronald G. Walters, "The Family and Ante-bellum Reform: An Interpretation," *Societas* 3 (1973): 221-32.

24. Quoted in Lawrence Foster, "A Little-known Defense of Polygamy from the Mormon Press in 1842," *Dialogue: A Journal of Mormon Thought* 9 (Winter 1974): 26; I am assuming here that a pamphlet, titled *The Peace Maker,* from which Foster quotes, represents the ideas of Joseph Smith.

25. Quoted in Foster, "Between Two Worlds," 258.

26. Alexis de Tocqueville, *Democracy in America,* trans. Henry Reeve, ed. Phillips Bradley, 2 vols. (New York, 1942), 2:105-106.

27. Joseph Lee Robinson, Journal, 22, archives, historical department, Church of Jesus Christ of Latter-day Saints, Salt Lake City, Utah.

28. Leonard Arrington has suggested that "the conditions under which Brigham Young and the Twelve Apostles assumed leadership assured a hierarchical structure designed along authoritarian lines. The theophanous works of Joseph Smith were canonized into doctrine, and the doctrine and organizational structure of the church became more dogmatic and inflexible" ("The Intellectual Tradition of the Latter-day Saints," *Dialogue: A Journal of Mormon Thought* 4 [Spring 1969]: 18; see also Ephraim E. Eriksen, *Psychological and Ethical Aspects of Mormon Group Life* [Chicago, 1922], 35-36).

29. *Journal of Discourses* 5:91 (herafter JD); James Edward Hulett, "The Sociological and Social Psychological Aspects of the Mormon Polygamous Family," Ph.D. diss., University of Wisconsin, 1939, 37.

30. Belinda Pratt, in Burton, *City of the Saints* (London, 1861), 520.

31. JD 5:49; *Millennial Star* 5:193.

32. *Millennial Star* 17:726; see also JD 2:83. Hundreds of wives were "sealed" to Smith posthumously, among them the Empress Josephine. See Thomas Milton Tinney, "The Royal Family of the Prophet Joseph Smith, Jr," 1973, typescript, Utah State Historical Society, Salt Lake City.

33. JD 3:356.

34. Ibid. 12:186; see also Sterling McMurrin, *Theological Foundations of the Mormon Religion* (Salt Lake City: University of Utah Press, 1965), 3-5, 49-57; D&C 93:29; Smith, *History of the Church,* 6:310-12. For a dissenting Mormon view, see Lowell Bennion, "This-Worldly and Other-Worldly Sex:

A Response," *Dialogue: A Journal of Mormon Thought* 2 (Autumn 1967): 106-108: "We do not know that [sex] is eternal. As we know sex it is physical and biological as well as social and spiritual. Who can speak of the resurrected state in physiological terms with any knowledge or meaning?"

35. JD 5:254; 6:101; James Talmage, *Jesus the Christ* (Salt Lake City, 1922), 30.

36. JD 2:210; 8:115, 211; 13:407. For a modern Protestant argument that Christ was married, see William Phipps, *Was Jesus Married?* (New York, 1971).

37. See Hymn no. 138, in *Hymns; The Church of Jesus Christ of Latter-day Saints* (Salt Lake City: Church of Jesus Christ of Latter-day Saints, 1948). Mormon apologists will no doubt find remarkable parallels if not confirmation of the Mormon position in the recently translated Gnostic gospels discovered in 1945 in the caves of Nag Hammadi in upper Egypt. See Elaine Pagels, "The Suppressed Gnostic Feminism," *New York Review of Books* 26 (22 Nov. 1979): 42-49; *The Gnostic Gospels* (New York, 1979).

38. *Millennial Star* 17:722-23; 19:717; 20:817; Ileen Ann Le Cheminant, "The Status of Woman in the Philosophy of Mormonism from 1830-1845," M.A. thesis, Brigham Young University, 1942.

39. The case of Sonia Johnson, who was excommunicated from the Mormon church because of her opposition to the anti-ERA stand of the hierarchy, received wide coverage in the news media.

40. *City of the Saints*, 529.

41. Leonard Arrington, "Blessed Damozels: Women in Mormon History," *Dialogue: A Journal of Mormon Thought* 6 (Summer 1971): 22-31.

42. "The Mormon Utopia," *The World of Nations* (New York, 1971), 57. The most influential interpretation is Barbara Welter, "The Cult of True Womanhood: 1820-1860," *American Quarterly* 18 (1966): 151-74.

43. Mark P. Leone, "The Economic Basis for the Evolution of the Mormon Religion," in Irving R. Zaretsky and Mark P. Leone, eds., *Religious Movements in Contemporary America* (Princeton, NJ, 1974), 751-52; Robert Bellah, *Beyond Belief* (New York, 1970).

44. Edward W. Tullidge, "The Godbeite Movement," *Tullidge's Quarterly Magazine* 1 (1880): 32.

45. U.S., Congress, Senate, *Proceedings before the Committee on Privileges and Elections of the United States Senate in the Matter of the Protest against the Right Hon. Reed Smoot, A Senator from the State of Utah, to Hold His Seat*, 4 vols. (Washington, D.C., 1904-1907), 1:97-99.

46. Quoted in Martin Marty, *A Nation of Behavers* (New York, 1976), 201.

47. See for example the minutes of the St. George Stake High Council, 1862-, as reported in Nels Anderson, *Desert Saints: The Mormon Frontier in Utah* (Chicago, 1942), 146-48.

48. According to the laws of the kingdom of God, adultery was punishable by death, though enforcement of the law cannot be documented.

Gustive O. Larson suggests the possibility of enforcement during "The Mormon Reformation," *Utah Historical Quarterly* 26 (1958): 60-63. The community, however, condoned and perhaps encouraged extra-legal action. See, for example, the celebrated case of The *United States v. Howard Egan,* in October 1851. Egan had tracked down and killed the seducer of his wife, James Monroe. In his plea for the defense Mormon apostle George A. Smith argued that by the standards of the community Egan had no choice but to kill Monroe. Egan was acquitted. See JD 1 (1854): 95-103; Lowry Nelson, *The Mormon Village: A Pattern and Technique of Land Settlement* (Salt Lake City, 1952).

49. JD 12:194; *City of the Saints,* 518.

50. "An Economic Interpretation of the 'Word of Wisdom,'" 47.

51. "Sexuality, Class and Role," 149.

52. Harold T. Christensen, "Mormon Sexuality in Cross-Cultural Perspective," *Dialogue: A Journal of Mormon Thought* 10 (Autumn 1976): 62-75; Harold T. Christensen and Kenneth L. Cannon, "The Fundamentalist Emphasis in Contemporary Mormonism: A 1935-1973 Trend Analysis of Brigham Young University Student Responses," privately circulated.

53. "From Satyr to Saint: American Attitudes toward the Mormons, 1860-1960," 23-25, paper presented at Annual Meeting, Organzation of American Historians, Chicago, 1973.

3.

# "They Shall Be One Flesh": Sexuality and Contemporary Mormonism

*Romel W. Mackelprang*

SEVERAL YEARS AGO I PRESENTED A SERIES OF GUEST LECTURES ON sexuality to undergraduate nursing classes at Brigham Young University's Salt Lake Center. My presentations were aimed at preparing students for their work with patients with severe neurological disabilities. During my first presentation I was dismayed at the lack of student interaction in a subject that in other settings usually met with lively discussion. I was even more surprised after the class by the number of students (all of them LDS) who wanted to talk privately about personal sexual matters. When it came to highly personal questions related to sexuality and church policy, students were extremely anxious to talk privately with someone who shared their religious beliefs but who did not know them personally or was not in an ecclesiastical position over them. As I spoke with these students I was struck by the uncertainty and in some cases guilt some were experiencing as they attempted to fit their sexuality with their religious convictions. In subsequent presentations at BYU, in speeches to church groups, and in counseling sessions with church members, I have noted the same phenomenon.

My experience in clinical practice has taught me that to help church members with sexual problems it is almost always essential to address contributing religious issues. My LDS clients' sexual problems seem to be no more severe or pervasive than those of members of other religions or of those who profess no religious affiliation. However, when sexual problems occur, religious issues are more likely to be a factor for LDS clients than for any others (with the possible exception of Catholics). However unintentional, church membership contributes to sexual problems for some people. This essay addresses sexuality in the context of Mormonism and explores ways to promote healthy attitudes about sexuality and sexual expression.

Church leaders sometimes convey conflicting messages to members regarding sexuality. On the one hand, they repeatedly and forcefully emphasize that sexual activity is to be reserved for marriage. They characterize masturbation and other autoerotic activity as sins and teach that sexual contact outside of marriage may be grounds for church action that can jeopardize membership. In fact, leaders stress that adultery is second only to the "shedding of innocent blood" in seriousness. Moral sins of a sexual nature require confession to the Lord and bishop or other ecclesiastical leaders for the transgressor to receive full forgiveness. Furthermore, some leaders consider homosexuality to be so grievous a sin that they do not differentiate between sexual orientation and sexual activity in calling for action against gay men and lesbians.

Church leaders strongly and frequently emphasize the serious nature of sexual sins to members, especially young members. Bishops conduct regular worthiness interviews with adolescents from the age of twelve through young adulthood. Moral cleanliness is a major focus of those interviews. Ironically, "sins of immorality" are almost always defined as sexual in nature, a position that ignores the plethora of other immoral acts in which people engage. These regular opportunities for teens to confess their sexual sins to church leaders are intended to help young members remain chaste. Some bishops have even "helped" them by requiring them to confess their sins to their parents as well. Unfortunately, some adolescents learn to avoid the potentially negative consequences of confession simply by withholding information. For example, in one ward in which I lived the bishop required deacons to tell their parents if they confessed to masturbation in priesthood interviews, whereupon several quickly learned to avoid this embarrassment by denying such activity.

An all-too-common societal double standard sometimes surfaces in LDS culture as well: while sexual immorality is wrong for members of both genders, it is especially bad for females. This attitude sometimes becomes apparent when my clients and I discuss their sexual histories. For example, LDS men frequently talk about premarital masturbation as though almost all boys have masturbated. LDS women, on the other hand, are far more likely to display embarrassment and guilt about masturbation.

On the positive side, church members are taught that sex in marriage is a special way of sharing with one's mate. The act of procreation is as close to being godlike as men and women can become. Sex is sanctioned in marriage, especially when the intent is to bring children into the world. Unfortunately, the messages urging restraint and the warnings against sexual sin, even between husband and wife, greatly outnumber positive messages. Rarely do church leaders affirm the pleasure and gratification brought about by satisfying intimate physical relationships, choosing instead to focus on the negative aspects of sexuality.

From the time of conception, humans experience the effects of gender. Genetics and, within weeks, hormone production begin a life-long process of sexual influence. Gender differences are present at birth and, through a combination of biological and environmental influences, continue throughout life. Infant exploration of the genitals is as common and natural as are other attempts to explore the environment. Some of the earliest negative messages about sexuality come from parents who, upon seeing this natural exploration, react adversely, even punitively. As children grow, they encounter similar messages. Boys and girls are taught to not touch themselves and are sometimes told that their genitals are undesirable or "nasty." This may be especially true for girls who, unlike boys, have no "legitimate" reason to regularly touch or view their genitalia. Girls may grow to womanhood without learning what their genitals look like or even the proper names of their sexual organs. An example of this was related to me by the nurse of a young, acutely disabled woman I was counseling. As the nurse began to teach this woman and her mother how to insert a catheter into the bladder, the mother asked about the "little mound of tissue" that was her daughter's clitoris. When the nurse offered an explanation, this mother of five adults expressed surprise, having always assumed that the clitoris was inside the vagina.

As children reach adolescence, they experience greater physiological, social, and psychological changes than at any other time in their lives. They develop new and confusing urges. The attitudes of parents and other adults help create either a positive sexual perspective or confusion and disproportionate feelings of guilt. When adults do not balance messages about the pitfalls of inappropriate behavior with reinforcement of the special nature of sexuality, adolescents who "fall" may believe that "all is lost," an attitude that can often lead to promiscuity among those who prematurely engage in sexual experimentation.[1]

Parents have a responsibility to teach their adolescent children not only about morality and the implications of sexual expression, but also about the physical processes their bodies undergo as they mature. Those who do so conscientiously will reap great benefits for their efforts. Teaching proper sexual terminology in toddlerhood and progressing to comprehensive sexual discussions in adolescence promote greater awareness and help circumvent future problems. Parents and church leaders should present information and counsel in frank, positive ways rather than in negative, moralistic terms. A possible consequence of such a negative, moralistic approach was evident in a woman I counseled who had an aversion to sexual intimacy. She related that the most powerful message about sex she received from her parents was, "I would rather see you dead than have you be immoral." Though she was now a married adult, her overwhelming fear of doing something forbidden, even with her spouse, continued to plague her.

Discomfort with sexuality is manifest in the numerous euphemisms we use to refer to sexual anatomy. We would not think of using slang to refer to an arm or leg, but sexual slang could fill volumes. Parents who have difficulty using words such as "penis" or "vagina" convey their discomfort to their children, who quickly learn to avoid using accurate sexual terminology. When parents are embarrassed by their children's questions about sex and reproduction, they teach their children to be likewise embarrassed. When parents neglect to discuss sexuality with their children, they almost ensure that their children's education will be inaccurate and inappropriate. Ironically, many of these same parents oppose any attempts by public schools or other groups to provide sexual information.

This negative attitude towards sexual education can be seen in a statement by Rodney Turner, an LDS author and BYU religion professor who contends, "It was the father of lies who introduced sex education into the world."[2] When parents do not inform and schools are not allowed to educate, where do young people turn to find answers to their very natural questions? They rely on movies, magazines, books, or older friends who provide information that is often as limited as it is inaccurate.

Some parents teach children that sex is dirty and undesirable. People from families where such attitudes are overtly taught or, more often, unwittingly conveyed may come to view sex as base and vulgar. I find this attitude most often in women who were taught as girls that sex is a responsibility and a duty to be borne solely for the satisfaction of their spouses or the begetting of children. The idea of sex for personal and mutual gratification is a totally foreign concept to them. Most church leaders would agree that this sentiment is destructive to relationships but seldom offer sexually affirming messages that would reinforce more positive attitudes.

Although there is no evidence that accurate sexual knowledge promotes premature sexual activity, it is clear that the lack of knowledge leads to problems. The 1989 *General Handbook of Instructions* for church leaders is clear on the subject of sex education: "Parents have primary responsibility for the sex education of their children. Teaching this subject honestly and plainly in the home really improves the chance that our people will avoid serious problems. To help parents teach this sensitive and crucial information, the church has published 'A Parent's Guide.' . . . When schools have undertaken sex education, it is appropriate for parents to seek to ensure that the instructions given their children are consistent with sound moral and ethical values."[3] Sex education, then, is the responsibility of parents. First, to provide information and, second, to monitor and supplement information children receive from others.

To help LDS parents fulfill this responsibility, specific, church-produced or -endorsed training materials seem essential. Unfortunately, church authorities have historically been reluctant to produce such materials. Kenneth Cannon, a Brigham Young University professor, wrote about a project commissioned by Alvin R. Dyer to produce for the Mormon church an educational manual entitled

"Human Maturity." Although hundreds of hours were devoted to its production, the manual was never published.[4] Cannon also reports that lessons on sexuality, developed for inclusion in church instructional manuals, were likewise never published. In 1985, however, the church published *A Parent's Guide*, a booklet that includes some open and frank discussions of sex and sexuality designed for parents of children ranging in age from infancy to young adulthood. To date, it is the best effort by the church to deal with the broad range of sexual issues confronting church members. Unfortunately, the vast majority of those members are unaware of its existence.

The problems of sexual ignorance and the rampant discomfort about sexuality could be ameliorated with a positive, concerted effort by church leaders to disseminate frank, comprehensive, and positive sexual educational materials. The *Parent's Guide* is a positive step, but much more information, more widely available, is needed.

Marriage is the ultimate experience for many Latter-day Saints, who look to it for the emotional and physical bonding it offers. Physical expressions of love have both scriptural and ecclesiastical sanction. In fact, the Lord's first commandment to men and women, recorded in Genesis 2:24, deals specifically with sex and marriage: "Therefore shall a man leave his father and his mother, and shall cleave unto his wife: and they shall be one flesh." There is little doubt about the meaning of this verse. Sexual intercourse was not only approved, it is strongly encouraged. It is important to note that this command was given independent of any reference to having children—becoming "one flesh" was an end in and of itself.

In the modern LDS church the purpose most often given for sexual relationships between husbands and wives has been procreation. Sex is approved to strengthen the spiritual bonds between spouses, but references by general authorities to sexual activity solely for enjoyment and physical pleasure are few. Far more common are references to marital sex as being appropriate if restrained and kept within "normal" limits. For example, in *The Miracle of Forgiveness*, Apostle Spencer W. Kimball devoted fifteen pages to the pitfalls of sexual impurity, added a line briefly condoning a "normal and *controlled* sex life,"[5] but offered no elaboration on what constitutes controlled sex. Church president Joseph F. Smith had earlier stated, "Sexual union is lawful in wedlock, and if participated in with right intent is honorable and sanctifying,"[6] a notion that President Kimball echoed when he wrote that "pure sex life in marriage is approved."[7] But while he sanctioned sexual expression as appropriate, in the same section of the book he stated, "The doctrine that the devil is so eager to establish [is] that sex relations are justified on the grounds that it is a *pleasurable experience in itself* and is beyond moral consideration."[8]

While few would deny that marital sex involves some moral consideration, many Latter-day Saints are confused as to whether sex for the "pleasurable experience in itself" is appropriate. Church leaders say little or nothing regarding the physical and emotional pleasure, satisfaction, and bonding that are possible in a healthy sexual relationship. In fact, many messages, whether explicit or not, seem to indicate that "pleasurable" sex is inappropriate. The section on "Sex Desires" in Bruce R. McConkie's *Mormon Doctrine* contains no information at all and directs the reader to "see Sex Immorality," the obvious implication being that sexual desires are sinful and "immoral."[9]

The primary message most church members hear is that sex is primarily for procreation. Church president David O. McKay stated, "In most cases the desire not to have children has its birth in vanity. Such feelings . . . often tend to put the marriage relationship on a level with the panderer and the courtesan."[10]

Rodney Turner takes this argument and concludes that "apart from parenthood, marriage has no eternal validity." He also emphasizes that marriage does not justify "unrestrained sexual activity" and argues that a couple's love for each other and their desire for sexual intimacy are inversely related. For Turner, the strongest sexual desires between spouses occur when "love is least present."[11] This line of reasoning suggests that something is wrong with a marriage when a couple feels strong physical attraction for one another. With messages such as this, it is no wonder that LDS couples become confused or even eschew the bonding and sharing that come from mutually satisfying physical relationships.

While Turner's claims seem extreme, church leaders, for their part, have taught similar ideas. For example, J. Reuben Clark, of the First Presidency, stated, "As to sex in marriage, the necessary treatise on that for Latter-day Saints can be written in two sentences: Remember the prime purpose of sex desire is to beget children. Sex gratification must be had at that hazard. You husbands: be kind and considerate of your wives. They are not your property; they are not mere conveniences; they are your partners for time and eternity."[12]

President Clark's statement contains several messages. First, he equates sex with procreation and implies that men enjoy sexual intimacy more than women, a popular belief shared by much of society. Second, he assumes that men control sexual relationships and activity rather than men and women having an equal partnership. Third, sexual gratification can be hazardous, especially if it is to be had without the concurrent desire to procreate. The important positive message in Clark's statement is that women are masters of their bodies and not men's possessions and that men have no right to subjugate women for their own desires. (This pronouncement, especially at the time it was given, was certainly not in keeping with the sentiment of a major segment of society.)

Related to the discussion of sexuality is the topic of birth control. Since the early days of the LDS church, contraceptive use has been condemned. The doctrine of premortal existence and the mandate to provide premortal spirits the opportunity to experience mortality are the foundations for this proscription. For example, Brigham Young stated: "There are multitudes of pure and holy spirits waiting to take tabernacles. Now what is our duty? To prepare tabernacles for them . . . It is our duty to prepare tabernacles for all the spirits they can."[13]

Referring specifically to birth control devices, Apostle John Widtsoe wrote: "Any contraceptive is unnatural and interferes in one way or another with the physiological processes of life. All of them are in varying degrees injurious to those who use them, especially women."[14] Speaking in the October 1965 general conference, President Joseph Fielding Smith reiterated this position, stating: "I regret that so many young couples are thinking today more of successful contraceptives than of having a posterity. They will have to answer for their sin when the proper time comes and actually may be denied the glorious celestial kingdom." However, a First Presidency letter dated 1 April 1969 takes a somewhat different tone: "We seriously regret that there should exist a sentiment or feeling among any members of the church to curtail the birth of their children. . . . Where husband and wife enjoy health and vigor . . . it is contrary to the teachings of the church to curtail or prevent the birth of children. . . . However, the mother's health and strength should be conserved. . . . It is our further feeling that married couples should seek inspiration."[15] While church leaders have repeatedly condemned the use of birth control, this 1969 statement left some discretion to couples and urged them to consult their own consciences when determining the spacing and size of their families.

Official pronouncements regarding birth control have become less strident with the passage of time, but some modern church writers are not so equivocal. Rodney Turner contends abstinence and natural methods are the only legitimate forms of birth control, and that women who experience menstrual irregularities do so as a result of the sins of their female progenitors. In this context, he writes: "Both husband and wife must exercise self-control . . . [to avoid using] some form of contraception other than that provided by the menstrual cycle. This may appear unfair to those women who are subject to irregular menstrual cycles. However, the admitted inequities of nature's method of birth control are, presumably, to be borne along with all of the rest of life's inequities until a better day comes. In all likelihood, menstrual irregularities . . . came about through the violation of God's laws of health and hygiene. If so, the sins of the mothers of past ages have been visited on their daughters living today. But again, are we to free ourselves of the natural consequences of the race's past sins by resorting to new sins [of contraception]?"[16] According to Turner, women are not only to be blamed for gynecological problems, they must also allow these problems to control their sex lives.

This "blame the victim" mentality degrades women and leads to unnecessary guilt. The LDS client who first showed me this passage had denied her husband and herself the closeness they had previously enjoyed because she feared the spiritual and physical consequences. Because of her menstrual irregularities, she and her husband had limited sexual contact. When they "couldn't help it" and had sexual intercourse using contraceptives, they felt guilty. Because they felt comfortable sexually only when she was pregnant or trying to become so, their marriage and family relationships were needlessly damaged. Another couple entered counseling after the husband announced to his pregnant wife that they would not engage in sexual intercourse or other intimate contact during her pregnancy to demonstrate their worthiness and devotion to the Lord. Since procreation was the purpose of sexual intimacy, he concluded, they had met that goal and were now to abstain.

Homer Ellsworth's remarkable comments in the church's August 1979 *Ensign* magazine differ dramatically from Turner's opinions. In response to a question on family planning in the "I Have a Question" section, Ellsworth, a gynecologist, recommended that couples counsel together and seek God's guidance in family planning matters. He discussed abstinence as one form of contraception, but one that could have potentially adverse "side effects" on the marriage relationship.[17]

The latest official guidelines regarding "Birth Control" in the *General Handbook of Instructions* are as liberal as have been provided to date: "Husbands should be considerate of their wives, who have a great responsibility not only for bearing children but also for caring for them through their childhood. Husbands should help their wives conserve their health and strength. Married couples should seek inspiration from the Lord in meeting their marital challenges and rearing their children according to the teachings of the gospel."[18]

This is markedly different from the 1969 First Presidency statement. In a subtle but important change from the 1983 *General Handbook*, the statement, "Married couples should exercise self-control in all their relationships" is deleted.[19] This deletion effectively rescinds the "doctrine" that "natural" birth control is the only legitimate form of contraception and that sexual pleasure should be avoided. It is addressed primarily to men but acknowledges the mutual responsibility of both men and women in sexual decision-making. Distributed only to church leaders, the statement would be extremely helpful if made available to members. In light of past statements regarding sexuality and the sexual culture that has prevailed in the church, many members would benefit from wide distribution of policy statements that contain even subtle attitude changes.

In recent years, church leaders and publications have presented a more positive view of sexuality. For example, in the October 1971 *Ensign*, President Kimball was quoted as saying, "We know of no directive from the Lord that proper sexual experiences between husbands and wives need be limited totally to the procreation of children."[20] On another occasion, he observed, "If you study the divorces, as we have had to do in these past years you will find . . . sex is the first [reason]. They did not get along sexually. They may not say that in court. They may not even tell that to their attorneys, but that is the reason."[21]

While *A Parent's Guide* offers perhaps the most affirming officially sanctioned sexual messages for married couples to date, it presents a conservative view of sexuality. It describes the sex drive as a myth, counsels engaged couples to seek sexual information separately rather than together, and warns against "sexual excess" on the honeymoon. Yet it also provides some positive sexual messages. Referring to sex throughout the duration of marriage, it states: "They [couples] must be the very best of friends on their first occasion when they are able to begin to know one another completely. . . . And they must realize that the greatest passions in marriage lie ahead, to increase over the years through experience and growth. . . . In virtuous marriage passions increase over the years between the couple."[22]

In the September 1986 *Ensign* Brent Barlow discusses the joy and intimacy in marriage that couples experience when they nurture their sexual relationships.[23] The 1989 Relief Society manual suggests that within marriage, "sexual expression is ordained of God. It is a strong force in strengthening love, unity, and companionship."[24] Priesthood lesson manuals of recent years offer no similar reinforcement regarding sexual relationships. For example, in the 1990 *Melchizedek Priesthood Personal Study Guide,* the one lesson devoted to marital relationships, "Live Joyfully with Your Wife," contains no mention of physical intimacy between spouses. In fact, even though the authors refer to the "one flesh" scripture, they do so in a completely unrelated context.[25] If it is true, as President Kimball suggested, that "sex is the first reason" for divorce among LDS couples, why is it neglected in church curricula?

Many church members still operate under the mistaken assumption that sexual self-denial is a virtue and that sexual passions are sinful. Many remain ambivalent as they interpret conflicting messages. Some people have little interest in sexual intimacy. Others display aversive reactions. Though this occurs in society in general, in LDS couples, sexually aversive attitudes are more likely to be justified for religious reasons. For example, one couple with whom I worked had had an essentially asexual marriage for five years. The couple had five children, and the youngest was four years old. At the onset of her last pregnancy, the wife informed the husband (just as her mother had done with her father) that since they were finished having children, their sexual life was terminated. In her mind, the gospel taught that sex was for procreation, and self-control was the ultimate virtue—a virtue she was determined to master.

When sexual problems of this nature occur with LDS couples, it is critical to redefine them as "sexual" rather than "doctrinal" problems. Individuals who rely on past statements of church leaders or other LDS writers could benefit from the most contemporary statements and references that affirm the role of sexuality in marriage and emphasize personal choice and free agency. By eliminating "doctrine" as the root of sexual problems and the justification for negative sexual attitudes, therapists are free to emphasize positive relationships, communication, and intimacy. Problems arising from guilt or fear can be ameliorated by emphasizing the mandate to become "one flesh." (One reframing technique could be to point out that the clitoris is the only anatomical structure with the exclusive purpose of sexual pleasure, and then ask if God would create such a structure if sexual pleasure was wrong.) Couples can be encouraged to seek divine guidance concerning the timing of bringing children into the world. They can view sexual intimacy and procreation as related, but not synonymous terms. Finally, it is important to emphasize couples' mutual responsibility for decisions regarding sexual intimacy and procreation and a reduced reliance upon outside advice.

A major concern for many LDS couples is determining appropriate and inappropriate methods of sexual expression. As I mentioned earlier, most of the BYU nursing students' questions revolved around whether or not the sexual activities they were engaging in (or those they thought they might want to try) were ecclesiastically sanctioned. A number of these young people were engaged, and others were married; but their concerns were the same: "What sexual practices can I engage in and not get into trouble with the church?" Whereas extramarital sexual contact is unequivocally prohibited, in marriage the question becomes somewhat ambiguous. The *General Handbook of Instructions* counsels, "To be morally clean, a person must refrain from adultery and fornication, from homosexual or lesbian relations and from every other unholy, unnatural, or improper practice."[26]

The uncertainty here comes from the "other" category. What is and what is not unholy and impure? President Kimball counseled, "There are some who have said that behind the bedroom doors anything goes. This is not true and the Lord would not condone it."[27] In recent years, some local church leaders have inquired into the specific sexual practices of married members and have subsequently denied temple recommends to those who, based upon the leader's interpretation, engaged in "unholy" sexual practices. Moreover, stake presidents and bishops have used church meetings to specify the "unholy and impure" practices members are to avoid within marriage.

A question I have frequently been asked concerns the propriety of oral sex. To address this question, one must first define the term. Is kissing oral sex? How about a mouth on a breast? Or is oral sex limited exclusively to oral-genital contact? (These questions have special significance for persons with disabilities who have paralysis and lack sensation in their genitals, arms, and legs and for whom sexual expression is different from that of persons without disabilities.) On 5 January 1982, in response to numerous queries about oral sex, the First Presidency distributed a letter to bishops and stake presidents.[28] In it, they characterized oral sex as impure. However, the letter specifically stated that church leaders were not to discuss intimate sexual matters with members. The letter was also not to be shared with the general church membership.

Apparently, a number of the local leaders read the first part of the letter but ignored the second, choosing instead to delve into members' intimate lives. After the 1982 letter, several of my clients and a number of friends reported experiences in which bishops or stake presidents made such inquiries. Some reported local leaders using church meetings to counsel members about sexual practices. Almost all of the inquiries and counsel dealt specifically with oral sex. As a result of these intrusions, many members wrote letters to church leaders, protesting ecclesiastical meddling. In response to these reactions, on 15 October 1982 a second letter was sent to stake and ward leaders that reiterated the 5 January directive to avoid inquiring into couples' intimate sexual practices.[29] Further, it directed leaders that even if asked by members about specific sexual matters in marriage they were to avoid giving direct counsel. The latest directive, in "Instructions for Issuing Recommends to Enter a Temple" (1989), instructs interviewers to ask only, "Do you live the law of chastity?" They are further counseled: "When interviewing an applicant for a recommend, do not inquire into personal, intimate matters about marital relations between a husband and his wife. Generally, do not deviate from the recommend interview questions. If, during an interview, an applicant asks about the propriety of specific conduct do not pursue the matter, merely suggest that if the applicant has enough anxiety about the propriety of conduct to ask about it, the best course would be to discontinue it. If you are sensitive and wise, you usually can prevent those being interviewed from asking such explicit questions."[30] This directive makes it clear that couples, not church leaders, are responsible for their sexual conduct. They should take their questions to God, not to ecclesiastical leaders. The suggestion to "discontinue" sexual practices they have questions about may unintentionally lead to unnecessary guilt and restriction of physical intimacy. The most beneficial recommendation for couples, from a therapist's point of view, is to counsel and decide together. When necessary, couples can then seek God's guidance.

In some relationships, couples use sex as a tool to manipulate or control. This type of behavior usually indicates serious marital problems. According to scriptural and ecclesiastical mandates, force or coercion are not condoned. Moses instructed that a man guilty of rape be put to death (Deut. 22:25). Church leaders and publications stress the importance of mutuality and sharing.[31] Sometimes one partner withholds sex and affection to hurt or punish the other. Sometimes sexual behavior is engaged in perfunctorily, without affection. A woman I counseled who had filed for divorce, but because of financial difficulties continued to live in the same house with her husband, explained that he continued to demand sexual contact despite the impending divorce. When the woman sought her bishop's help, he told her that until the divorce was final, she should meet her husband's sexual requests. Every time he had sex with her, she felt violated; but because of her bishop's counsel she also felt helpless to stop his advances. Loving sexual expression carries the possibility of great intimacy, but when used coercively or as a punitive tool it can be extremely damaging.

Related to the discussion of sexuality is the prevailing attitude toward heterosocial relationships between men and women in the LDS church. The belief expressed by Billy Crystal in the movie *When Harry Met Sally*—that men and women can never become "just friends" because sex always gets in the way—holds sway in the church. Most members have known or at least heard of people who have committed adultery and have lost church membership as a result. (Bishop-Relief Society president adultery stories are probably far more prevalent than their actual incidence.) The tragedy of broken families and damaged relationships that stem from infidelity needs no elaboration.

Some church members therefore take the position that all extramarital male-female contacts or friendships are wrong. The following examples clearly illustrate this point. A man and a woman, neighbors in their ward, attended a series of church-related meetings approximately twenty-five miles from their homes. They drove to these meetings separately and never considered car-pooling. When queried about this, the woman spoke of the impropriety of being alone with someone of the opposite sex and the importance of "avoiding the very appearance of evil." The implication was that during these drives, the two of them might be sexually tempted or at least give others the impression that they were romantically involved. This same heterosocial discomfort is evident in the common practice in assigning older men as home teachers to young divorced women rather than sending men of a similar age. At a time when closeness and support of people of the opposite sex are most needed, in the church they are often least available. Another therapist has discussed this frustration and suggested that we need to distinguish emotional closeness from erotic feelings.[32] Sexualizing heterosocial relationships creates the very atmosphere that is feared simply because people do not have opportunities for platonic intimacy.

The belief that friendships with members of the opposite sex automatically lead to romantic feelings or sexual relationships effectively separates members along gender lines. This especially damages women, who already have little access to leadership and the decision-making process. Gender separation in interpersonal relationships deprives male church leaders of female perspectives and opinions. Married men and women must then rely solely on their spouses for opposite-sex interaction and feedback. Access to unmarried individuals is further restricted, especially when they are seen as potential threats to marital relationships. Removing heterosocial taboos would empower both women and men in the church to take full advantage of the resources offered by others, regardless of their gender. For women to share a more equal voice, intergender desexualization of relationships is necessary, a process that will mitigate some of the pain and isolation felt by many single members of the church.[33]

Another negative byproduct of sexualized heterosocial interaction is an environment in which single men and women relate to each other primarily as romantic objects or potential mates. After marriage, members avoid male-female friendships because they have not learned to relate to each other on a purely social basis. This predominantly masculine avoidance of the (nonwife) feminine results in a knowledge deprivation which devalues women's ways of knowing and being. Women, on the other hand, must daily acknowledge men's ways of knowing and doing since men hold virtually all authority over their spiritual lives. If we could create a culture that validates nonthreatening relationships, people could socialize and work together without sexual interference. Gender imbalances might begin to disintegrate, especially as men become more aware of and responsive to women's needs and respond to them as intellectual, spiritual, and social equals. Developing healthy heterosocial relationships after marriage may, in fact, reduce marital infidelity and enhance marriages as men and women replace suspicious, fearful attitudes with affirming, nonsexual ones.

Sexuality permeates much of what people do and think. The LDS perspective on sexuality is unique: like our heavenly parents, we have the potential to experience and enjoy eternal marriage relationships, one component of which is sexuality (we can eternally procreate). Attitudes toward sexuality and sexual expression have undergone marked changes in the more than 160 years since the LDS church was organized, many of which parallel similar changes in society at large.[34] Although church leaders have historically championed sexual expression for the purposes of procreation, they have only recently begun to sanction physical sexual fulfillment as ends in themselves.

More than a decade ago, Kenneth Cannon called for an "LDS philosophy of sex" that emphasizes the full realm of sexuality rather than focusing almost exclusively on chastity.[35] Whether an institutional "philosophy" on sex is needed, it is certain that a church culture that provides moral guidelines yet allows individuals and couples to fully develop as sexual beings is preferable to current ambivalence.

Though sexually affirming statements are gradually appearing in some LDS publications, their numbers are few, and most members are unaware of them. Moreover, of the sexually affirming articles and statements, very few are by general church authorities, whose statements emphasizing restraint and chastity are voluminous.

Latter-day Saints need to adopt a comprehensive approach to sexuality that includes positive messages emphasizing the joys and rewards of physical intimacy rather than focusing exclusively on the pitfalls of immorality. Ecclesiastical messages, whether in conference addresses, books, or other church publications, condoning appropriate sexual relationships engender a healthy environment wherein young people feel free to seek information and adults feel unencumbered by needless shame for legitimate expression of marital passion.

While it is important for members to obtain positive sexual information, for the most part educational materials have yet to be produced. In 1976 Shirley B. Paxman reviewed sexually-related books written by LDS authors.[36] The list was sparse at that time, and few titles have been added since. An increased ecclesiastical openness toward sexuality would no doubt encourage writing on the subject. Sexual literature written within a gospel context would teach people about such subjects as sexual anatomy, the physiology of sexual response, sexual intimacy, and common sexual problems and strategies to alleviate them. This information would help dispel myths and reinforce positive sexual attitudes. Priesthood and Relief Society manuals could include lessons about teaching sexuality to children and enhancing intimate relationships in marriage. Educational materials designed for youth could provide information about physical growth and development and lessons teaching restraint and chastity.

An environment that emphasizes the positive aspects of sexuality and promotes the acquisition of accurate sexual information would prepare church members to teach their children healthy attitudes, beginning with respect for and knowledge of their own bodies. As children mature, parents can balance messages about chastity with a celebration of the wonders of human development. This value-centered education in the home deals with young people having the tools necessary to counter the explosion of sexual information they receive from larger society and likewise prepares them for dating and, eventually, marriage.

An affirming sexual culture would likely prevent sexual problems for many church members. As leaders and parents complement the teaching of chastity with messages about the satisfactions of intimacy and healthy sexual expression, they can shift the emphasis away from restraint and focus on helping couples develop open and honest communication skills. Personal responsibility and spiritual guidance (when necessary) could replace ecclesiastical proscriptions. Couples could feel free to make their own decisions regarding method and frequency of sexual expression, contraception, family planning, and childbearing. This increased openness and awareness would confirm that sexuality and sexual expression are sacred, not shameful. It would affirm the idea that sexuality is much more than sexual arousal and physical desire. As we institutionally learn to appreciate sexuality, we could reduce artificial gender separations and enhance our ability to address the full range of sexuality-related issues. A culture that embraces all members could be created.

This essay only scratches the surface in dealing with LDS notions of sexuality. Ongoing discussion on the broad range of sexual issues is needed. It has been said that procreation brings us closer to God than anything else we do. We are taught that we have perfect Heavenly Parents. We assume, therefore, that their love for each other must be equally perfect. They created us in their images with the desire that we emulate them. It follows then, that the perfection we seek includes a perfect capacity to love our spouses completely in every way. One step on this road is an understanding and respect for our own sexuality and sexual expression, which is a prerequisite to becoming eternally "one flesh."

*NOTES*

1. Harold T. Christensen, "Mormon Sexuality in Cross-cultural Persepctive," *Dialogue: A Journal of Mormon Thought* 10 (Autumn 1976): 62-75.

2. Rodney Turner, *Woman and the Priesthood* (Salt Lake City: Bookcraft, Inc., 1976), 55.

3. *General Handbook of Instructions* (Salt Lake City: Church of Jesus Christ of Latter-day Saints, 1983), 11-5.

4. Kenneth L. Cannon, "Needed: An LDS Philosophy of Sex," *Dialogue: A Journal of Mormon Thought* 10 (Autumn 1976): 57-61.

5. Spencer W. Kimball, *The Miracle of Forgiveness* (Salt Lake City: Bookcraft, 1969), 74, emphasis added.

6. Joseph F. Smith, *Gospel Doctrine*, 5th ed. (Salt Lake City: Deseret Book, 1939), 309.

7. Spencer W. Kimball, *Faith Precedes the Miracle* (Salt Lake City: Deseret Book, 1975), 155.

8. Ibid., 154, emphasis added.

9. Bruce R. McConkie, *Mormon Doctrine*, 2d ed. (Salt Lake City: Bookcraft, 1976), 709.

10. Quoted in Turner, 227.

11. Ibid., 226, 263.

12. Ibid., 227.

13. Brigham Young, *Discourses of Brigham Young*, ed. John A. Widtsoe (Salt Lake City: Deseret Book, 1941), 197.

14. John A. Widtsoe, *Evidences and Reconciliations* (Salt Lake City: Bookcraft, 1943), 247.

15. *Conference Report of the Church of Jesus Christ of Latter-day Saints, October 1965* (Salt Lake City: Church of Jesus Christ of Latter-day Saints, 1965).

16. Turner, 235.

17. Homer G. Ellsworth, "I Have a Question," *Ensign* 9 (Aug. 1979): 23-24.

18. *General Handbook of Instructions*, 11-4.

19. Ibid., 77.

20. Spencer W. Kimball, "The Lord's Plan for Men and Women," *Ensign* 5 (Oct. 1975): 4.

21. Spencer W. Kimball, *The Teachings of Spencer W. Kimball*, eds. Edward L. Kimball (Salt Lake City: Bookcraft, 1982), 46.

22. *A Parent's Guide* (Salt Lake City: Church of Jesus Christ of Latter-day Saints, 1985), 46.

23. Brent Barlow, "They Twain Shall Be One," *Ensign* 16 (Sept. 1986): 49-53.

24. *Relief Society Personal Study Guide* (Salt Lake City: Church of Jesus Christ of Latter-day Saints, 1989), 137.

25. *Melchizedek Priesthood Personal Study Guide: Lay Hold upon the Word of God* (Salt Lake City: Church of Jesus Christ of Latter-day Saints, 1988).

26. *General Handbook of Instructions*, 11-4.

27. Kimball, *Teachings*, 312.

28. First Presidency to local leaders, 5 Jan. 1982, copy in my possession.

29. First Presidency to local leaders, 15 Oct. 1982, copy in my possession.

30. *Instructions for Issuing Recommends to the Temple* (Salt Lake City: Church of Jesus Christ of Latter-day Saints, Apr. 1989).

31. *A Parent's Guide.* See also Kimball, *Miracle of Forgiveness,* and Barlow, "They Twain Shall Be One."

32. Marybeth Raynes, "Getting Unmarried in a Married Church," *Dialogue: A Journal of Mormon Thought* 14 (Winter 1981): 75-90.

33. Delmont R. Oswald, "A Lone Man in the Garden," *Dialogue: A Journal of Mormon Thought* 23 (Spring 1990): 139-46 (reprinted in this compilation); Lawrence A. Young, "Being Single, Mormon and Male," *Dialogue: A Journal of Mormon Thought* 23 (Spring 1990): 146-51; Raynes, "Getting Unmarried."

34. Klaus J. Hansen, "Mormon Sexuality and American Culture," *Dialogue: A Journal of Mormon Thought* 10 (Autumn 1976): 45-56 (reprinted in this compilation).

35. Cannon, "Needed," 57.

36. Shirley B. Paxman, "Sex Education Materials for Latter-day Saints, *Dialogue: A Journal of Mormon Thought* 10 (Autumn 1976): 113-16.

# 4.

# The Persistence of Chastity: Built-in Resistance in Mormon Culture to Secular Trends

*Harold T. Christensen*

SOME TWO DECADES AGO A REPORT OF MINE WHICH SHOWED AN INcrease in premarital coitus among the females of my Mormon-based sample created concern among authorities of the Church of Jesus Christ of Latter-day Saints. In a letter to me dated 5 February 1971 Elder Alvin R. Dyer, a counselor in the First Presidency, cited the following sentence from a news release: "Christensen said the percentages of college women who had premarital coitus increased from 10 percent in 1959 to 32 percent in 1968 at a western university 'which represents the highly restrictive Mormon culture.'" President Dyer went on to say, "It would be helpful to us to have further information of this alarming condition." A little later he asked, "How and by whom was the survey made which produced these percentages?"

I answered him, in part, as follows: "Much as I would like to comply with your present request, I am unable to do so because of my responsibility as a researcher to protect the anonymity of the individuals and institutions studied; and indeed my commitment to do so in the case of the Intermountain sample. To do otherwise would violate my sense of integrity, and so I must ask that you respect my commitment and responsibility as a scientist. One would not ask the physician to betray the confidences of his patients nor the marriage counselor, to give another example, to reveal the secrets of his clients. The researcher has a similar responsibility to his subject. . . .

"All questionnaires were administered in classes, by permission of those in charge, and were returned anonymously. I do want you to know that this research has been done either by me or under my direction and that I take full responsibility. If there are ways in which I can be of help within the framework of this position, I am not only willing but anxious to do so." With that, the matter apparently was dropped for I heard no more.

I mention the above incident because it throws light on the sensitivity regarding sexual research. This sensitivity explains why, in reports dealing with my cross-cultural sex research, I consistently refer to my Mormon-based samples as "Intermountain," without further identification.[1]

This report focuses on the LDS portion of responses to a questionnaire concerning premarital sexual attitudes and behavior which was administered in 1978 to students at an "Intermountain" university located in the western United States. For comparative purposes non-Mormon responses from that same university, as well as additional non-Mormon responses from a large Midwestern university, are also examined. Furthermore, with respect to premarital coitus, 1978 data are viewed alongside equivalent data for 1968 and 1958 to give a twenty-year picture of this narrow but important facet of contemporary Mormon history.

It should be pointed out that the analysis reported in this essay represents one phase of an ongoing, long-range, cross-cultural investigation dealing with the phenomenon of premarital sex. It has involved samples from sexually-permissive Denmark, moderately-restrictive Midwestern United States, and highly-restrictive Mormon culture within the Intermountain region of the western United States. To date, some two dozen journal articles reporting on one or another aspects of the study have appeared.[2] This present report is the first to involve the 1978 data with a focus on the Mormon condition.

Research data rather consistently have shown lower rates of premarital coitus among Mormons than the surrounding culture.[3] But the contemporary American scene has been dominated by a so-called "sexual revolution" of perhaps unprecedented proportions. So the questions become: How is the Mormon norm of chastity holding up under modern conditions? Is the church able to successfully resist current trends toward sexual permissiveness? And, if so, to what extent and how is it accomplished?

Even though the central concern is with Mormon responses, it is important to know how these compare with non-Mormon responses in order to assess where we are. For present purposes, I shall ignore the Danish segment of my investigation, for it represents a different culture—one with a long history of sexual permissiveness—and shall compare Mormon responses against non-Mormon data from two American subsamples: my Midwestern samples and the non-Mormon portions of my Intermountain samples.

Most of the data to be reported are structured within the framework of *non*-coitus—that is, virginity or chastity—rather than sexual activity. This is because premarital chastity is the norm in Mormon culture.

There are a few additional points concerning the present data which need to be made. In Figure 1, I deal with each of the three time periods in order to measure trends; whereas in Tables 1 through 3, I restrict myself to 1978 data alone. Furthermore, in the first instance I report responses from sociology classes only. This refinement was necessary in order to achieve comparability from year to year.[4]

It may be presumed that sexual permissiveness, or lack of it, will vary within a university from academic department to academic department.[5] The 1978 Intermountain sample presented a problem in this regard, for each of the others had been derived from sociologically-oriented classes. In the 1978 Intermountain sample were circumstances beyond my control which cut off sociology class responses at just under 100. Fortunately, I was able to supplement that small group with more than 200 additional returns from classes in the Department of Family and Human Development. Since comparability is not a key issue in the tables (as it is in Fig. 1) I have combined sociology and non-sociology responses for the sake of larger numbers.

We turn now to the results of this investigation. They are to be reported in terms of four data-induced propositions, with some attempt at interpretation even when this takes me a little beyond the examined evidence. Statistical evidence seldom tells the whole story. This is especially true in this instance since some of my Intermountain samples are small and my classroom approach to data-gathering even throws the criterion of representativeness into question. The statistical "purist" is left plenty of room to raise questions. Still, my data are comparable from culture to culture and from one time period to the next. Furthermore, the findings seem to demonstrate a certain consistency and logic. Nevertheless, I would like to emphasize that I regard the evidence given here as only suggestive, not conclusive. I present my generalizations at the level of hypotheses—reasonable speculations that invite further empirical testing.

*Proposition 1. Mormon premarital sex norms are strikingly conservative.* Evidence of sexual conservatism in Mormon culture can be found at two levels: attitude and behavior. Attitudes describe what one believes or feels about something, while behavior indicates what he or she does. Figure 1 presents one important measure of each: percent virgin, which, of course, reflects behavior; and percent preferring to marry a virgin, which is a good indicator of attitude. These are shown separately for the three years studied and for both the Mormon and the two non-Mormon subsamples used as reference groups.

First to be noted is that for each time period and within each sample actual virginity is lower than preference for marrying a virgin. This seems to reflect a general human tendency to be more demanding in choosing a marriage partner than in governing one's own premarital sexual behavior.[6] While keeping this differential in mind, it is worth noting that these two measures form similar patterns; in broad outline they vary together, both across cultures and from one time period to the next. Since attitude is a precursor to behavior, this is expected.

The most striking generalization to be derived from Figure 1—and most important—is that Mormon percentages are considerably and consistently higher than those for the non-Mormon respondents. This is true with respect to both measures and within each of the sample years.

It is of particular significance, I think, that while premarital virginity (chastity) dropped to a minority position in one of the non-Mormon groups as early as 1968 and in the other by 1978,

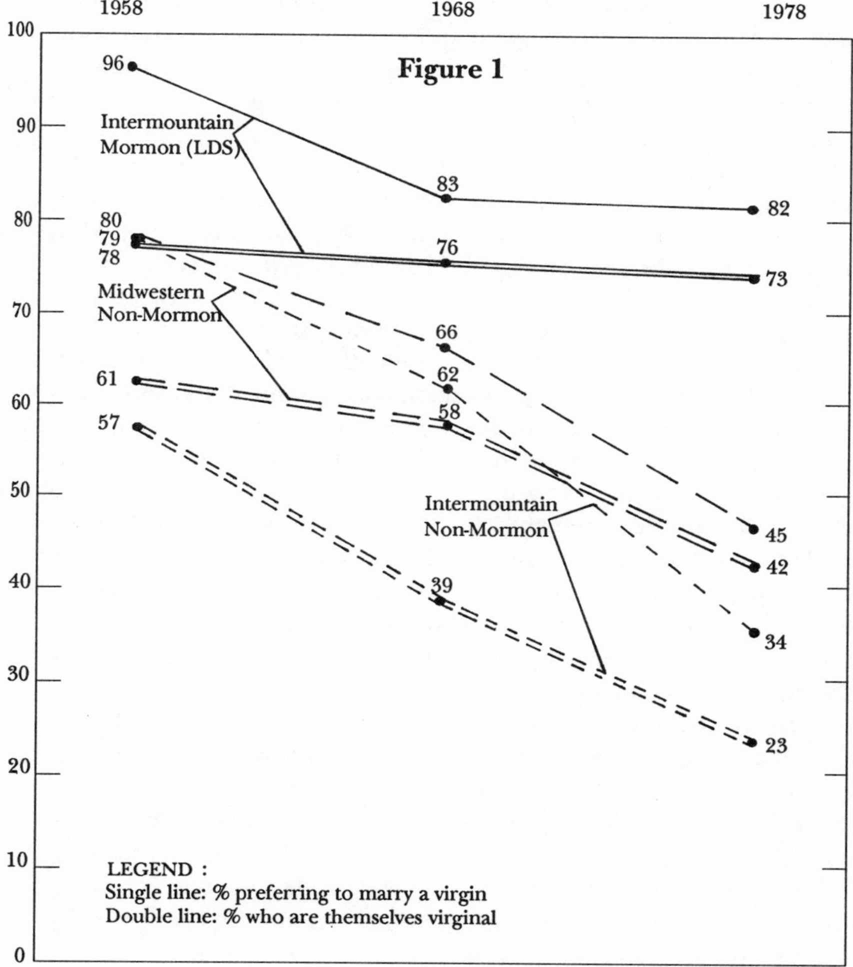
1958
1968
1978
Figure 1
96
83
82
80
79
78
76
73
66
62
61
58
57
45
42
39
34
23
Intermountain Mormon (LDS)
Midwestern Non-Mormon
Intermountain Non-Mormon
100
90
80
70
60
50
40
30
20
10
0
LEGEND :
Single line: % preferring to marry a virgin
Double line: % who are themselves virginal

chastity in the Mormon group always was and is now a majority phenomenon. In 1978 nearly three-fourths of Mormon respondents still claimed to have abided by the chastity standard. This proportion is more than three times larger than for the Intermountain non-Mormon group and nearly two times larger than for the Midwestern non-Mormon group. Surely differences of such magnitude cannot be viewed as occurring by chance.

Parenthetically, I would like to call the reader's attention to a tendency for Intermountain non-Mormons to stand out in even sharper contrast to the Mormons than the Midwestern non-Mormons. This can be seen in Figure 1 and in most of the comparisons presented in the tables. Apparently, living in close proximity to Mormons has the effect of turning some non-Mormons on an opposite course, perhaps as a reaction against the perceived ultraconservatism of the church. Perhaps conservative non-Mormons more often yield to conversion efforts than their liberal neighbors, as well.

Table 1 presents three additional measures of attitudes that bear on sexual behavior. First are the percentages of respondents who disagreed with the statement, "It is best not to try to prohibit erotic and obscene literature and pictures by law, but rather to leave people free to follow their judgments and tastes in such matters." By rejecting that statement they, in effect, favored censorship of pornography. As might be expected, many more Mormons than non-Mormons were found to favor censorship.

The next percentages address the question of intimacy in dating. The questionnaire defined necking as "light kissing and embracing," petting as "body fondling below the neck," and coitus as "complete sexual intercourse." Respondents were asked to consider a hypothetical eighteen-month dating period characterized by normal love development and to mark on an appropriate scale the points at which they would approve of necking, then petting, and finally coitus. By subtracting the point on the scale at which necking is first approved from the point at which coitus is first approved, it is possible to come up with a rough measure of what students considered an ideal love relationship offering promise of marriage. According to this measure, Mormon respondents perceive intimacy development as best when spread out over a twelve-month period, which is two-thirds of the hypothetical eighteen-month courtship span they were asked to

TABLE 1. SELECTED INDICES OF ATTITUDINAL CONSERVATISM (1978 DATA: TOTAL SAMPLES)[a]

| | Males | | | Females | | |
|---|---|---|---|---|---|---|
| | Intermountain | | Mid-Western | Intermountain | | Mid-Western |
| | LDS (N=60) (1) | Non-LDS (N=34) (2) | Non-LDS (N=225) (3) | LDS (N=182) (4) | Non-LDS (N=50) (5) | Non-LDS (N=320) (6) |
| *I. Attitude Toward Pornography* | | | | | | |
| Percent Favoring Censorship | (1) 75.0 | 14.7 | 25.6 | 72.4 | 18.0 | 42.6 |
| *II. Attitude Toward Length of Time for Intimacy Development* | | | | | | |
| Average Number of Months | (2) 12.2 | 5.9 | 8.8 | 12.0 | 8.7 | 10.1 |
| *III. Attitude toward Premarital Coitus* | | | | | | |
| Percent Who Disapprove | (3) 88.1 | 20.6 | 20.1 | 92.2 | 25.0 | 28.0 |

a Overall sample Ns are sdhown in the column headings. However, the statistics given in this and subsequent tables are based upon the numbers of respondents answering the respective questions. Non-responses to the questions of Table 1 varied from 0 to 3.

consider. In contrast, non-Mormon respondents see a more rapid development as being appropriate—some nine or ten months in most instances or a period extending over about one-half of the hypothetical courtship time-span.

On the scale just described, many—especially the Mormon respondents—checked first coitus as occurring only after marriage (Table 1, line 3). Again we see the Mormon response standing in sharp contrast to the non-Mormon response; fully nine-tenths of the former declare themselves on the side of premarital chastity as compared with about one-fifth to one-fourth of the latter.

Thus we have four attitudinal measures (disapproval of premarital coitus, preference for marrying a virgin, favoring a gradual pattern of sexual development, and favoring censorship of pornography) and one behavioral measure (remaining virginal until marriage) all pointing to the same conclusion: Mormons are disproportionately high on the chastity norm. Considered together, these comparisons clearly underline the fact that Mormons are more apt to opt for a temptation-reduced environment and self-control in their personal lives. Typically, they see the most intimate forms of sexual expression as belonging only to marriage and they commit themselves to putting on the brakes, so to speak, in order to "keep the law of chastity" which they regard as a commandment from God. While premarital sex now characterizes a "new majority" in American culture generally, the Mormon subculture continues to stand out as an exception.

*Proposition 2. Mormon conservatism tends to be remarkably resistant to change.* Up to this point we have stressed Mormon/non-Mormon differentials regarding sexual conservatism but with almost no attention given to the phenomenon of movement over time. Yet every one of the trend lines in Figure 1 moves downward. Whether with reference to attitudinal or behavioral measures, movement over the two decades covered by the study has been consistently away from the chastity norm. This means, of course, that the sexual revolution has taken a toll.

Each of the trend lines for Mormon respondents declines only slightly between 1958 and 1978 whereas the non-Mormon lines—all four of them—drop dramatically. This suggests that, with respect to chastity, Mormons and non-Mormons may be pulling farther apart.

Support for these findings comes from a parallel study of several thousand student responses drawn from seven different colleges and universities in the northwestern United States. The researcher was Wilford E. Smith, and the years covered are 1950, 1961, and 1972. Smith's data, like my own, show much higher percentages of Mormon than non-Mormon respondents reporting no coitus out of wedlock and also show a trend away from chastity for non-Mormons.[7]

Still another investigation relevant to this phenomenon was carried out by Christensen and Cannon comparing more than 1,000 Brigham Young University Mormon student responses between 1935 and 1973. Every one of the thirty-six topics which were reported (and which pertain to attitudes and behavior in the areas of religion and ethics) showed a shift toward greater conservatism over the more than one-third of a century that was covered by the study. We interpreted this as a swing back toward fundamentalism, which we did not feel was typical of American culture in general. And while we could not be certain how much of this conservative movement was due to increasing religious selectivity and socialization at BYU and how much of it represented change that was churchwide, it was our strong feeling that the latter played a prominent role. The Mormon church as a whole is believed to have been moving toward greater uniformity. Three of the thirty-six questions have particular relevance to our present concern: attitudes toward premarital necking, premarital petting, and premarital coitus. Percentages who considered these levels of sexual intimacy morally wrong were for 1935 and 1973, respectively: necking, 16 and 35; petting, 77 and 90; and coitus, 88 and 98. This upward shift rather clearly indicates that at the attitudinal level Mormon sexual conservatism is more than holding its own—it appears to be increasing.[8]

In an earlier paper based on parts of my cross-cultural data, I noted for both my Danish and my Intermountain Mormon groups an almost level trend line in premarital coitus for the decade 1968-78. While premarital coitus within my Midwestern samples continued to increase over the second as well as the first decade of the study, in the other two cultures there was practically no movement over the second decade. With respect to the Danish samples, I explained this as very likely due to a ceiling effect: rates were so near their upper limits (around 95 percent) that there was little room for further increase. But percentages showing coitus in my Intermountain Mor-

TABLE 2. TWO INDICES OF THE CONSEQUENCES OF PREMARITAL COITUS (1978 DATA: COITAL SUBSAMPLES)[a]

| | Males | | | Females | | |
|---|---|---|---|---|---|---|
| | Intermountain | | Mid-Western | Intermountain | | Mid-Western |
| | LDS (1) | Non-LDS (2) | Non-LDS (3) | LDS (4) | Non-LDS (5) | Non-LDS (6) |
| *I. Value-Behavior Discrepancy* | | | | | | |
| Percent of Coitally Experienced Who Disapprove Premarital Coitus | (1) 44.4 | 14.3 | 5.1 | 47.6 | 3.2 | 6.2 |
| *II. Negative Effects* | | | | | | |
| Percent Negative Reactions to First Premarital Experience [b] | (2) 68.0 | 30.6 | 43.5 | 83.8 | 59.6 | 66.2 |

a Premarital coital subsample Ns are 9, 28, 136, 21, 33, and 178 respectively.

b Percentage here represent the composites of eight feeling responses: tenseness, guilt, remorse, disgust, fear of religious punishment, fear of others knowing, fear of pregnancy, and fear of disease. remaining categories in the check list are indifference, happiness, relaxation, and conquest.

Respondents were asked to check as many terms as applied and then circle the one that they felt had been their strongest feeling on the day following the first premarital coital experience. The Ns used to calculate percentages were in this instance, total checks (rather than number of respondents) with the circled items given double weight. The resulting Ns are 25, 85, 402, 74, 99, and 582 respectively.

mon samples remained at the 25 percent level. I explained the almost-no-trend phenomenon observed within my Mormon data as likely due to a braking effect resulting from religious teachings and pressures.[9]

*Proposition 3. Mormon deviants, although proportionally fewer, pay a heavier price.* Evidence for this somewhat surprising finding comes from the value-behavior discrepancy exhibited by Mormon respondents (Table 2, line 1) coupled with negative reactions following premarital coitus (line 2). "Value-behavior discrepancy" is a term that I earlier coined to describe the violation of one's own standards.[10] It is measured here by using participation in premarital coitus as the base (coital percentages were obtained by subtracting Fig. 1 values from 100) and calculating percentages of participants who disapproved of such behavior even though they themselves had been involved.

Value-behavior discrepancy and negative effects are different sides of the same coin. When a person violates his or her standards, it stands to reason that he or she will experience more guilt or other undesirable feelings. The important thing to observe is that proportionately more Mormon than non-Mormon respondents found themselves caught up in this syndrome.

This is not to say that the overall effects of promoting chastity are harder on Mormons, for the church's efforts do produce lower indulgence rates. My present investigation does not carry over into marriage and possible effects that may derive from conformity with sexual norms. But nonconformity does produce negative effects in societies where the behavior in question is strongly condemned–in this case, premarital sex in the Mormon culture.

The situation in some ways is analogous to alcoholism among drinkers. During the mid-1950s in a book called *Drinking in College* Mormon college students were reported to have the lowest drinking rate among religious groups. But of drinkers, Mormon students showed up with an extremely high rate of alcoholism.[11] In an earlier attempt to explain this phenomenon I wrote: "In a sexually restrictive culture, such as the Mormon of the Intermountain region of the United States, morality tends to be rigidly fixed; things are regarded as either black or white, good or bad. In judging an act, little allowance is made for conditions or circumstances; hence a thing that

TABLE 3. TWO INDICES OF THE "BREAKING EFFECT" OF RELIGION (1978 DATA: NON-COITAL SUBSAMPLES IN 1; TOTAL SAMPLES IN II)

| | Males | | | Females | | |
|---|---|---|---|---|---|---|
| | Intermountain | | Mid-Western | Intermountain | | Mid-Western |
| | LDS (1) | Non-LDS (2) | Non-LDS (3) | LDS (4) | Non-LDS (5) | Non-LDS (6) |
| *I. Stated Reasons of the Non-Coital Group for Not Going on to Coitus* [a] | | | | | | |
| Percent "Moral or Religious Teachings" | (1) 56.8 | 23.1 | 30.8 | 56.1 | 36.0 | 54.1 |
| *II. Frequency of Church Attendance* [b] | | | | | | |
| Percent "Once a Week or More" | (2) 88.3 | 8.8 | 24.6 | 83.0 | 14.0 | 27.3 |

a. In addition to "moral and religious teachings," the checklist included the following: lack of desire, lack of opportunity, fear of others knowing, wanting to avoid getting serious or making a commitmnent, and held back out of respect for the person I was going with. respondents were asked to check as many items as applied and then circle the one that they felt had the strongest influence. Ns–which represent total checks with the circled checks counting double, just as explained in footnote b of Table 2–are 162, 13, 224, 460, 25, and 279 respectively.

b. Sample Ns in this instance are the same as shown in the column headings of Table 1. Number of non-responses varied from 0 to 4.

is considered wrong is wrong—period! This results in a narrow range of tolerance and discourages deviation and the development of subcultures."[12]

While continuing to work for conformity, perhaps it is time that our religious culture directs increasing attention to the offender—preventing, if it can, some of the more devastating aspects of the trauma and finding improved ways for helping him or her to cope in the face of culturally induced guilt.

*Proposition 4. Religious socialization is the major variable.* After looking at these various unique aspects of Mormon sex standards—the conservative stance, the successful resistance to secular trends, the greater negative effects when standards are violated—one asks, "Why?" My data suggest a particular kind of religious socialization to be the reason.

But before discussing that, permit me to mention two other studies that have reached essentially this same conclusion—the first with reference to religiosity in general and the second, like our own, focusing on Mormon culture. From his voluminous body of research, Alfred Kinsey found that religiously devout men and women participate less than the non-devout in virtually all socially disapproved forms of sexual behavior. He concluded that religion is the "most important factor in restricting premarital activity in the United States."[13] In the Wilford Smith study previously cited, religious activity in the Mormon samples was found to be associated with increasing chastity levels between 1950 and 1972, whereas the reverse was true with both the inactive Mormon groups and the non-Mormon groups. Smith said, "Mormons of both sexes who reported infrequent church attendance reported increasing heterosexual activity right along with the non-Mormon, especially in 1972."[14]

My own study supports these others by, first of all, demonstrating a positive relationship between church attendance (presumed to represent overall religious commitment) and the absence of premarital sex.[15] It then goes on to compare Mormons and non-Mormons on frequency of church attendance, the presumption being that differences would reflect and help explain differences in chastity maintenance. The attendance differences were of high magnitude: well over four-fifths of Mormons attended church once a week or more as compared with only about one-fourth of non-Mormons (Table 3, line 2).

An equally important finding is that "moral or religious teachings" was named by substantially more virginal Mormons than virginal non-Mormons as their reason for stopping short of coitus (Table 3, line 1). Overall, this item stands out as the major explanation that respondents give for refraining.[16]

When these two different approaches are viewed together—high church attendance and high motivation from moral and religious teachings—it is not difficult to understand why premarital sexual indulgence is as well controlled as it is in Mormon culture. From infancy on Mormons are socialized into viewing unchastity as a sin and chastity as one of the highest virtues. This is continually stressed: in the home, from the pulpit, in programs of the several church organizations, and in articles carried by church publications. Promiscuity carries severe sanctions ranging from disapproval to being denied entrance into the temple to being either disfellowshipped or excommunicated. Of course repentance followed by forgiveness provides a way back into the full graces of the church. But overstepping in the sexual area is not taken lightly and the perspectives the church holds on these matters, together with the pressures that it exerts, provides a powerful means of social control. Thus there exists a kind of built-in resistance to secular influence.

Interestingly, it is the Mormon male, in comparison to other males, who lays disproportionate claim to moral and religious motivation. It happens that this item is not the only one in my study where the Mormon male reveals himself to be uniquely conservative—more so than normally expected. This characteristic shows up in several of the comparisons: most notably with respect to favoring censorship of pornography (Table 1), disapproving premarital coitus (Table 1), and attending church frequently (Table 3). In addition—although not shown in Figure 1—I have run separate male and female percentages for both virginal preference regarding a marriage partner and being virginal oneself and found that here too the Mormon male, in most instances, stands out as being uniquely conservative. With respect to these six items at least, intersex difference is less with Mormon than non-Mormon respondents. It appears that there is something operating in Mormon culture to religiously socialize the Mormon male disproportionately to other males and in this manner make him less like other males and more like Mormon females. While the evidence from present data is not final, it certainly is suggestive.

Mormon males are made to feel important and to function in ways that are religiously meaningful to them. Leadership in the church is drawn from lay membership. Females may serve in one or more of the church auxiliary organizations, but they can neither hold the priesthood nor serve in the central governing structure as men do. Girls and women are told to honor the priesthood and to share in its blessings through their husbands, but they cannot be ordained as most men are.

I believe that it is because of this program for keeping the male religiously active and the female supportive of him that so many of the sexual measures which we have employed show male-female differences to be less in the Mormon than the non-Mormon segments of our samples. The Mormon male—probably because of his role as holder of the priesthood—is more effectively socialized into religious conformity, including observance of the chastity norm, than is true with males generally. The norm in Mormon culture is chastity for both sexes. It is a restrictive single standard, approached by means of "taming" the male, not a permissive single standard, achieved by means of liberalizing the female (such as in Scandinavia, for example).

## *NOTES*

1. George R. Carpenter, my collaborator, met with resistance as he gathered data from the Mormon-oriented university. In order to proceed, we agreed with administrators to protect their anonymity in all our publications. But these early difficulties—and similar problems in follow-up studies—resulted in smaller samples from the Intermountain segment. No such difficulties were experienced with either the Midwestern or the Danish universities. The resistance encountered at the Intermountain university is believed to be prima facic evidence of sexual conservatism in Mormon culture.

2. For a complete listing, see my "Mormon Sexuality in Cross-Cultural Perspective," *Dialogue: A Journal of Mormon Thought* 10 (Autumn 1976): 62-75; bibliography on 74-75.

A number of graduate students and faculty members worked with me during different phases of the investigation. Their collaborations have been acknowledged in the publications that apply. Invaluable assistance in gathering the 1978 data came from Kathryn P. Johnsen, Erik Manniche, Jay Schvaneveldt, and Kaare Svalastoga.

Questionnaires were administered during regular class periods. Introductory explanations stressed the scientific nature of the investigation and the anonymity of responses. Students were urged to answer honestly for the purpose of helping enlarge society's understanding of an illusive area of behavior. They were told that participation was strictly voluntary and that, if they so chose, they could either leave early or hand in the questionnaire blank. Very few did.

3. Ibid. See also Harold T. Christensen and Christina F. Gregg, "Changing Sex Norms in America and Scandinavia," *Journal of Marriage and the Family* 32 (Nov. 1970): 616-27; and Wilford E. Smith, "Mormon Sex Standards on College Campuses, or Deal Us Out of the Sexual Revolution," *Dialogue: A Journal of Mormon Thought* 10 (Autumn 1976): 76-81.

4. Since this has resulted in rather small samples, I have based Figure 1 on total or combined male-female responses. The combined numbers, from which the percentages of this figure were calculated, are as follows for 1958, 1968, and 1978 respectively: Intermountain Mormon, 135, 154, and 56; Intermountain non-Mormon, 35, 63, and 43; and Midwestern non-Mormon, 352, 480, and 544.

5. The Family and Human Development (FHD) portion of my 1978 Intermountain sample proved to be considerably more conservative on most items than did the sociology portion. For example, percentages for premarital coitus are as follows for the FHD and sociology respondents, respectively: males, 22.5 and 51.7; females, 18.2 and 44.4. When just the 1978 data are used—as is the case in Tables 1 through 3—it does not appear that combining the FHD and sociology portions biases the results.

6. This, however, seems to be much less true of females. A separate analysis from my data has revealed that many more females are willing to marry a non-virgin. When there is a discrepancy between what one does and what one wants in a marriage partner, it typically is the female who accepts and the male who rejects a partner with greater sexual experience.

7. See the Smith reference cited in n3. Smith limits himself to reporting data pertaining to present premarital sexual activity (coitus, petting, masturbation, and homosexuality) explaining his reason for omitting total or cumulative data as being that the two data sets are very similar.

I have in my possession an earlier and expanded draft of his *Dialogue* article which is titled "Sexual Behavior Reported by Mormon and non-Mormon College Students over Three Decades by Church Attendance." In Table III of that paper Smith does give the cumulative percentages for non-coitus. These are as follows for 1950, 1961, and 1972 respectively: Mormon males,

66.4, 70.7, 76.9; non-Mormon males, 41.0, 58.4, 27.3; Mormon females, 87.1, 85.9, 87.2; non-Mormon females, 79.8, 87.4, 43.1. It is interesting to observe that these percentages are not greatly different from those shown in my Figure 1. But the most meaningful parallels from these two studies lie in the identical directions and similar magnitudes of our Mormon/non-Mormon and our over-time comparisons.

Still additional data from Smith's valuable research on this subject may be found in his "The Constancy of Mormon Chastity," in Glenn M. Vernon, ed., *Research on Mormonism* (Salt Lake City: Association for the Study of Religion, Inc., 1974), 624-41.

8. Harold T. Christensen and Kenneth L. Cannon, "The Fundamentalist Emphasis at Brigham Young University: 1935-1973," *Journal for the Scientific Study of Religion* 17 (1):53-57.

9. Harold T. Christensen, "Two Measures of Premarital Sexual Behavior Compared Across Cultures and Over Time," paper presented at the annual meeting of the California Council on Family Relations, Santa Barbara, California, 27 Sept. 1980.

10. See Harold T. Christensen, "Value-Behavior Discrepancies Regarding Premarital Coitus in Three Western Societies," *American Sociological Review* 27 (Feb. 1962): 66-74.

11. Robert Strauss and Selden D. Bacon, *Drinking in College* (New Haven, CT: Yale University Press, 1953), passim.

12. Harold T. Christensen, "A Cross-Cultural Comparison of Attitudes Toward Marital Infidelity," *International Journal of Comparative Sociology* 3 (Sept. 1962): 124-37, quote from p. 137.

For a more recent exposition of the leveling and perhaps dysfunctional effects of overriding orthodoxy in Mormon culture, see Marvin Rytting and Harold T. Christensen, "The Effect of Religious Orthodoxy: A Statistical Analogy," *Journal of Psychology and Religion* 8 (Winter 1980): 314-22.

13. Alfred C. Kinsey et. al., *Sexual Behavior in the Human Female* (Philadelphia: Saunders, 1953), 324, 686-87, and passim.

14. See the Smith reference in n3; quote from p. 78.

15. This relationship held for both the Mormons and non-Mormons. With respect to the former, over nine-tenths of frequent church attenders (once a week or more) were virginal compared to about half of infrequent attenders. For non-Mormons the proprotions were approximately two-thirds and one-third, respectively.

My study tested other factors to determine if they associated with premarital chastity: age and happiness in one's parent's marriage, for example. With age, there was found to be a slight relationship: the younger respondents reflected greater chastity. With parental happiness, there was a somewhat stronger relationship: respondents from a happy family environment showed greater chastity. No factor, however, reflected an association as strong as church attendance.

16. See table note for a description of how this index was constructed and for a listing of additional factors.

# 5.

# Exhortations for Chastity: A Content Analysis of Church Literature

*Marvin Rytting*

BASED ON HIS STUDY OF THE SEXUAL ATTITUDES AND BEHAVIOR OF college students, Harold T. Christensen has concluded that Mormon premarital sex norms are "strikingly conservative" compared to the broader American culture and "remarkably resistant to change."[1] If anything, the data he presented probably underestimated both the conservatism and resistance to secularization.[2] In fact, other studies have shown this increasing conformity.[3] Christensen hypothesized that one of the important factors in the Mormon ability to resist the permissiveness of the society is the strong religious socialization which the church provides and suggested that the emphasis on chastity in the church is increasing. In order to test this hypothesis, we performed a content analysis of one aspect of religious socialization: exhortations for chastity in official church publications. We chose a random sample of articles appearing in the *Improvement Era, Ensign, New Era, Instructor, Church News*, and talks given in general conference from 1951 to 1979. Because of the difficulty of obtaining this material in Indiana, there are a few deviations from strict randomness, but they are minor and we have attempted to account for them.[4]

If anything, our results underestimate the actual frequency of admonitions to be chaste. First, it is our impression that only a relatively small percentage of chastity injunctions in Mormon culture come from the official materials which we sampled since chastity is usually preached in youth firesides, standards nights, and interviews—and possibly in the home. In addition, there were many general statements about being moral, clean, pure, or faithful or about resisting temptation, gratifications, or animal instincts—all of which we are reasonably certain were both meant as exhortations to be chaste and interpreted by the audience in a sexual context. But we used a strict criterion for inclusion of an article as a reference to chastity, and if the statement was so general that another interpretation was possible we did not include it. Many subtle reminders to be chaste are therefore not reflected in these data.

It is important to know the Mormon moral code in order to identify exhortations because most references employ euphemisms—overtly sexual words are rare. One of the most interesting parts of this code is the use of the term *morality* as a synonym for chastity. While moral philosophers would find this usage disconcerting, most Mormons know that when the Brethren advise us to be moral, they mean for us to avoid sexual misconduct. This use of the word *morality* was evident in the indexes where most of the entries under this heading referred to sexual conduct. And it seemed to become more firmly entrenched over time. Starting in 1976 the index notation under morality reads simply "see chastity." Even more intriguing was the notation under immorality, which reads "see homosexuality." These simple index references reflect much about sexual attitudes in contemporary Mormon culture.

We rated approximately 500 articles or speeches. Of these, about 400 referred to chastity. We identified the source, publication date, and author of the articles; evaluated them on several criteria such as how explicit they were, to whom they were directed, and how strict the tone was; and identified specific topics mentioned within them.[5]

*There was an overall increase in the number of references to chastity over time* (see Fig. 1). After a slight decline during the 1950s and possibly into the early 1960s, admonitions increased during the mid-1960s and became dramatic during the 1970s. The explicit references show a fairly steady increase while the implicit references fluctuate. If the total impact can be thought of as the midpoint between the explicit line and the total line, there is a fairly smooth

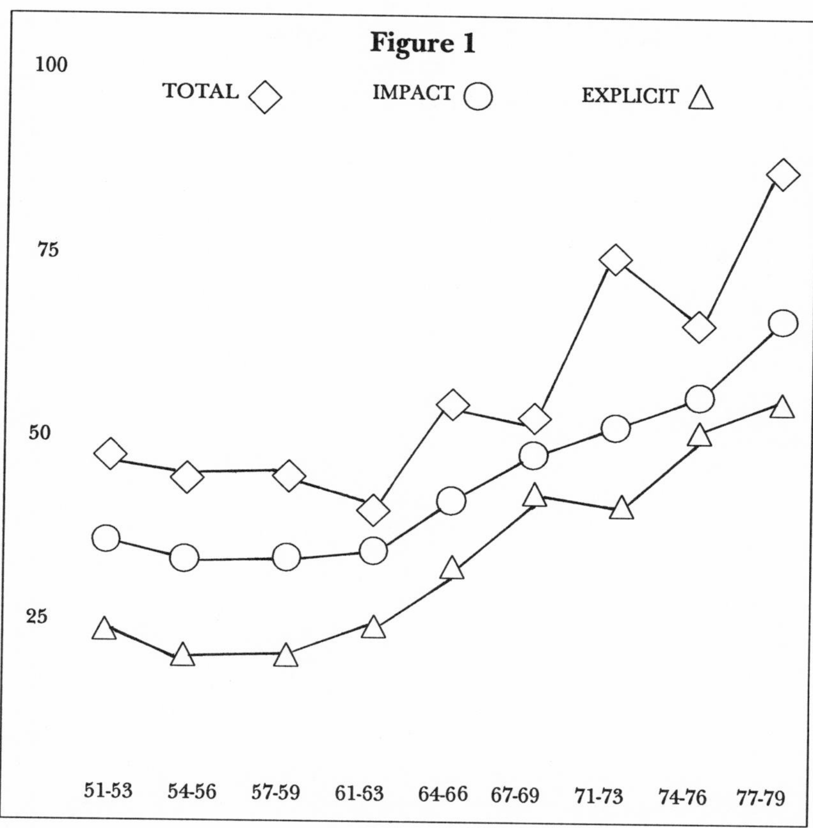


increase. This result provides support for the hypothesis that there has been an intensified socialization promoting the chastity norm.

*Statements about chastity have become more explicit.*[6] In the 1950s it was most common to make veiled references to chastity or at most to make very general statements about being clean and pure and chaste or saving oneself for marriage. By the 1960s it was still most common to make general statements, but there were also many specific injunctions about what not to do. In the 1970s, most admonitions were specific. Before the mid-1960s chastity was typically alluded to in passing or was a minor theme within the article or talk.

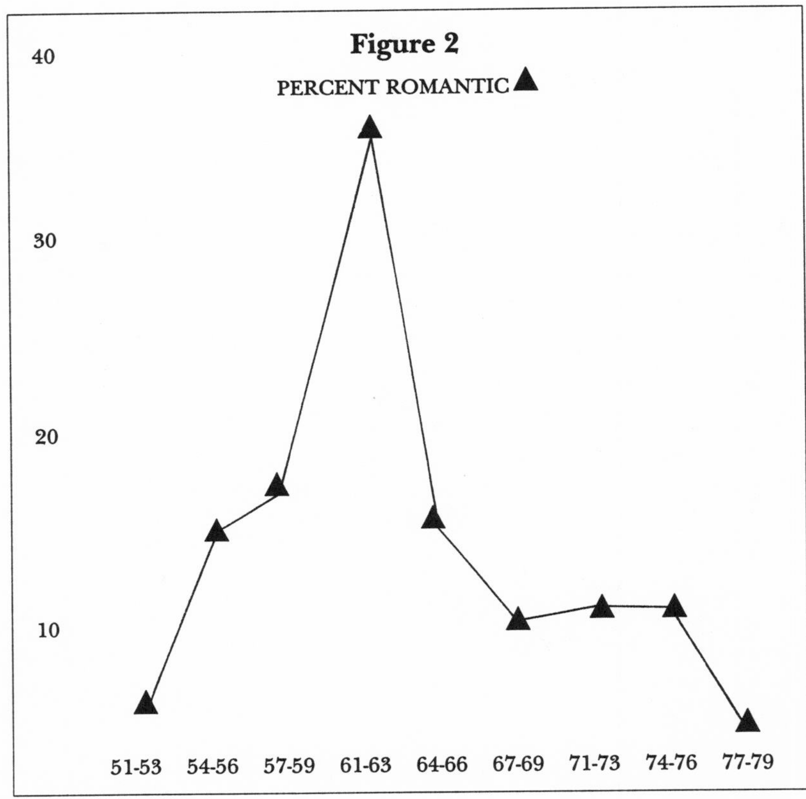


More recently chastity is likely to be a major theme and often the only theme of the article.

*The rhetoric is much stronger than it used to be.* Although it would be misleading to call any of the statements lenient, the tone of the 1950s was certainly more moderate. Chastity was generally presented in positive—almost romantic—terms as the best way to be happy and to make others happy. More recently the focus has been on negative effects of sexual activity because to be unchaste is sinful and those who indulge unlawfully will suffer punishment and misery.

The romantic portrayal of chastity peaked in the 1961-63 period and had almost disappeared by the 1970s (see Fig. 2).

*The focus of the admonitions–to whom they are directed–has also changed.* In the 1950s most of the statements were to individuals to

**Figure 3**

| | | | |
|---|---|---|---|
| 123 | Premarital Sex | 20 | Necking |
| 88 | Extramarital Sex | 20 | Prostitution |
| 70 | Lust/Impure Thoughts | 20 | Cohabitation |
| 57 | Pornography | 14 | Sex Education |
| 55 | Immodesty | 14 | Illegitimacy |
| 49 | Birth Control | 11 | Equal Rights Amendment |
| 48 | Divorce | 11 | Early Marriage |
| 44 | Abortion | 10 | Sex in Music |
| 41 | Dating | 10 | Mixed Marriage/Dating |
| 35 | Homosexuality | 9 | Delayed Marriage |
| 35 | Sex in Movies | 8 | Rape |
| 34 | Vulgarity | 6 | Dancing |
| 30 | Petting | 5 | Sterilization |
| 28 | Sex on TV | 5 | Nudity |
| 27 | Promiscuity | 4 | Staying Out Late |
| 25 | Perversions | 3 | Incest |
| 25 | Venereal Disease | 3 | Masturbation |
| 22 | Grooming | | |

maintain purity or to parents to teach their children to be chaste. Over time more and more statements are directed toward or against society. Expressions of dismay about the sexual excesses of society and dire warnings about the consequences of cultural permissiveness are coupled with exhortations for the Saints to refrain from worldly pleasures and to actively work to clean up society. Being chaste before marriage is no longer sufficient: we must take care to avoid unwholesome connubial practices, and we must fight the social evils of pornography, abortion, homosexuality, and perversion.

*The frequency with which specific themes have been mentioned has changed.* The most common theme was premarital sex. We counted 123 specific references and there were at least that many more indirect references to remaining chaste before marriage. Other common themes are listed in Figure 3. It is interesting to note that masturbation is at the bottom of the list. This should serve as a warning not to interpret the placement of a specific topic on this list as an indication of how strong the sanctions against these behaviors are in Mormon culture. The strong condemnation of masturbation is inculcated more in personal interviews than in public discourse.

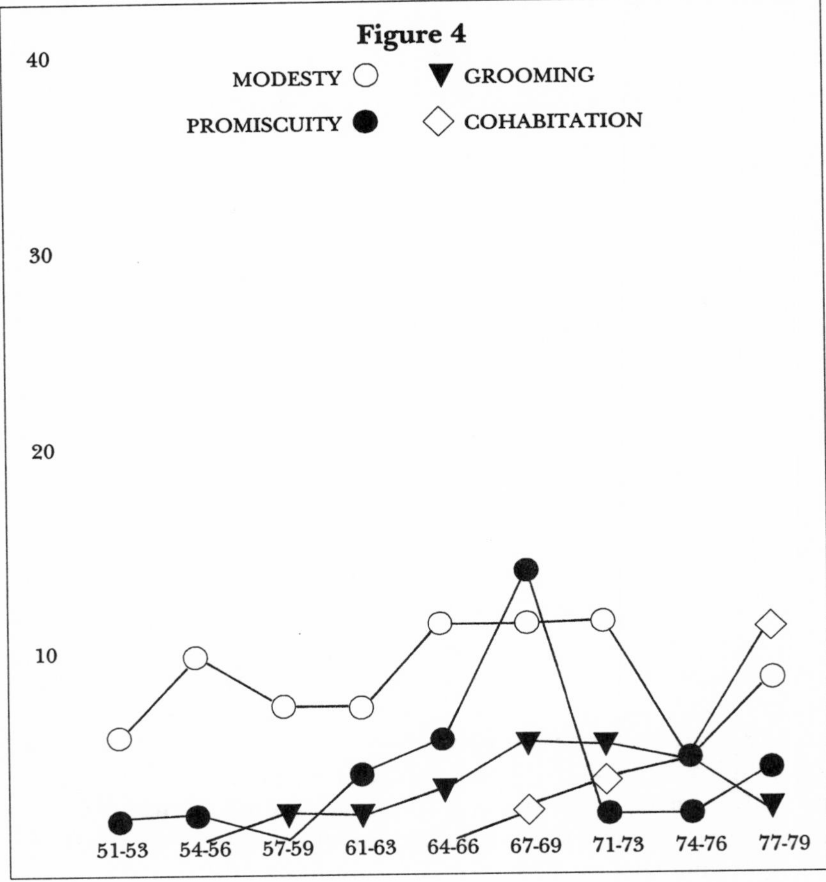


The lack of references is probably due to a feeling that it is not an appropriate topic for open discussion, and this applies also to the lack of any specific definition of the general term "perversions." These are better not discussed in public. In fact there is some indication that the private injunctions sometimes become too explicit. In the late 1970s, bishops were warned to avoid having "pornographic interviews," with the implication that mentioning perversions specifically might lead people to try them.

The most general change over the years has been the increasing tendency to mention specific themes. During the 1950s the typical

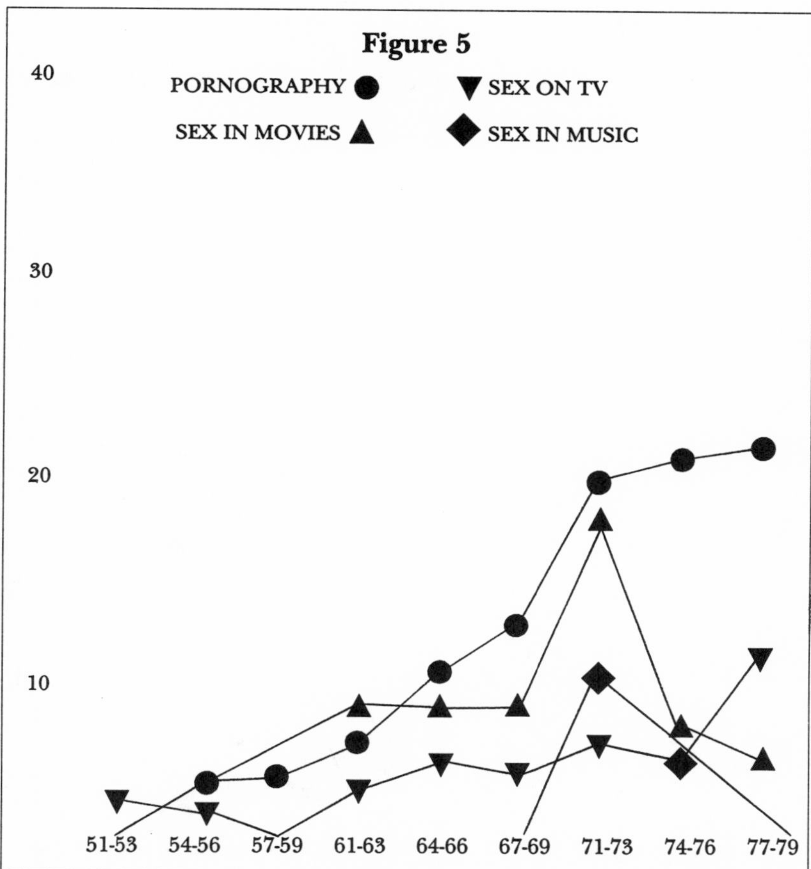


article mentioned two or three, but one-third contained no specific theme at all and only 10 percent referred to four or more specific examples. In contrast, during the 1960s and 1970s only 20 percent contained no specifics, and one-third mentioned four or more themes. There were no themes which were mentioned significantly more often during the 1950s than they have been since. There were several topics which were not referred to during the 1950s, including perversion, homosexuality, pornography, sex in the movies and on TV, and venereal disease.

Specific references to premarital sex hit their peak during the

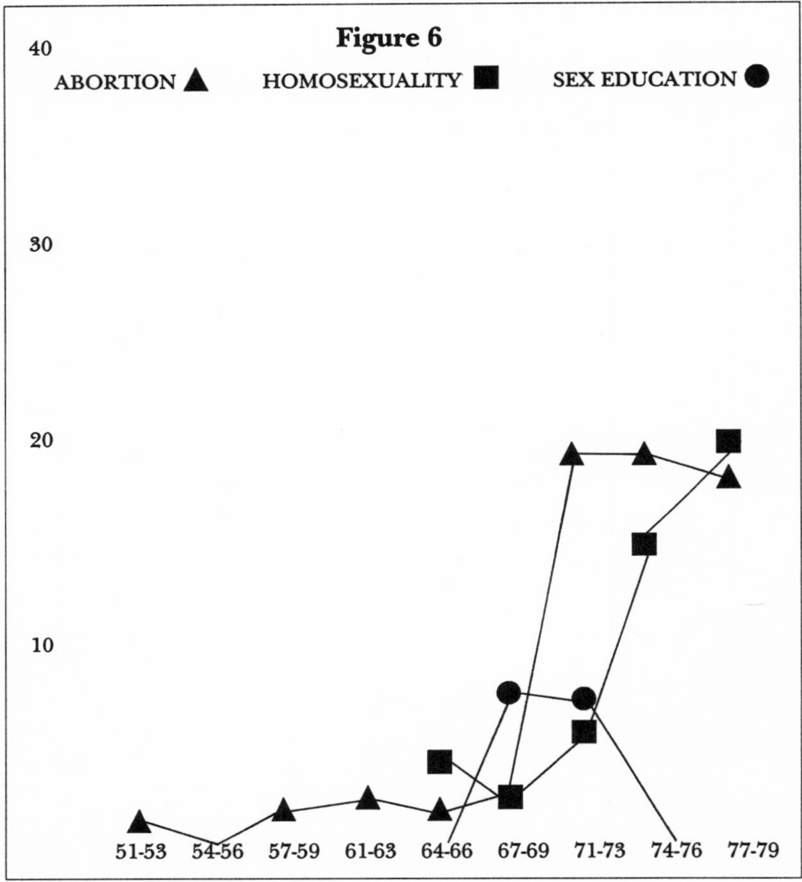


1960s when analyzed as a percentage of total citations, although the gross number of references continued to rise throughout the 1970s. Also hitting peaks during the 1960s were immodesty, illegitimacy, free love or promiscuity, and venereal disease—all associated with salient facets of what is sometimes called the sexual revolution of the 1960s, the fairly widespread and highly publicized experimentation with sex by young college students (see Figure 4).[7]

During the 1970s the focus broadened from premarital sex to include marital sex, with references to issues such as birth control and unwholesome connubial excesses (including the only mention of

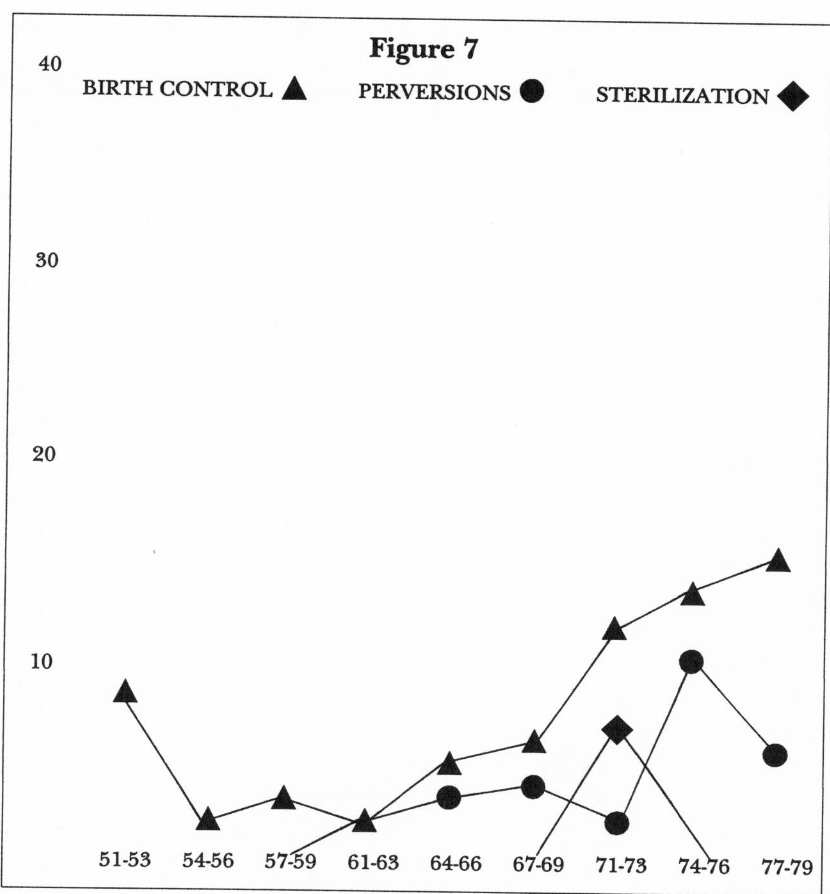


sterilization and incest) and sociopolitical issues such as pornography, homosexuality, living together without formal marriage, and moral dangers inherent in the Equal Rights Amendment. Note the gradually increased concern with the pornography issues (see Fig. 5) and the rather precipitous jump in political issues (see Fig. 6) and marital injunctions (see Fig. 7).

Several variables can explain the dramatic change in official rhetoric. Our data provide some support for four factors, and as firm believers in multi-causal explanation, we suggest that all of these processes—and possibly others—have had an impact.

*Changes in publication format have had an influence on the content and frequency of statements about sex.* Throughout the 1950s and 1960s, for example, President David O. McKay wrote a monthly editorial in the *Instructor.* This provided a regular outlet for his views on chastity. Another regular outlet for his statements came in articles for the *Church News* which seemed to report on almost every talk he gave—even in ward sacrament meetings, particularly during the early and mid-1950s. This regular exposure in the media helped him dominate the scene and was again true for President Kimball in the *Church News.*

Publications also became larger and dropped advertising so that more articles could be published. In 1961 the *Improvement Era* started a new section called the "Era of Youth." In the first few years, there was an increased number of references to chastity which then tapered off. When the *New Era* began as a separate publication for church youth in 1971, there was an even more dramatic increase in references to chastity augmented by the practice of carrying "The Spoken Word" by Richard L. Evans and reprinting church positions directed to youth.[8] Once again over time the references tapered off somewhat, but not as much.

The consistency of a publication can also become an important factor. The editorials in the *Church News*, for example, have consistently been—most notably since the mid-1960s—the most outspoken on sexual conduct in the Mormon media. The admonitions in these editorials are more explicit, more emphatic, and more negative in tone than the other publications. They are the most likely to preach about avoiding excesses in marital sexuality and to warn of the dangers of sexual permissiveness in society. They are also the most inclined to portray sex as disgusting and the least inclined to present any positive context for chastity.

*Trends in the broader culture have resulted in a hardening of the rhetoric about chastity.* The overt sexuality of the late 1960s and early 1970s had a strong impact on church leaders. Advocacy of free love and living together without marriage and the rise in illegitimacy and venereal disease prompted scathing denunciations. The advent of mini-skirts prompted increased emphasis on modesty, surpassing efforts in the early 1950s to stamp out strapless formals. In reaction to the counterculture, admonitions began to include injunctions not only to be modest but to be well groomed (beardless) and neatly dressed to avoid the appearance of evil.[9]

The rapid proliferation of pornography in society was a factor in the increased concern expressed about not only hard-core pornography but about sex in movies, television, and popular music. The emergence of the gay liberation movement produced increasingly harsh statements about homosexuality. This was particularly evident in 1978 when one article about homosexuality in a California newspaper served as the impetus for several editorials in the *Church News*. The abortion issue looms larger after the Supreme Court ruled that it was legal. Early statements about abortion seem moderate in comparison to recent rhetoric, and the increased number of references is dramatic. The church obviously responded to the social milieu. There is potential irony here. Church leaders seem to be more vociferous about the evils of sexuality at a time when church members seem to be very strict in sexual behavior and conservative in their attitudes.

*There was a perception that members of the church were becoming less observant of the law of chastity*. A hint of this comes from Christensen's article.[10] He interpreted his 1968 findings as indicating that the chastity norm was alive and well in Mormondom compared with what was happening in the Midwest and particularly Scandinavia. Still, the fact that the rate of premarital sex among Intermountain women in the sample had tripled in the previous ten-year period would not have been comforting to church leaders. The letter that Alvin R. Dyer wrote to Christensen indicates that the church found the data alarming. Whether or not Christensen's study had an impact, it seems evident that the perception in 1971 was that the sexual permissiveness which was sweeping the country may have been leading the youth of Zion astray. Within this context, it is interesting to note that in the year 1971 there were more references to chastity than in any other year in the sample. This year differed from other years also in that statements came from the Quorum of the Twelve and the First Presidency. It seemed to have been a concerted effort. There was an unusually large number of articles and talks devoted exclusively to chastity. Many of the references were from general conference, and these tended to be more explicit, emphatic, and strict than normal.

Although there were obviously other factors operating, it seems likely that the research reported in Christensen's essay contributed heavily to these results. This is a sobering thought about the role that research in the social sciences plays in influencing the very phenomena being studied. There is a circular flow of causality: socialization affects attitudes and behavior, but attitudes and behavior can also affect socialization.

*The most salient factor in the tone of chastity exhortations was the changing style of successive church presidents.* David O. McKay clearly dominated the rhetoric in the 1950s through the mid-1960s, both in the number of statements about chastity and in setting the tone and establishing the point of view. Likewise, the feel of the 1970s rhetoric reflected the perspective and style of Spencer W. Kimball. Joseph Fielding Smith and Harold B. Lee did not dominate the chastity dialogue during their presidencies—the apostles did.

There are some similarities between presidents McKay and Kimball. For both, chastity was a compelling issue. Even when it was not the subject of a talk or article, they often made passing references to it. In their presidencies, they traveled throughout the church with one basic talk on the subject which they repeatedly gave, only slightly changing versions of the same message. They dominate our analysis mainly because they dominated the press. The *Church News* reported almost weekly on talks given by President McKay, and almost all contained some reference to chastity. President Kimball was undoubtedly preaching the law of chastity at the same time—and in his own style—but the *Church News* did not start reporting on all of his talks until he became president.

The style of the two men was radically different. When McKay became president in 1951, there were two types of statements about sexuality. On one hand, there were reasonable and moderate statements by men like Apostle John A. Widtsoe. There were also, however, several references back to an official statement from the 1940s which included the line, "better dead clean than alive unclean."

President McKay enthroned the first approach, and by the mid-1950s it was dominant. While he was adamant about the necessity for chastity, he focused on positive reasons for remaining virtuous and made chastity seem romantic. He spoke of the joy of a young man and woman, deeply in love, meeting at the temple altar with the full assurance that they both brought with them bodies and minds which were clean and pure because they had heeded the admonition to "be faithful to your future spouse." He used images of classic chivalry: a flower growing by the roadside is covered with dust, a young man passes it by and instead risks his life to scale the perpendicular cliffs in search of the sweet and lovely flower that grows in the high mountain meadow, untouched by human hands.

McKay's major theme was the importance of self-control. We need to have spirituality rather than succumb to animal instincts and gratifications. Among the passions which we are to control are anger, selfishness, greed, and lust. Chastity was rarely singled out as the most important part of self-control, but it was usually mentioned. McKay rarely went into detail but rather talked in general about the importance of maintaining virginity. He seldom mentioned necking and petting or sex in marriage and never dealt with perversions. He did become somewhat more direct and strict in the late 1960s, but less than 5 percent of his statements come from that time period, and by then he was no longer the main spokesman on the subject of chastity.

In comparison with the statements of President McKay, the exhortations of President Kimball were more explicit, more emphatic, more direct, more specific, and stricter. They were more likely to describe sexual misconduct rather than discuss sex in a positive or romantic context. Kimball had a litany of abominations which usually included homosexuality, perversion, abortion, pornography, adultery, and birth control. More than half of the time, he mentioned at least six different specific topics (McKay mentioned that many only once), sometimes as many as thirteen or fourteen.[11]

It is tempting to explain the differences between the rhetoric of presidents McKay and Kimball as merely personality differences, but that would not paint a complete picture of why Kimball was so much more severe. One explanation would be Kimball's adoration and emulation of his father who was strict and rebuked people pointedly in his sermons.[12] But this would not account for the importance which chastity had assumed for Kimball. There were hints that his seeming obsession came as much from his experiences as an apostle as from his personality. In 1947 Kimball was assigned to interview members who had in various ways violated the sexual rules of the church. He was disturbed by this experience, and it is likely that the recurring theme of chastity sprang largely from this assignment as a member of the Quorum of the Twelve. In 1951 he spoke out strongly on modesty at BYU, and chastity has been a common theme ever since. In 1959, along with Apostle Mark E. Petersen, he received a special assignment to counsel homosexuals, and in 1968 he was so concerned with this issue that he asked President McKay to enlarge the committee. His jurisdiction in the sexual areas may have kept the issues uppermost in his mind and made him feel as though sexual problems were indeed rampant.[13]

In a broader context, the differences in the approaches reflect different attitudes toward sex in American society at large. The *Puritan* perspective on sex was strict, but the rhetoric was relatively calm. The focus was on maintaining premarital chastity through social sanctions, but sex per se was seen as good; marital sex was a legitimate and beautiful—even holy or sacred—expression of conjugal love. The *Victorian* view focused on the evil nature of sex itself and the need for control of every manifestation of sexuality—extending to "the supposedly ubiquitous sexual excesses practiced within the privacy of the marriage bed or, even worse, by the individual alone."[14] The rhetoric of the Victorian sexual reformers exhibited frantic, even fanatic, fervor.

Each perspective developed against the unique challenges and anxieties of a specific era. Social control worked for the Puritans in a world which was relatively stable and secure. The near-hysteria of the Victorian era, according to Klaus Hansen, probably came from the anxiety generated by a cosmic confrontation with the possibilities of individual freedom coupled with a breakdown of social control.[15] John Barth has called this sense of cosmic confrontation "cosmopsis" or "a sense of possibility so overwhelming that [a person] is unable to choose at all for fear of eliminating alternative choices."[16] This kind of confrontation leads some to resist commitments or limits and paralyzes them. The Victorians reacted by trying to eliminate as many of the options as possible. Since social restraint was not working as it had done in Puritan times, Victorian morality demanded severe individual restraint.

President McKay's discussions of chastity were an intriguing mixture of Puritan and Victorian themes. His tone was principally Puritan, but his focus on the need for individual self-control and the importance of avoiding excesses of any kind, particularly sexual excesses, contained a remnant of Victorianism. This was tied to a capitalistic metaphor which stressed the economic virtues of saving oneself for marriage and arriving at the marketplace with undamaged goods.

In the 1950s, however, capitalistic individualism (which helped bring on the original Victorianism) was no longer the exciting but anxiety-producing new wave of the future. It was an old established system and seemed to be working. An underlying assumption of the 1950s was that rational self-control was as successful as social control had been for the Puritans—and one of the basic assumptions behind McKay's treatment of sexuality was that sex is controllable, and therefore a moderate and rational appeal to maintain chastity was sufficient. In a stable time, we did not need the harsh denial of sexual possibilities to give us security.

But capitalism had another assumption which led to problems. Philip Slater points out that capitalism is based on the assumption of scarcity.[17] It is an economic system for the distribution of scarce resources. But with prosperity came abundance, and the old rules of capitalism no longer worked. Economic progress was no longer dependent upon saving to generate capital but rather on consumption of no-longer scarce goods. As we were constantly reminded by the advertisers, the American way was to consume as much as possible. To a generation raised on conspicuous consumption, the assumption of scarcity did not make sense and the need for control was far from obvious. If it is good to indulge in material gratifications, why not indulge in sexual gratification also? It was a small step from middle-class conspicuous consumption to anti-middle-class overtly excessive gratification of any impulse. Rejection of any type of control became a symbol which provided a sense of identity for rebellion against middle-class morality.

American society was faced with another crisis. With a rejection of both social and individual control, untold options unfolded and massive anxiety resulted. No wonder church leaders were dismayed and concerned. We had lost control. In American society social control had broken down and individual self-control was rejected. There were hints that control was slipping among Mormon youth, and the government was trying to impose its will upon us by taking away BYU's ability to control the sexual behavior of its students.[18]

In this context, it is not surprising that Mormon rhetoric again adopted a Victorian flavor. In contrast to McKay's message, we are now told that we are not really able to control our sexual urges. Social control by the church is needed to help us avoid temptation. But we also need to control the larger society. We must stamp out pornography, outlaw abortion, and send homosexuality back to the closet so that we can avoid contact with the overpowering force of sexual desire. But still, we cannot leave out self-control. Even making it to marriage unscathed is no guarantee of safety. We must have eternal vigilance lest we are seduced by excessive enjoyment of marital sex. In the midst of our deep concern to avoid evil, there is little room for sex to be a beautiful and natural expression of affection.

Victorianism is basically a secular sentiment rather than a religious view. Although it may adopt the language of religion, it was in the nineteenth century, and it is today, a social reaction to the anxiety produced by a loss of control or a cosmoptic crisis. It is not intrinsic to Mormonism. In addition, it is an emotionally charged response and blurs distinctions which are necessary for mature moral reasoning. It may be the basis for a code of proper behavior, but it is not the source of a meaningful morality.

Just as there are multiple causes of the change in rhetoric about chastity, there are surely several different effects which come from it, some positive and some negative, as Harold Christensen points out in his essay. It is important to examine carefully what the effects of our sexual attitudes might be and search for an approach which will encourage responsible, healthy sexual behavior.

One place to begin might be with the economic metaphor, already discussed, which Slater used to analyze the counterculture and explain the "sexual revolution." The belief in abundance that he described lasted a relatively short time. With the energy crisis and environmentalism, we are again aware of scarcity. We need not return to the grasping selfishness of capitalism, however. There is not enough to squander—we need some controls—but there is enough to share. This is true of intimacy also. We need some control (enough to reduce the number of options from the infinite to the manageable), but we do not need the Victorian rejection of sexuality altogether. The no "control" position is currently being discredited both in professional circles and in our society. What we need—both individually and as a culture—is a well-managed intimacy which values sexuality but also controls it.

*NOTES*

1. Harold T. Christensen, "The Persistence of Chastity within Contemporary Mormon Culture," paper presented at the meeting of the Mormon History Association, Rexburg, Idaho, May 1981, and reprinted in this volume.

2. Christensen attempted to maintain comparable samples across time, which resulted in basing the results on more liberal students in sociology classes. Using his total sample, the percent virginal is 87 percent rather than 73 percent. If the true comparison sample lies somewhere between the sociology classes and the total, the 1978 students are not merely maintaining a conservative standard but observing the sexual prohibitions more strictly.

3. Harold T. Christensen and Kenneth L. Cannon, "The Fundamentalist Emphasis at Brigham Young University: 1935-1973," *Journal for the Scientific Study of Religion* 17 (1):53-57; Wilford E. Smith, "Mormon Sex Standards on College Campuses, or Deal Us Out of the Sexual Revolution," *Dialogue: A Journal of Mormon Thought* 10 (Autumn 1976): 76-81.

4. The biggest variation in the selection of material is between the time before and after 1960. Starting with 1961, the church has published an index to church publications: *Index to the Periodicals of the Church of Jesus Christ of Latter-day Saints*, 1961-70; 1971-75; 1976; 1977; 1979. (We could not find the 1978 index, so we did a random sample of the publications for that year.) Indexes before that time are incomplete and inconsistent. Therefore, for the years since 1960 we sampled one-third of the index references dealing with any category which was potentially related to chastity, but we took a one-third sample of the publications themselves during the 1950s. There is a possible distortion with this strategy because the indexes might not include some references to chastity which we would pick up while specifically looking for them. To verify the adequacy of the indexes, we sampled 1979 from the periodicals as well as from the index and concluded that the index sample underestimates the number of references by at least one-third. To make the indexed and nonindexed years comparable, we multiplied the former by 1.5 when reporting the basic frequency of chastity exhortations.

This correction was done only for Figure 1, the total number of chastity references. The only difference in interpretation of the data without this correction would be that the number of citations would show a more pronounced drop from 1957-59 to 1961-63. The references in 1961-63 are probably underestimated still because many of the index references sampled came from the early issues of the "Era of Youth" and sounded like chastity messages but did not meet our criteria.

5. All of our ratings were performed by two raters. We randomly divided the years and sources. In checking the reliability of the ratings, we found a general agreement, especially in identifying the specific topics. There are a few ratings which we had trouble agreeing upon but we do not report those results. The patterns we report, however, are true for both raters.

6. All of the comparisons which we report have differences which are significant at the .05 level, using either a chi-square, t, or F statistic (the latter for a one-way analysis of variance).

7. In the graphs, articles which expounded on the specific topic rather than merely mentioning it were counted as two references.

8. The reprinting of official statements in the *New Era*, the *Church News*, and the *Ensign* increased the number of references which could be sampled. Some conference talks were also reported in the *Church News* as well as the *Ensign* in the early 1970s, many area conferences were held and the proceedings were referenced in the indexes. We did not have access to these, so the 1971-74 period, especially, is probably still underestimated.

9. At one point there was even an injunction not to wear the extremely modest long dresses because they had been associated with the hippie culture.

10. See n1.

11. As an example of this style, see Kimball's special article on morality in the November 1980 issue of the *Ensign*.

12. Edward L. Kimball and Andrew E. Kimball, Jr., *Spencer W. Kimball* (Salt Lake City: Bookcraft, 1977).

13. Ibid.

14. Klaus J. Hansen, *Mormonism and the American Experience* (Chicago: University of Chicago Press, 1981), 149; reprinted in this volume.

15. Ibid.

16. Cynthia Davis, "Heroes, Earth Mothers and Muses: Gender Identity in Barth's Fiction," *The Centennial Review* 24 (Summer 1980): 311.

17. Philip E. Slater, *The Pursuit of Loneliness: American Culture at the Breaking Point* (Boston: Beacon Press. 1976).

18. It is likely that the strength of the church opposition to the Equal Rights Amendment comes partly from its experience with government attempts to enforce Title IX regulations at BYU—ERA is a moral issue because it can break down social control.

# 6. Fidelity, Polygamy, and Celestial Marriage

*Eugene England*

In this essay I explore an idea—the general Mormon expectation of polygamy in heaven—that has important religious and moral implications but about which there is little definite scriptural direction and no clear official doctrine. I attempt a reconsideration of our traditional popular thought that is, of course, unauthoritative—but serious. I suggest some new, possibly beneficial, ways we might think and feel about monogamous marriage—both as it is and as it might be. My essay is not a critique of official Mormon practice or doctrine but an invitation to reexamine some unofficial ideas and expectations which persist among most Mormons because of a past practice—a practice I believe was divinely inspired but also believe was divinely, and permanently, rescinded.

Shakespeare's *Julius Caesar* contains a crucial scene after Brutus has decided to join the conspiracy and kill Caesar. Brutus is reflecting on that decision in his orchard in the early morning when his wife Portia joins him. Awakened when Brutus has left her side and alarmed by the voices and cloaked figures of the departing conspirators, she worries that all this may be related to his "musing and sighing" at dinner the night before and the "ungentle looks" and "impatience" with which he had waved her aside. Even now Brutus claims he is merely "not well in health" and tells her to "go to bed." But Portia will not be dismissed and speaks straight to the heart of his real illness:

You have some sickness of offense within your mind,
Which, by the right and virtue of my place,
I ought to know of. . . .
I ask you, by my once commended beauty,
By all your vows of love, and that great vow
Which did incorporate and make us one,
That you unfold to me, yourself, your half,
Why you are heavy. . . .
Within the bond of marriage, tell me, Brutus,
Is it there stated I should know no secrets
That appertain to you? Am I yourself
But, as it were, in sort or limitation,
[That is, am I one with you in only a limited way?]
To keep with you at meals, comfort your bed,
And talk to you sometimes? Dwell I but in the suburbs
Of your good pleasure? If it be no more,
Portia is Brutus' harlot, not his wife.[1]

Portia then reminds Brutus of the qualities of lineage and character that first drew him to her and, as further proof of her firmness and courage to bear his painful and intimate secrets, reveals that she had wounded herself in the thigh but had suffered patiently all night without troubling him. Brutus exclaims, "O ye gods. Render me worthy of this noble wife!" But he does nothing to achieve that worthiness. A knock at the door signals an additional conspirator to be won over, and Brutus readily allows this crucial opportunity with his wife to be interrupted. Although he promises Portia that "by and by thy bosom shall partake/ The secrets of my heart," he never keeps that promise. Had he shared his deepest self with his other half, his wife, and had then been advised by her better perspective, this man, whom Marc Anthony later calls "the noblest Roman of them all," might have been deterred from bringing greater evil on Rome than the evil he sought to cure. Instead, he destroys the life of Portia, who kills herself by swallowing hot coals after she learns what he has done and sees what his fate will be. And Brutus finally takes his own life after Octavius and Anthony defeat his armies at Philippi.

Shakespeare thus shows how well he understood the importance of *fidelity*, the complete faithfulness, loyalty, and sharing that is possible only when a man and a woman join their full lives–physical, mental, and spiritual–in what he called "the marriage of true minds"[2]. He saw fidelity as central to married love, which he portrayed as the supreme form of human happiness and wholeness at the end of each of his comedies–and the violation or interruption of which lies at the heart of most of the tragedies and late romances.

I believe Shakespeare is right. Marital fidelity is central to mortal joy and eternal life, and great catastrophes are already resulting from our current neglect of it, in society generally and in too many Mormon marriages. It is the key to our concepts of sexual morality before and after marriage. And there is, I believe, a serious danger to the ideal of fidelity–and thus both to our sexual morality and to our concepts of ourselves as eternal men and women–in the expectation, shared I fear by many Mormons, that the highest form of marriage in the celestial realm is what is technically called polygyny, plural wives for a single husband.

*I believe official Mormon polygyny, as it was practiced in the nineteenth century, was inspired by God through his prophets.* (I emphasize this point because some, who have heard about but not read this essay carefully, have assumed the opposite.) I am the descendant of polygynists. I honor those literal ancestors and my many spiritual ancestors who lived that law–faithfully, morally, and at enormous costs to themselves and the church. Those costs included alienation from American culture and from their own moral training, martyrdom for a few, and nearly the total destruction of their church and culture by the United States government, which was willing to use brutal and in my view unconstitutional means to force Mormon conformity. I believe that the good achieved by polygyny–including probably the cohesion forced by the extreme social and moral isolation and persecution it provoked–outweighed those costs and made possible the establishment and success of the church during its beginning period. And when that practice had achieved its purposes, limited to a specific historical period and place, God took it away.

*I believe God removed polygyny by inspiration to his prophets because it was no longer worth the costs it exacted.* It was not removed because our ancestors lacked the courage or ability to continue to pay those costs or merely wanted to accommodate themselves to mainstream American values. I believe that anyone who honestly examines the evidence will conclude that there were terrible difficulties and mistakes, embarrassing vacillations and equivocations, even transgressions and deceptions (by both church leaders and lay members), that accompanied both the beginning and the end of polygyny. But I do not believe that the problems accompanying plural marriage came, as some have alleged, because Joseph Smith was uninspired or lustful or because Brigham Young and John Taylor persisted in a mistake against God's will. As I read their letters, journals, and sermons and the accounts and testimony of those who knew them best, I find evidence, despite mistakes and problems, that Joseph Smith had great self-control and that all three prophets were divinely inspired leaders who would not persist in a form of marriage—the supreme sacrament of Mormon theology—that was contrary to God's will.

The anguish, mistakes, and problems that instituting polygyny brought to Mormons came because most people involved were trying to respond to what they believed was undeniable new revelation that nevertheless directly countered their own moral inclinations and Christian training. And I believe that in that clash of the old moral code with new revelation lies the best answer to the question of *why*. Why would God require such a strange practice, one counter to standard Christian morality and inherited rationality, one that contradicted sensible and God-given moral laws—and thus could be practiced only at enormous cost?

There are parallels in other difficult questions, such as: Why would God command his faithful prophet Abraham to kill his son Isaac, when God condemned human sacrifice as immoral? or, Why would God deny priesthood blessings to blacks, counter to his own teachings about universal equality? Polygyny was, as the Lord in Doctrine and Covenants 132 indicates, an "Abrahamic" test, that is, a command by God to violate an earlier commandment: "God commanded Abraham, and Sarah gave Hagar to Abraham to wife. . . . Was Abraham, therefore, under condemnation? . . . Nay; for I, the Lord, commanded it. Abraham was commanded to offer his son Isaac; nevertheless, it was written: Thou shalt not kill. Abraham, however, did not refuse, and it was accounted unto him for righteousness" (v. 35; see vv. 34-37).

God apparently uses such a unique and uniquely troubling test to teach us the crucial but paradoxical truth that personal experiences with divinity must outweigh our rational assumptions about morality. Obedience to divine commands sometimes supersede our understanding of earlier commands. If we are to transcend the human limitations of even our best inherited culture and religion, we must learn, sometimes painfully, to be open to change. Truth and history are too complex to be reduced to simple, irrevocable commandments—even from past prophets—like "Thou shalt always have only one spouse." Truth must be ultimately "rational," but its logic is not always or immediately clear to our present reason.

Our ancestors' obedience to the new and "contradictory" revelation of polygyny, I believe, both tested and confirmed their worthiness to build God's kingdom. They learned, as Shakespeare also knew, that "Sweet are the uses of adversity".[3] And they learned that lesson from the most wrenching human adversity—when contraries are posed by God himself. But if polygyny was an Abrahamic test, and thus a means to reveal and develop qualities necessary in one particular and unusual historical setting, it is not necessary to project this lifestyle into the eternities as the basis for a celestial order, as many Mormons now do. Heaven is, by definition, a place where cultural limitations and historical peculiarities of earth life no longer prevail. Abrahamic tests and other special historical requirements, such as "lower" laws like the Levitical priesthood for the ancient Israelites and tithing for us, teach us much about God's flexible dealing with human limitations and historical conditions but little about a supernatural celestial order, beyond such temporary mortal conditions.[4]

What then could such a supreme order be like? What *should* be our model of celestial marriage? Though we are given very little direct description of that highest heaven, the scriptures clearly support a theology of absolute fidelity between equal partners as the basis for sexual morality, marital happiness, eternal increase and, in its fullest implications, for godhood itself, the creative relationship and resulting power that makes all existence possible:

> Neither is the man without the woman nor the woman without the man, in the Lord (1 Cor. 11:11).
>
> And Adam said, This is now bone of my bones, and flesh of my flesh. . . . therefore shall a man leave his father and his mother, and shall cleave unto his wife: and they shall be one flesh (Gen. 2:23-24).

> For it must needs be, that there is an opposition in all things (2 Ne. 2:11).
>
> Black and white, bone and free, male and female . . . all are alike unto God (2 Ne. 26:33).

The theology of eternal, faithful sexuality as the foundation of divinity itself based on these and other scriptures is unique to Mormonism and is profoundly attractive to me. Just as the atonement of Jesus is the key to our salvation from sin and death in this life, so celestial marriage seems to be the key to exaltation, or eternal progression, both now and in the life to come.

The Mormon theology of marriage has two main characteristics. First, it implies that complementary oppositions lie at the heart of physical, moral, and social existence. The most fundamental of these is the male-female polarity. That fundamental opposition, when it is tamed and matured into physical and spiritual unity, makes possible the creation and proper nurture both of mortal children and of spirit children to populate new universes. Female-male unity (which God has powerfully imaged in the concept of becoming "one flesh") ideally involves complete sharing—between separate, co-eternal individuals and without loss of our own individuality—of all our singularity, vulnerability, trust, hopes, and potentialities.

Since celestial marriage is a crucial requirement for exaltation to godhood, Mormon theology suggests that the maturity essential to discovery and exaltation of the self is ultimately possible only in a fully equal, bi-polar but thus complementary, individual-to-individual synthesis. The supreme figure for this ideal, powerfully reinforced each time faithful Mormons attend temple or sealing ceremonies, is that of the earth's first lovers and parents: We are each invited to become, figuratively, Adam or Eve. We are thus imaginatively united in that perfect one-to-one unity established in the beginning by God, because "it is not good that the man should be alone" (Gen. 2: 18). The Hebrew word for "alone" means incomplete, unfulfilled, rather than lonely. We are united that we might "know" each other, meaning in Hebrew to fully comprehend and share our being, sexually and in all other ways.[5] The highest model for marriage, then, established in Eden and reinforced in the most sacred LDS ceremonies, is monogamous and centered in full one-to-one fidelity.

The image of becoming one flesh is realized most literally, of course, in conception, when our bodies actually unite to make new life. The sexual relationship perfectly represents spiritual union within polarity, that one-to-one sharing that ultimately makes possible the creativity enjoyed by the gods themselves. We can violate that creative union of two opposites in various ways—by immature haste or promiscuity, by self-gratification or lust (outside marriage or even within it if sex is indulged in selfishly), by lying to each other, by not sharing fully and often our deepest feelings and hopes, by refusing to be vulnerable and thus walling off parts of ourselves, or by not working constantly to justify and build complete trust.

The second main idea about marriage in Mormon theology is that since the fullest and highest form of love in the universe, the love that makes godhood possible, is the fully sexual and exclusive love of a man and a woman eternally committed to each other, it is the key to our highest joys and exaltations—or our greatest pains and failures. That love, even if the accidents of mortal life may prevent children, is the love that will continue the work and glory of God through eternal increase and creation in the hereafter. Therefore heterosexual married love is the ideal held out for all and eventually made available to all: Mortal probation continues for a long time after death in order to provide equal opportunities to all, and our theology promises that any genetic, developmental, or cultural problems or physical accidents that prevent marriage or children in this life will be resolved and opportunities for such marriages and children will be provided *everyone* in the next life.

But, as I understand it, Mormon theology also promises serious consequences if we oppose or neglect that ideal. There are prohibitions against homosexual activity and extramarital intercourse and discouragements against lust—of promiscuous, selfish, or obsessive eroticism—even in marriage. The only rational explanation, it seems to me, for such warnings and prohibitions is that by their nature certain practices either tend to center on self rather than on relationship and to deny the creative integrity of sexual intercourse—that is, its unique capability, at least in potential, to produce new life—or they violate the trust and fidelity that the vulnerability and creative power of male-female union both nurture and need.

What then about polygyny? It, in my view, does not fit the model of one-to-one fidelity I have described. First, we must consider the possibility that polygyny really does not violate fidelity, that if people are good enough they can have trust and sexual wholeness with more than one person. If this were true of our polygynous ancestors, as it could have been, might it be even more likely in the celestial realms where the conditions and our capabilities will be much better than what we know now? I have found that this is the hope and assumption of many, perhaps most, Latter-day Saints who have seriously considered the possibility they might eventually live in plural marriage.

I find two problems with such a hope. First, it is based on a dangerous notion: that getting more of a good thing is an improvement, that great love for one person is better if extended to great love for many people. Consider, however, the differences between the various elements that make up truly complete love. They include charity or unconditional, Christlike love—but also friendship and erotic love, love that makes choices, love that is based on differential desires. The unconditional, *redemptive* love God has for all his children and commands us all to learn is certainly capable of being multiplied to many people. But such unconditional love is only a *part* of married love. And the other elements of a complete, married love, including restrictive obligations, covenants of complete and exclusive sharing, and the creative sexual love that makes new children and universes possible, are not improved by multiplication. In fact, they seem to be destroyed or at least weakened by it. Romantic, married love is, I believe, strengthened by being *exclusive*, even for the gods.

Eternal marriage uniquely includes all the elements of love: the exclusive, the inclusive, and the unconditional. Although it can expand greatly, even to include Christlike sacrificial love for populous worlds of spirit children, it will nevertheless be injured by forces that weaken by division powerful bonds of filial obligation and sexual fidelity. In other words, celestial married love differs from mortal love not because it includes a larger group of individuals but because it includes a greater degree of the same kind of love required for earthly relationships—sexual love and idiosyncratic "liking" as well as greater charity or Christ-like love. But those unique and exclusive extra qualities, which give married love the greatest potential of any relationship, require the fully mutual fidelity only possible between one whole woman and one whole man bound together by covenant.

Such fidelity, I believe, moves us beyond polygyny or polyandry, beyond patriarchy or matriarchy, beyond priesthood in its usual functions and meaning. It seems to me that those are all lower laws, serving their inspired purposes—but only during certain mortal times with their cultural limitations. The ideal celestial order of marriage—of power, of creation, and of administration—will be the one the temple marriage sealing ceremony invites us to look forward to if we are faithful: a full and equal complementarity of queen and king, priestess and priest. It will be what church president Ezra Taft Benson has said is the *third* priesthood order, "described in modern revelation as an order of family government where a man and woman enter into a covenant with God—just as did Adam and Eve—to be sealed for eternity, to have posterity, and to do the will and work of God throughout their mortality."[6]

Just as the lower Aaronic (or Levitical) priesthood is superseded by the Melchizedek when historical conditions or individual maturity warrant, so I believe Melchizedek priesthood is a preparatory order that will be to some extent superseded by the fully equal order that men and women receive when sealed in the temple. And though we are apparently not yet mature enough to implement that order fully and administratively on earth, we should, it seems to me, try to imagine it for the future, at least in the celestial kingdom, and prepare ourselves for it by living it as fully as possible now.

That brings me to a second problem with the dubious argument that in celestial marriage we will be more able to love inclusively. Such an expectation can tempt us to love inclusively and thus superficially—even promiscuously—in this life. Mormons sometimes joke about looking forward to polygamy—because it will be more sexually diversified for men or less sexually demanding or psychologically intense for women (or will simply allow a division of labor in a household to the advantage of women). The serious edge under these jokes sometimes emerges in open longing for something "better" than we know in monogamy, perhaps a wider circle of easy friendships, unfettered by the full demands and resultant exclusions of being one flesh with one individual.

The trouble with these jokes and serious hopes is their projected flight from the full responsibilities of married love right now, which includes loving unconditionally—but also being an intimate friend, having children, sharing one's deepest self, and being fully vulnerable. In Michael Novak's words, "Seeing myself through the unblinking eyes of an intimate, intelligent other, an honest spouse, is humiliating beyond anticipation."[7] And we are tempted to avoid that humiliation, however redemptive it is. Having comparatively shallow, friendly, intellectual, artistic relations with a group of people, even having merely sexual adventures with a variety, is not as difficult as developing a full relationship of fidelity with one person. And I fear that many Mormon men and women let the expectation of polygyny as the ideal future order justify their inclination to be vaguely promiscuous or superficial in sexual relationships, to flirt or share their identity with a number of people, or simply to withdraw from the struggle into blessed singularity—and there too often to be satisfied with some version of love of self. In short, I fear some Mormons, assuming future polygyny, practice for it now by diverting their affections and loyalties away from the arduous task of achieving full spiritual and physical unity with the one person they would otherwise inescapably have to face, an imperfect spouse.

The nineteenth-century Mormon experience shows that such temptations are intrinsic to polygyny. Those who lived it best, most devotedly and successfully, apparently found they could do so only by making the relationships more superficial—that is, less romantic, less emotionally intense and focused. Zina Diantha Huntington Jacobs Smith Young, wife of three men, including Joseph Smith and Brigham Young, and one of the strongest public advocates of polygamy, was quoted in the *New York World*, 19 November 1869, as saying, "A successful polygamous wife must regard her husband with indifference, and with no other feeling than that of reverence, for love we regard as a false sentiment: a feeling which should have no existence in polygamy."[8] Vilate Kimball, first wife of Heber C., counselled an unhappy plural wife that "her comfort must be wholly in her children; that she must lay aside wholly all interest or thought in what her husband was doing while he was away from her."[9]

Diaries, letters, and reminiscences of polygynous wives and children reveal that suppressing the romantic dimension of married love was indeed one of the costs of polygyny, whatever its compensating values. Even the best relationships appear to have been bittersweet. But I fear that such a flight from the complete love that includes romance may actually appeal both to overly idealistic unmarried

Mormons and to Mormons who are not completely happy in their marriages now. If so, it is an unfortunate compromise, one without genuine compensating values and one to be repented of rather than rationalized by the hope that eternal marriage will be polygynous. One of the most horrifying results of this idea, conveyed by some teachers of LDS youth, that polygyny is a "purer" love, is that they prepare some young women to be persuaded by Mormon fundamentalists that they can engage in that "higher" order right now. Such thinking can also encourage promiscuity in the young married, who may share their deepest feelings, even sexual interests, too broadly; it can encourage passivity in the middle-aged, who may thus neglect the constant struggle for full fidelity, which includes romance and friendship; and it can encourage irresponsibility in the old, who may finally retreat from their life-long task of building a deep and full celestial love into bored tolerance or silent alienation.

Now let me turn to a consideration of why, in addition to the serious danger to fidelity, I believe polygyny, though it was once an inspired practice, is not an eternal principle. I have five main reasons.

1. A requirement so central and important to our eternal salvation should be firmly grounded in the scriptures, but it is not. In fact, the clearest scriptures state that polygyny is only an occasional requirement, otherwise extremely dangerous. In the Book of Mormon, the prophet Jacob reports the Lord's insistence that David's and Solomon's polygyny was "abominable," apparently, as the Lord suggests in Doctrine and Covenants 132:37-38, because they went beyond what he commanded them. The Lord tells the Nephite men categorically to have one wife only and no concubines—no divided fidelity of any kind (Jacob 2:27). In this general exhortation to chastity and monogamy, God offers only one exception: "For if I will . . . raise up seed unto me, I will command my people" (v. 30). The only such exception we know about since that time is documented in Doctrine and Covenants 132, where the Lord commanded his young church to practice polygyny, and we must assume that commandment was given for that fundamental purpose stated in the Book of Mormon.

I think the operative words in the Lord's statement of his one exception, "to raise up seed," are "*unto me.*" Polygyny, historical evidence indicates, did not produce a larger *number* of children; it was more likely instituted because of the Abrahamic test and because it concentrated children in well-organized and elite families. My sense is that it produced a *more devout and religiously well-trained* progeny. That is certainly what some leaders, such as Brigham Young[10] and Erastus Snow,[11] believed was a central purpose and effect of polygyny. My chief evidence that they were right is the subjective one that well into the 1950s and 1960s, when the surge in new convert members began, I was present at a number of meetings where standing count indicated that a huge majority of active Mormons, especially leaders, were descendants of polygynists, a much larger percentage than the percentage of Mormons who actually practiced polygyny.

At any rate, Doctrine and Covenants 132 does not say or imply that polygyny is anything more than an exception, commanded for a specific purpose relevant to a specific historical circumstance and, by implication, to be rescinded when those circumstances changed or when the costs began to outweigh the benefits.

All of the passages in section 132 about eternal conditions and promises relate to "the new and everlasting covenant," to what will happen "if a man marry a wife . . . and it is sealed unto them by the Holy Spirit of promise" (v. 19), that is, to *eternal* marriage, *not to plural* marriage. The language concerning plural marriage, it seems to me, simply grants permission to engage in this practice when required, with precise conditions: "If any man espouse a virgin, and desire to espouse another [by the law of the priesthood], and the first give her consent, and if he espouse the second . . . then is he justified" (v. 61).

Only two verses of section 132 could be read as support for eternal polygyny. Verse 39 declares that David will not inherit his wives "out of this world" because of his sin against Uriah and Bathsheba, possibly implying that had he *not* sinned he would have inherited those wives in the next life. And verse 63 states that plural wives are given to a man "to multiply and replenish the earth . . . and to fulfill the promise which was given by my Father before the foundation of the world, and for their exaltation in the eternal worlds, that they may bear the souls of men; for herein is the work of my Father continued, that he may be glorified." At most these verses suggest that polygyny might continue for those sealed into it here on earth, not that it will be required of others.

However, if we interpret verse 63 to imply polygyny in heaven, it requires that we see the purpose of celestial plural wives as primarily to bear *more* spirit children, more of "the souls of men." One of the popular concepts of eternal polygyny is that each male god will keep his plural wives pregnant most of the time to produce those billions of spirit children for "the eternal worlds" referred to in Doctrine and Covenants 132:63. This notion seems so obviously wrong, so demeaning to women, that I am tempted to simply dismiss it, but I have found that enough Mormons, including teachers of religion, espouse such an argument that I must respond.

The assumption is that it would take a woman nine months to bear each spirit (which would be about 60 billion years to produce the 80 billion spirit children for an earth like ours). To try to reduce that time to, say, 20 billion years, through requiring plural wives and turning them into birth machines, is absurd on the face of it. To imagine such an inefficient way to produce spirit children insults God and to imagine such a limited, unequal role for women in eternity insults and devalues them—and our Heavenly Parents.

Though the scriptures are at most ambiguous, it is true that a number of nineteenth-century Mormon apostles and prophets, in their defense of polygyny, indeed clearly claimed it was the celestial order of marriage, including Brigham Young[12] and Joseph F. Smith.[13] However, in the same sermons they asserted or implied, with the same conviction, one or more of the following: that the wives of those who do not practice polygamy will be, in the next life, given to those who do[14]; that the more wives and children one has in this life, the greater one's future glory[15]; that if Utah did not receive statehood before polygamy was abolished, it never would[16]; and that the practice of polygyny by the church would *never* be taken away.[17] Since we no longer believe—or accept as inspired—those other claims, the associated claim, that celestial marriage is polygynous, is at least called into question.

The situation is similar to that of denying priesthood to blacks. Some apostles and prophets until recent times stated that the policy was rooted in pre-existent choices and the eternal nature of blacks or their ancestors.[18] But in the same sermons or writings they also recorded their equally firm beliefs that interracial mixing with blacks would bring death[19] or that the Civil War would not free the slaves[20] or that blacks would never receive the priesthood in this life until all whites had.[21] All of those claims have been proven false–and thus uninspired. We should all aspire to the courage of Elder Bruce R. McConkie, who, after the 1978 revelation flatly contradicted his (and other prophets') earlier teachings that blacks would never receive the priesthood on earth, declared: "Forget everything that I have said, or what President Brigham Young or President George Q. Cannon or whomsoever has said in days past that is contrary to the present revelation. We spoke with a limited understanding and without the light and knowledge that now has come into the world [about how 'all are alike unto God . . . black and white' (2 Ne. 26:33)]."[22]

The same Book of Mormon passage states that "all are alike unto God . . . male and female." We now have additional light and knowledge, because of the 1890 revelation and subsequent church teachings, to overcome our "limited knowledge" of what *that* means. Because God spoke in the 1978 revelation to end the practice of priesthood denial to blacks we should seriously question the rationale that well-meaning church members developed to explain that practice: the racist and unscriptural notion that blacks were not "valiant" in the premortal world. And because God spoke in 1890 to end the practice of polygyny, we should also question the rationale that well-meaning church members developed to justify it: the sexist and unscriptural notion of post-mortal plural marriage. Analogies are not proofs, but this one should encourage us to reassess our post-Manifesto understanding of marriage.

I realize this is a troubling position: If we start questioning some statements of church leaders, why not all? Though I sympathize with–and share–this anxiety, the assertion that revelation is either totally true or totally untrue is a false dichotomy. We simply do not believe, as Mormons, that we must accept all scripture and prophetic teaching as equally inspired, and we have no doctrine of prophetic infallibility. The scriptures and modern church leaders themselves have made this point again and again and have given us guidelines for distinguishing binding truth from good advice–and both of these from "the mistakes of men."[23] Polygyny served certain valuable historical purposes and then was rescinded, thus proving questionable some statements which were made in the process of defending it–especially that it would be permanent on earth because it is based in an eternal requirement. Such statements can now be thoughtfully and prayerfully reassessed in relation to other fundamental scriptures and doctrines (as I am trying to do here) without opening the Pandora's box of complete skepticism. Modern prophets themselves have explicitly renounced or modified specific practices and teachings of earlier prophets (the Adam-God theory, for instance), without thereby calling into question those prophets' general inspiration or prophetic authority.

2. My second reason for questioning eternal polygyny, in addition to the lack of scriptural support for such a doctrine, is that if polygyny were the highest order of marriage, surely God would want us to practice it whenever and wherever we could on earth. A serious effort by the church to strike down the anti-polygamy laws as unconstitutional would probably now succeed. But such an effort is not made, and even in countries where polygyny is legal, Mormons, even converted polygynists with living wives, cannot be members of the church if they practice it.

3. There is a general Mormon assumption that the plural wives who were in the past sealed to polygynists (and additional wives sealed to widowers today) are bound by an eternal sealing that cannot be broken—so at least *those* marriages must be plural in eternity. Yet the modern church practice, initiated by President David O. McKay, of sometimes *sealing a woman to more than one man* (polyandry)—which occurs in temple work done for a deceased woman who was married to more than one man during her life—undermines this assumption. Such a woman is now sealed to all her husbands without our presuming to make a choice for her—and, of course, her choice in the spirit world of one of those husbands for an eternal companion must then invalidate the other sealings and leave those men free to find their own eternal companions. Sealings thus seem to guarantee bonds only when they are subsequently agreed upon by both parties—and do not forcibly bind anyone.

But if this is so in such polyandrous sealings, then it must as well be the case in polygygnous ones. The man involved could have the opportunity to work out a one-to-one relationship as the basis for celestial marriage from among the women to whom he was sealed, and the other sealings must then be invalidated by mutual consent, thus freeing those women to form one-to-one celestial marriages with others.

What would become of all the "extra" plural wives freed from earthly sealings in such a scenario? Possibly the "extra" husbands of widows released by their choice of an eternal companion, the many single men who have lived on earth, and infants who have died and inherited celestial glory will be available as partners. One must trust in the principle of continued life and development after death, before judgment, to see that *all*, including both those who marry on earth to more than one person and those who marry no one, will be able to find their eternal companions if they so choose.

4. Another popular rationale for polygyny is that there will be more righteous women than men in heaven. This patronizing sentiment cloaks a sexist assumption, demeaning to both men and women. A fine satire on the matter, "In the Heavens Are Parents Single? Report No. 1," by the "Committee on Celestial Demographics," published in the spring 1984 issue of *Dialogue: A Journal of Mormon Thought*, makes a plausible case that there actually will be *more men than women* in the highest degree of the celestial kingdom. We know that 104 males are born for every 100 females and 47 percent of males born into the world have died before age eight, as opposed to only 44 percent of females. If we accept the popular Mormon idea that all children who die under eight are exalted–then already we have a surplus of nearly 2 billion males![24]

I believe it is more likely–certainly more consistent with the concept of free agency–that children who die and are thus, in the words of Doctrine and Covenants 137:7, "*heirs* of the celestial kingdom," are not guaranteed exaltation but only guaranteed an opportunity for exaltation and that the number of males and females in the celestial kingdom will be essentially the same. In fact, I believe it will be *exactly* equal, because those who achieve celestial glory will arrive there partnered, two-by-two as into the ark, after having achieved, as part of their righteousness, a celestial marriage. Arguments about relative numbers are irrelevant; the highest degree of the celestial kingdom will be, by definition, a place made up of eternal male-female couples.

5. My fifth reason for believing celestial marriage is not polygynous–and main reason for thinking that we must not simply say,

"We can't possibly imagine what it will be like in heaven and so shouldn't worry about it"—is that it seems to me, from reflection and from talking with Mormon women, includng my wife and five daughters, that the devaluation of women inherent in the expectation of polygyny is destructive of their sense of identity and worth *now*. For instance, the argument considered above, that there must be polygyny because there are more celestial women than men, sounds on the face of it complimentary to women. But if we reflect a bit, it is simply a way of saying that one good man is in some sense the equivalent of more women than one, however "righteous" those women are compared to the average man. Can one man emotionally and sexually satisfy more than one woman? Is he capable of being "equally yoked" to more than one woman—spiritually or intellectually or managerially or whatever? In either case, the implications seem to diminish women, reducing them to less than full equivalence with men.

If we believed that the celestial order would be truly more inclusive, then we should allow for the possibility of polyandry. If all were capable of a "higher," more inclusive love, then the rational and nonsexist arrangement would allow for plural husbands, as well. However, both the historical order Mormons once practiced and the celestial order many Mormons anticipate accept only plural wives, not plural husbands. Since there is no good reason to believe that polygyny will be needed to accommodate an excess of women in the celestial kingdom, then the expectation that there will be plural wives but not plural husbands cannot help but imply fundamental inequalities between men and women that have to do with their most central qualities and feelings, those invovlving sexual and spiritual identity and relationships.

I believe we can remove that vague implication of inferiority without becoming alienated either from nineteenth-century Mormonism or from our present faith in the gospel and the church. It is possible and spiritually healing, I believe, to affirm our polygynous ancestors for their obedient sacrifices and courageous achievements, which made the foundations of the restored church secure—and yet to reject the expectation of future polygyny. For too many of us, that expectation undermines the foundations of our present identities as women and men and diverts us from the difficult struggle for complete fidelity in our marriages that both the earthly gospel standard of morality and the expectation of celestial marriage as the basis of godhood require.

I do not presume to speak for others or authoritatively. My intent is simply to help free us, as Mormon men and women, to think about our marriages in the afterlife without the anxiety-ridden and, I believe, morally corrosive expectation of future polygyny. Let us not be limited to our past understanding. In the speech I referred to earlier, Elder McConkie observed, "Since the Lord gave this revelation on the priesthood, our understanding of many [scriptures] has expanded. Many of us never imagined or supposed that they had the extensive and broad meaning that they do have."[25] And though he then discussed only our understanding of how blacks and whites are "alike unto God," I suggest that we also need to consider that our understanding of how men and women are alike and equal unto God may still be narrow, in need of further expansion. Men who harbor an unhealthy sense of superiority and women who have felt degraded by the assumption of future polygyny should feel free to seek the inspiration that may help unburden them.

Certainly none of us can presume knowledge of the celestial order and what we will be capable of there, but our whole religion is built on the assumption that this life is, in its essentials, very much like that future life and a direct preparation for it. We have been commanded to try to develop perfect one-to-one fidelity in our marriages here, and in the temple marriage sealing ceremony we have been given, I believe, a clear vision of what the highest future order of marriage will be: a full and equal, one-to-one partnership of a king and a queen, a priestess and a priest, a perfectly balanced and yet dynamic bi-polar union that makes possible "a fulness and a continuation of the seeds forever and ever" (D&C 132:19).

Difficult as complete married fidelity and unity is to achieve, there is nothing sweeter than our approximations of it. And we have been given no clear evidence that it will not continue to be the sweetest thing in heaven, the foundation of godhood and a blessing available to all who, freed from this world's limitations, really want it.

*NOTES*

1. William Shakespeare, *The Riverside Shakespeare*, ed. G. Blakemore

Evans, et al. (Boston: Houghton Mifflin, 1974), *Julius Caesar*, 2.1.268-75, 280-87.

2. Ibid., sonnet 116.

3. Ibid., *As You Like It*, 2.1.12.

4. Joseph F. Smith, in a discourse in the Salt Lake tabernacle, 7 July 1878, suggested the danger of polygyny, a powerful principle "that savors of life unto life, or of death unto death," if misunderstood or misused. He believed it was applicable "when commanded and not otherwise" and was "particularly adapted to the conditions and necessities . . . the circumstances, responsibilities, and personal, as well as vicarious duties of the people of God in this age of the world." *Journal of Discourses*, 26 vols. (Liverpool, Eng.: LDS Bookseller's Depot, 1855-86), 20:26 (hereafter JD).

5. David J. Whittaker, "A Covenant People: Old Testament Light on Modern Covenants," *Ensign* 10 (Aug. 1980): 36.

6. Ezra Taft Benson, "What I Hope You Will Teach Your Children about the Temple," *Ensign* 15 (Aug. 1985): 8. Joseph Smith listed on 27 August 1843 three priesthoods: Melchizedek, Patriarchal, and Levitical. See Joseph Fielding Smith, ed., *Teachings of the Prophet Joseph Smith* (Salt Lake City: Deseret Book Co., 1964), 323; Joseph Smith, Jr., *History of the Church of Jesus Christ of Latter-day Saints*, ed. B. H. Roberts, 7 vols., 2d ed. rev. (1949; rpt. ed., Salt Lake City: Deseret Book Co., 1951), 5:555; and Andrew F. Ehat and Lyndon W. Cook, comps. and eds., *The Words of Joseph Smith* (Provo, UT: Brigham Young University Religious Studies Center, 1980), 244-45.

7. Michael Novak, "The Family Out of Favor," *Harper's* 252 (Apr. 1976): 41.

8. Quoted in Richard S. Van Wagoner, *Mormon Polygamy: A History* (Salt Lake City: Signature Books, 1986), 102.

9. Ibid., 102-103.

10. JD 3:264.

11. Ibid. 24:165.

12. Ibid. 11:269, 271; 16:166.

13. Ibid. 20:28.

14. Ibid. 16:166.

15. Ibid. 1:61; 20:29-31.

16. Ibid. 11:269.

17. Especially John Taylor. See Van Wagoner, 128.

18. JD 11:272. See also First Presidency Statement, 17 Aug. 1949, archives, historical department, Church of Jesus Christ of Latter-day Saints, Salt Lake City, Utah; and Bruce R. McConkie, *Mormon Doctrine* (Salt Lake City: Bookcraft, 1958), 102.

19. JD 10:110.

20. Ibid., 250.

21. Ibid. 7:291; 11:272; First Presidency Statement, 1949; and McConkie, *Mormon Doctrine*, 476.

22. Bruce R. McConkie, "All Are Alike unto God," speech given 18 Aug. 1978, in *Charge to Religion Educators* (Salt Lake City: Church of Jesus Christ of Latter-day Saints, 1982), 153.

23. Preface to the Book of Mormon; see also D&C 1:24-27.

24. Committee on Celestial Demographics, "'In the Heavens Are Parents Single?': Report No. 1," *Dialogue: A Journal of Mormon Thought* 17 (Spring 1984): 85-86.

25. McConkie, "All Are Alike unto God," 152.

# 7.

# "The Abominable and Detestable Crime Against Nature": A Brief History of Homosexuality and Mormonism, 1840-1980

*Rocky O'Donovan*

AT THE OUTSET OF THIS ESSAY I FEEL IT IS IMPORTANT THAT READERS know of my agenda, since I do not subscribe to the theory of academic objectivity. First, I am Gay, and by that I mean that I participate politically, socially, and intellectually in a community of men-loving-men.[1] Second, while I am academically trained as a historian, that is not a role with which I am comfortable. Rather, I consider myself a social activist, theorist, and poet. Third, I was raised a Mormon, completed an LDS mission, and married in the Salt Lake temple, but due to the homophobia and heterosexism I encountered in the church, I came to realize that for me the only viable solution was to explore spirituality on my own path.[2] I was later officially excommunicated from the church for my stance in opposing the oppression of Lesbian, Gay, and Bisexual people. Fourth, I am a liberationist: I do not seek "equal rights" for my people. I do not desire equal access to power. Rather, I actively explore different paradigms in which we can all move away from and forget "power relationships."

In the following essay I explore how Mormon leaders have confronted and tried to eradicate first sodomy and later homosexuality—and conversely how Lesbian, Gay, and Bisexual Mormons have responded to their religion and its doctrines. In doing so, it is apparent to me that Mormon women found that the intensity of female homosociality[3] available in Mormon structures created a vital space in which they could explore passionate, romantic relationships with each other. At the same time I have uncovered some of the problematics of male homosociality—its power to arbitrarily defend or exile men accused of entering into erotic relationships with other men.

During the early 1840s Mormon founder Joseph Smith deified heterosexuality by making the god of Mormonism a male heterosexual, or as Mormon bishop T. Eugene Shoemaker recently posited: "The celestial abode of God is heterosexually formed."[4] At the same time Smith also eternalized heterosexuality by creating secret temple rituals which extended opposite-sex marriages (heterogamy) into "time and all eternity" and multiplied heterosexuality through polygamy. In fact, Smith's own heterosexism is revealed when historian Richard S. Van Wagoner explains that Smith's "emphasis on procreation became the basis for the Mormon concept of humanity's progress to divinity. All of Smith's . . . doctrinal innovations fell into place around this new teaching. Smith explained that God was an exalted man and that mortal existence was a testing ground for men to begin to progress toward exalted godhood. Salvation became a family affair revolving around a husband whose plural wives and children were sealed to him for eternity under the 'new and everlasting covenant.'"[5]

Polygamy thus bound together all of Mormon theology and cosmology, while simultaneously defining early Mormon sexuality and setting Mormons off as a "peculiar people"—a separate and elite community of believers and practicants. This separatism—which the sexual deviance of polygamy created—was an effective means for Mormons to gain social and political power. However, while practicing their own sexual perversion (i.e., polygamy), Mormons disavowed other sexual perversities (such as sodomy)—especially if by doing so persecution could be deflected from themselves onto others.

I believe the Mormon temple ceremony offers a useful metaphor for exposing the ambiguities and problems inherent in Mormon sexualities. During the endowment ritual men, cross-dressed in feminine-like attire, and women, dressed as brides, sit separately in two distinct, homosocial groups. The female homosociality of the endowment ceremony is only temporary, for every woman must eventually break from her all-female group and embrace a man (representing "God").[6] Thus women's world is fractured while their sexuality is funnelled through men. However, men's homosociality is only confirmed when at the close of the ceremony they embrace other men (again representing "God") and reaffirm their procreative potential as part of the embrace.

Patriarchy at its core is homosocial. It is a society of men whose power exists solely at the expense of the authenticity of femaleness. In a patriarchy, and especially a religious patriarchy, men have social, emotional, spiritual, intellectual, and political intercourse almost exclusively with other men. But sexual intercourse between men in a patriarchy is not allowed. In a world where sex is constructed to be power, men are internally and externally unable to have sex with anyone equal to themselves. Any man who dares enter into sexual relations with other men is sent off, exiled, excommunicated, stripped of priesthood authority and membership in the kingdom of white, heterosexual males.

*"The Sisterhood of the Loving": Mormon Polygamy, Sorority, and Lesbian Desire.* In feminist Adrienne Rich's ground-breaking 1980 essay "Compulsory Heterosexuality and Lesbian Existence," she describes her theory of a "lesbian continuum" on which she believes all women exist, whether they identify themselves as Lesbian or not. This continuum is "a range–through each woman's life and throughout history–of woman-identified experience." For Rich, this Lesbianism easily encompasses many forms of emotional "intensity between and among women, including the sharing of a rich inner life, the bonding against male tyranny, the giving and receiving of practical and political support."[7]

This intense female bonding (or homosociality) was present in the parameters of Mormon polygamy. While some critics see polygamy as a form of male tyranny over women, I find that many Mormon women subversively reconstructed polygamy as a means of escaping male domination on many other levels, in what I call heroic acts of Lesbian resistance.

The potential for female homosocial relationships is found among the polygamous "sister-wives" of Milford Shipp.[8] His first wife, Ellis Reynolds Shipp, earned a medical degree at the Woman's Medical College of Pennsylvania in 1878. This was possible only because her sister-wives cared for her three children in Utah while she was studying back east, pooling their resources to pay her tuition. Her sister-wives also wrote her encouraging letters, while she described those from her husband as "harsh," "bitter," and "sharp." When Dr. Shipp returned to Salt Lake City, she set up a thriving medical practice and made enough money to send her other sister-wives through medical college or midwifery training. Indeed her biographer claims that her sister-wives' "role in ensuring Ellis's professional advancement stands as a moving testimony to the close relationships possible among Mormon plural wives."[9]

Milford Shipp was almost entirely uninvolved in the lives of his wives. He gave them important marital status and fathered their children. Otherwise, "in polygamy the wives and children learned to fend for themselves."[10] Dr. Shipp recorded in her private journal, "How beautiful to contemplate the picture of a family where each one works for the interest, advancement, and well-being of all. *Unity is strength.*"[11] Given that her husband only nominally participated in the lives of these women, I believe this quote must be interpreted in the context of Rich's Lesbian continuum. Even more to the point is Ellis's statement, also from her journal, about "how pure and heavenly is the relationship of sisters in the holy order of polygamy." That these women not only shared a husband, but also surnames, lives, hopes, education, political views, economic status, child-rearing, etc., indicates a depth of homosocial and homophilic intercourse typifying the "Lesbian" relationships (in Rich's definition) of Victorian Mormonism.

Despite the fact that Joseph Smith deified, eternalized, and pluralized heterosexuality through polygamy and temple ritual, early Mormon women found that their bodies, sensuality, and desires were neither tamed nor contained by obedience to the institution of polygamy. I believe that many women found creative, unique, and intensely meaningful ways to confess and express their desire for other women.

Feminist historian Carol Lasser has documented that Victorian women in America, in order to formalize "Romantic Friendships" with other women, sometimes married brothers, becoming sisters-in-law and sharing a surname. She theorizes that marrying brothers "deepened their intimacy extending it in new directions, further complicating the intricate balance of emotional and material ties, and perhaps offering a symbolic consummation of their passion" for each other.[12] Interestingly, Mormon women had the unique ability to take this one step further by marrying the same man and becoming sister-wives. Thus the unique arrangements of polygamous households provided a potential medium for Lesbian expression among women, who could easily (albeit covertly) eroticize each other's bodies through the gaze of their shared husband.

Indeed at least one Mormon woman went so far as to request that her husband marry polygamously after she fell in love with another woman, so that the two women could openly live together. Sarah Louisa (Louie, the masculinized name she preferred) Bouton married Joseph Felt in 1866 as his first wife, but according to a 1919 biography, around 1874 she met and "fell in love with" a young Mormon woman in her local LDS congregation named Alma Elizabeth (Lizzie) Mineer.[13] After discovering her intense passion for Lizzie, a childless Louie encouraged Joseph to marry the young woman as a plural wife, explaining "that some day they would be privileged to share their happiness with some little ones." Joseph conceded in 1876. But Lizzie's new responsibilities of bearing and raising children evidently proved too great a strain for her and Louie's relationship. Five years later Louie fell in love with "another beautiful Latter-day Saint girl" named Lizzie Liddell, and again Joseph obligingly married her. Thus Louie "opened her home and shared her love" with this second Lizzie.[14]

In 1883 thirty-three-year-old Louie met nineteen-year-old May Anderson, and they also fell in love. This time, however, May did not marry Joseph. In 1889 May moved in with Louie, and Joseph permanently moved out of the house Louie had built and bought on her own.[15] Thus began one of the most intense, stable, and productive same-sex love relationships in turn-of-the-century Mormonism. These two women lived together for almost forty years, and together presided over three of Mormonism's most significant institutions: the

General Primary Association (for children), the *Children's Friend*, and the Primary Children's Hospital.[16]

Louie and May were fairly open about the romantic and passionate aspects of their relationship, as reported in their biographies published in several early issues of the LDS *Children's Friend*. According to their recent biographer, Felt and Anderson's relationship was a "symbiotic partnership with each compensating for the weaknesses and complementing the strengths of the other." The 1919 *Children's Friend* more bluntly declared that "the friendship which had started when Sister Felt and [May Anderson] met . . . ripened into love. Those who watched their devotion to each other declare that there never were more ardent lovers than these two." The same biography also calls the beginning of their relationship a "time of love feasting," and makes it clear that the two women shared the same bed.[17] Twice in the *Children's Friend*, Anderson and Felt were referred to as "the David and Jonathan" of the Primary, which, the magazine explained, was a common appellation for the two women. For centuries David and Jonathan had signified male-male desire and eroticism because their love for each other "surpassed the love of women."[18] That two women were described as David and Jonathan masculinizes their love while firmly encoding it within a homoerotic context.

While polygamy was instigated by Mormon men (but subsequently appropriated by their wives as a powerful source of homosociality), the women created structures and discourses of sorority on their own which allowed Lesbian expression. The all-female Relief Society and Young Ladies' Mutual Improvement Association, as well as other early expressions of Mormon feminism, are all examples of homosocial enclaves within the larger, male-dominated structures of power. In the papers of Mormon Lesbian poet Kate Thomas is the clipping of a poem that appears to have been printed in the *Young Women's Journal* at the turn of the century. The poem, written by Sarah E. Pearson and entitled "Sister to Sister," beautifully describes the intensity of homosocial sorority that Pearson encountered "in the sunlight of the Gospel of Christ." For Pearson, Mormonism did not divide women against each other but made them sisters, "congenial, life-long friends with like, true aims to bind us;/ With a glimpse of a tender heart shown in compassionate feeling–/ The bleeding scars from the smart of death's pangs half revealing;/ The comradeship of the true, the sisterhood of the loving;/ The voice of my heart to you and the cry my soul is giving."[19] Lillie T. Freeze, a fifty-year veteran of both the Young Ladies' Mutual Improvement Association and Primary general boards, recalled in 1928 that "through these [all-female] agencies the women were seeking 'the life more abundant,' desiring to bless and comfort each other and to cultivate the longing for higher things than the social pleasures of the day could afford," again recalling Rich's definition of the Lesbian continuum.[20]

While Louie Felt and May Anderson apparently had no trouble reconciling their passionate relationship with their religion, other early Mormon women found it more difficult. For example, Kate Thomas, a prolific turn-of-the-century Mormon poet and playwright, withdrew somewhat from Mormonism while exploring her attraction to other women. Thomas, who never married, left Utah for New York City and Europe in 1901 but still maintained contact with Mormonism by writing lessons and poetry for the Relief Society and Young Women's manuals and magazines while on her extended absences. However, some of her poetry from that period reflects growing disaffection with Mormonism.

At the age of nineteen Thomas began keeping a private journal of "love poetry" while attending LDS Business College in Salt Lake City. This journal consists almost entirely of poems written to other women. When she moved to Greenwich Village (by then a homosexual mecca) in New York City in 1901 she explored not only Lesbian desire, but religious and spiritual traditions as diverse as Catholicism and Buddhism. Thomas also became an outspoken peace activist, anarchist, supporter of the League of Nations, and practitioner of Yoga.[21]

While having difficulties with her religion, it is clear that Thomas was able to reconcile her sexuality with her spirituality, and thus had no trouble asking God to bless her loving unions with other women. In the fall of 1901 Thomas wrote the following love poem to an unnamed woman:

This morning how I wished that I might be
A poet even for a little while
Just long enough to write one heart-felt rhyme
To one so near that she seems a part of me.

But were I all the bards that ever sung
Turned into one transcendent immortelle
It seems to me I still would lack the tongue
To say how long I'd love her or how well!
May every blessing that God has in store
Fall on her daily doubled o'er and o'er
When world on world and worlds again shall roll
God grant that we two shall still stand soul to soul![22]

In other poems written about the same time, I believe, she used the word "gay" as a double entendre to mean both happiness and same-sex desire. The following short poem is an example:

A scarlet West;
An East merged into eventide.
A brown plain
And by my side
The one–the one in all the world
I love the best!
Last night's gay mask–
The outward wildness and the inward ache
I cast off forever; from her lips I take joy never-ceasing.
Brown plain and her kiss
Are all I ask.[23]

The word "gay" was used in the United States as early as 1868 to describe same-sex male desire.[24] Five years after Thomas wrote this poem, American writer Gertrude Stein wrote "Miss Furr and Miss Skeen" in which she repeatedly used "gay" to signify same-sex *female* desire.[25] I suspect that Kate Thomas discovered this underground meaning while she was living in Greenwich Village and used it throughout her poetry. That it meant homosexual desire to her is supported by the fact that the only time she used the word "gay" outside of poems written to other women was in a poem about "Gay Narcissus," who has traditionally signified same-sex (especially male) desire.[26] Another lengthy poem entitled "A Gay Musician" is about Thomas's love for a woman named Illa. The following is a brief passage: "That dear white hand within my own I took/ 'Illa,' I whispered, 'May I keep it so?'/ My eager blood my anxious cheek forsook,/ Fearing my love that loved me might say no. . . ./ She raised her eyes. There looking I beheld/ The Sound of Music through the eyes of love."[27] One historian commented that in this poem "the poet is speaking in the voice of one female to another . . . and as in many others in the journal, makes clear the sensuality of fantasy and desire."[28]

Cornelia (Cora) Kasius was another Mormon Lesbian who left Utah and ended up in Greenwich Village, where she could explore her sexuality. A prominent social worker from Ogden, Utah, Kasius was assistant general secretary to the LDS Relief Society as early as 1923.[29] In 1928 she moved to New York and by 1930 was on the faculty of Barnard College. By 1945 she also served on the faculties of New York University, Columbia University, and New York School of Social Work.[30] At that time she was appointed "Welfare Liaison Officer" to aid in the reconstruction of Holland after World War II. She later returned to Greenwich Village, where she remained until her death in the 1980s.[31]

These women found avenues for exploring passion between women within official Mormon structures such as the Relief Society. It thus comes as no surprise that the most radical discourse of Mormon sorority, that of early Mormon feminism, also created vital space in which women could desire other women romantically and sexually. Historian of Mormon feminism Maxine Hanks has recovered one of the most important early documents relating to Lesbianism in Victorian America: what appears to be the earliest published statement on Lesbianism. In the 1870s Mormon women began publishing an ecclesiastically-sanctioned feminist periodical called the *Woman's Exponent.* The 15 April 1873 issue reprinted from a New York paper an article by the pseudonymous "Fanny Fern," entitled "Women Lovers."[32] The essay comments on the current fashion of "smashing" without actually using the term.[33] Smashing involved passionate, sometimes sexual, friendships between women before the turn of the century. To clarify the possibly confusing wording of the document, I should explain that two kinds of "women lovers" are being described: the innocent, victimized pursuer (called Araminta) and the manipulative, passive-aggressive pursued woman (called "the other party" as well as the "conquering 'she'"). The complete text of this remarkable article follows:

*WOMEN LOVERS*

> Perhaps you do not know it, but there are women who fall in love with each other. Woe be to the unfortunate she, who does the courting! All the cursedness of ingenuity peculiar to the sex is employed by "the other party" in tormenting her. She will flirt with women by the score who are brighter and handsomer than her victim. She will call on them oftener. She will praise their best bonnets and go into ecstasies over their dresses. She will write them more pink notes [love letters], and wear their "tin-types" [photographs], and when despair has culminated, and sore-hearted Araminta takes to her bed in consequence, then only will this conquering "she" step off her pedestal to pick up her dead and wounded. But then, women must keep their hand in. Practice makes perfect.[34]

This significant article colors the women of the *Exponent*, and indeed of the entire early Mormon feminist movement, a distinct shade of lavender. As Mormon historian D. Michael Quinn has pointed out, Louise L. Greene's decision, as editor of *Woman's Exponent*, to reprint this brief essay "indicates her assumption that 'Women Lovers' was of interest to Mormon women."[35] The language is casual but calculated. The author warns women to be careful when loving other women—not to be victimized by exploitive and destructive women. The closing statement "practice makes perfect" indicates that Lesbian desire is complete and perfect in and of itself, and is not a precursor to heterosexuality.

*Sodomy, Faggotry, and Heterosexual Panic in Early Mormonism.* One of the most dramatic events in the history of Mormonism and homosexuality occurred in the 1840s. John C. Bennett, a recent convert, arrived in Nauvoo, Illinois (then LDS headquarters), and immediately began his rise to ecclesiastical prominence.[36] Within months of arriving, he became a chief advisor to Joseph Smith. After Sidney Rigdon's refusal to allow his daughter to marry Smith polygamously, Bennett was given the title of Assistant President to the Church, placing him above either first counselor Rigdon or church patriarch Hyrum Smith. Bennett also became chancellor of the

University of Nauvoo, mayor of Nauvoo, and a general in the Nauvoo Legion. But Bennett had a mysterious past, for he had risen to high positions in other cities, other social circles, only to be cast out and forced to move on. Rumors of Bennett's past soon began to circulate in Nauvoo. Men were sent by Joseph Smith to other towns where Bennett had lived, and they returned with sober news: Bennett also had a long history as a "homo-libertine," according to Mormon historian Sam Taylor.[37] When the news broke in the leading councils of the church, Bennett drank some poison in what appears to have been a carefully planned suicide attempt. Being a physician, he would have known exactly how much to take to get him sick but not to kill himself. This sham suicide quickly brought forgiveness and sympathy from both Joseph Smith and the church at large.

Soon, however, more rumors circulated of Bennett's practices in Nauvoo: that he was courting several women simultaneously, that he had performed abortions on various Mormon women, that he frequented "the brothel on the hill," and that he was giving out high-ranking positions in the Nauvoo Legion in return for sexual favors with men under his command. Rumors of sodomy even reached non-Mormons. Reverend W. M. King accused Nauvoo of being "as perfect a sink of debauchery and every species of abomination as ever was in Sodom and Nineveh." Samuel Taylor felt that Bennett's "sexual antics" with men in the Nauvoo Legion cast aspersions of sodomy on "hell knows how many revered pioneers."[38] However, another Mormon historian, T. Edgar Lyon, thought that Bennett could not have been homosexual since he was also accused of seducing women. "From my limited knowledge of homosexuals," Lyon wrote, "it seems to be out of character of the man [Bennett] to be so deeply involved with girls and women in town and at the same time practicing homosexuality."[39]

As Taylor speculated, Joseph Smith could overlook just about anything but disloyalty. And Bennett turned disloyal, publicly espousing plural marriage, arguably Mormonism's best-kept secret during these years. Taylor also felt that Smith dared not use accusations of sodomy against Bennett for fear of destroying the reputations of the young men Bennett had seduced, as well as not wanting the public to know that their prophet had put a sodomite in a high position. Instead, Smith claimed that Bennett had tried to enlist the legion to murder Smith during one of their musters. After his plot failed, Bennett was publicly humiliated and privately threatened, then given a chance to recant. Fearing for his life, he signed a statement saying that Smith had never taught or practiced polygamy, and left Nauvoo in May 1842. He was immediately released as Assistant President, excommunicated, and lost his university chancellery and mayorship. But Bennett went on to write one of Mormonism's most scathing exposés, *The History of the Saints.*

In July 1842 Joseph's younger brother, William Smith, editor of a Mormon newspaper, *The Wasp,* tried to silence Bennett's accusations by sarcastically writing that Bennett only saw Joseph Smith as "a great *philanthropist* as long as Bennett could practice adultery, fornication, and–we were going to say, (*Buggery,*) without being exposed."[40] Two years later a slander suit brought against Joseph Smith by Francis Higbee implied that he and his brother, Chauncey, had been sexually involved with Bennett in the Nauvoo Legion where Higbee had been a colonel. During Higbee's suit, Brigham Young testified that he had "told Dr. Bennett that one charge against him was leading young men into difficulty–he admitted it. If he had let young men and women alone it would have been better for him." Hyrum Smith also testified that Higbee had been "seduced" by Bennett. Other testimony indicated that Bennett "led the youth that he had influence over to tread in his unhallowed steps." Although deleted in the printed version, the original notes of Bennett's church trial indicate that in addition to charges of sex with women, other testimony about Bennett was "too indelicate for the public eye and ear," an allusion to the "unspeakable crime" of sodomy.[41]

Accusations of buggery or sodomy (and later of homosexuality) have been used throughout European and American history in religious and/or political attacks to malign one's opponents. Bennett was vilified publicly as a bugger because he publicly admitted that Mormon leaders were practicing polygamy. This is an important factor in understanding Mormon sexuality and Mormon heterosexual panic, as I call it. As stated earlier, Joseph Smith had just begun to deify heterosexuality. Mormons found themselves in the ironic position of having to protect this deification, eternalization, and multiplication of heterosexuality by exposing Bennett's acts of buggery with men. This is not the only time accusations of homosexuality, whether true or not, were used by Mormons in their political battles.

In 1886 Mormon leaders used homosexual accusations to politically destroy the character of one of their own elite. Thomas Taylor, the wealthy polygamous bishop of Salt Lake City's 14th Ward, was excommunicated for masturbating with several young men in southern Utah. Behind this accusation, however, lay years of conflict between Taylor and church leaders. Twenty years earlier Taylor had paid $15,000 to help bring a group of Mormons from Europe to Utah, with the understanding that the church would repay him. Brigham Young neglected to pay the sum back, and when Young died Taylor went to John Taylor (no relation) for payment. However, the new Mormon president judged Thomas Taylor's claim to be invalid and asserted that Taylor had secured the money illegally in the first place. Thomas called this accusation libelous and through adjudication won payment of the money owed him. Then came accusations from Richard Williams of Parowan, brothers Simeon and William Simkins of Cedar City, and a fourth teenager who alleged that Thomas Taylor had on several occasions slept with them and during the night had used their hands to masturbate him.[42] Taylor was immediately disfellowshipped from the church, and news of the proceedings reached the columns of the *Salt Lake Tribune.* The *Tribune* went so far as to accuse Taylor of being "guilty of a horrible and beastly sin" and interestingly reiterated that he "is a polygamist." In another editorial the *Tribune* asked if Taylor should be "prosecuted in the courts? Or is there no law against sodomy, either, in this most lawless of Territories."[43] Here the anti-Mormon *Tribune* identifies Taylor's "beastly sin" as sodomy (which same-sex masturbation technically was not) and then obliquely compares sodomy to the "lawlessness" of Mormon polygamy.[44] In a letter to church president John Taylor on 22 September 1886, Thomas confessed his "sins" and asked to be reinstated into full fellowship in the church: "I am sending consent to day for my [first] wife to obtain a divorce, she never has appreciated the addition of [other] wives to my family, and now I have sinned, her patience is exhausted, and I fear for my children.

"I am ashamed to think that I have been so weak and I feel to cry God be merciful to me, and I want my brethren to be merciful to me. I want to be humble and live so that I can purify my thoughts and words and actions . . . Oh, help me to come back to [God's] favor. I expect to have offended you greatly I humbly ask your forgiveness.

"I am suffering terribly. My nerves are unstrung I have such throbbings of the heart, and headache. I cannot sit still, nor sleep, when I doze off to sleep, I wake and see before me excommunicated, and my wife suffers almost if not quite as much as bad, and I feel for her because it is my doing and I ought to be alone the sufferer, and I will try to endure. I do not want to apostatize I want to return to my allegiance to God and his work and I pray you to grant me this favor as soon as you can in righteousness, and I will try to live so as to be worthy of so great a favor."[45] Despite this plea for forgiveness, none was forthcoming, for Thomas Taylor had committed two unspeakable crimes: he had challenged a church president and he had dared to desire other men.

Even lay Mormons accused members of their own families of sodomitical practices, ostensibly for political gain. In 1893 Lorenzo Hunsaker went through two ecclesiastical trials in Honeyville, Utah, for alledgedly having sexual relations with two younger half-brothers. Rudger Clawson, the local LDS stake president, fortunately left a verbatim account of these proceedings in his journal. Clawson recorded in 1894 that "One of the most extraordinary cases that ever arose in the Church of Jesus Christ of Latter Day Saints was that of Peter and Weldon Hunsaker versus Lorenzo Hunsaker in the Honeyville Ward."[46] He then quotes for the next 150 pages from private conversations, letters, petitions, church court records, and personal testimonials.

Evidently just after October 1893 general conference Lorenzo Hunsaker told Clawson that "[recently] Peter and Weldon, his [half-] brothers had circulated a story in that Ward to the effect that [Lorenzo] had been guilty of sucking their penis . . . [for] a period of some two or three years. . . . The question, therefore, was what, under the circumstances had best be done." Clawson said "that if I were in his place, I should treat the whole affair with silent contempt and gave as a reason that the charge was so monstrous and ridiculous that he would be degrading himself in the eyes of sensible people to follow it up. . . . My confidence in the purity of Lorenzo's life and faithfulness as a Latter-day Saint," Clawson confided, "was such that I felt it would be an insult to ask him if he were guilty."[47] Had Clawson asked Hunsaker that question, events might have turned out differently.

Lorenzo did as suggested, ignoring the accusations, and found himself quickly excommunicated by the bishop of the Honeyville Ward. Lorenzo appealed the action to the stake presidency and high council. Eventually other half-brothers and male neighbors added their own accusations of attempted or accomplished oral and anal sex and masturbation with Lorenzo. But as Clawson indicated in his journal, Lorenzo was a Mormon in good standing: he was a polygamist, a full tithe-payer, a temple attender, a high priest, and close friend of local church leaders, while his accusers were known to swear occasionally, miss church services, or drink now and then. Thus the question came down to Lorenzo's piety versus the impiety of some ten accusers. But behind all this lay the issue of the family inheritance.

Abraham Hunsaker, the patriarch of a family of some fifty children, had recently died but had made it clear that Lorenzo was to be the fiscal and spiritual head of the family even though he was not even close to being the oldest of Abraham's sons. After Abraham's death, there had been some petty bickering and power struggles, and the accusations of homosexuality against Lorenzo must be viewed in the context of that power struggle among Abraham's heirs. While Peter, Weldon, and others probably used their accusations against Lorenzo to erode his familial power and social influence, it seems clear after reading all the testimonies that Lorenzo was engaging in sexual relations with his half-brothers and perhaps a neighbor or two. However, because of his standing in the church, Lorenzo eventually won readmission into the church and managed to have Peter and Weldon excommunicated for lying. The other accusers, when faced with similar action against them, recanted. During this period the local ward structure fell apart as people picked sides. A petition was circulated by the women of the ward, protesting the church's action against Peter and Weldon, but when they presented it to Clawson, he curtly replied they "could do as they pleased, but if they wished to do right, they would invariably vote to sustain the propositions of the Priesthood."[48] Clawson eventually released all local ward leaders for disobedience and for "humiliating the Priesthood."[49] He then replaced them with men who would follow counsel and withheld the sacrament from the ward for several months as punishment.

For Thomas Taylor, secular judicial proceedings and media attention were minimal, while for Lorenzo Hunsaker, no such exposure occured at all, suggesting that the church carefully controlled the public responses in both situations. In Taylor's case, judicial proceedings were brought against him in the form of a grand jury investigation that took place several months after his excommunication. The grand jury convened in southern Utah, where it predictably received a minimum of press coverage. Although the ecclesiastical investigation found enough evidence to excommuniate Taylor, the grand jury concluded that "there was no evidence of the crimes he was accused of" and dropped the case.[50] It seems apparent that Mormon leaders wanted to humiliate Taylor, while avoiding a full-blown scandal that could damage the church's image if all the details, notably Taylor's business dealings with the church, became well publicized—especially when the eyes of the nation were turned to Mormonism during these tumultuous years of anti-polygamy sentiment.

The fear of yet more scandal perhaps helped keep Lorenzo Hunsaker out of the courtroom and media, as Hunsaker was a good Mormon polygamist like Thomas Taylor.[51] If a male polygamist could be sexually active with men as well as women, then perhaps the hierarchy of gender would be blurred when the rigidity of Mormon gender structures was brought into question. Even acknowledging homosexual desire among church members was unthinkable. Little profit would have come from pulicizing these cases in open court with the media filing sensationalized reports on an already battered church.

However, Mormon leaders could be ruthless when uncovering sodomy among non-Mormons, as occurred when Private Frederick Jones was brought to trial in 1864 for raping a nine-year-old boy. According to accounts published in the *Salt Lake Daily Telegraph* and the *Daily Union Vedette*, in October 1864 Jones, stationed at what is now Fort Douglas, raped a boy named Monk (allegedly at knife-point) in a ravine between downtown Salt Lake City and Fort Douglas. The boy then told his father, who pressed charges against Jones. A week later Jones was in the Salt Lake City jail awaiting trial for sodomy.

When he was examined by a justice of the peace, Jones pled not guilty. During the hearing a week later the justice determined that the "evidence was clear and conclusive against Jones," went into recess to "examine the law on the subject," but then discovered that Utah had no anti-sodomy law. When Jones appeared for sentencing, he was released. He set off on foot for Fort Douglas but only reached the corner of First South and State Street, where he was killed. Witesses heard gun shots, saw the flash of pistol fire, and heard the sound of retreating footsteps, but no one reported to have actually witnessed the murder.[52]

Although the Jones suit actually dealt with violent pedophilia (an adult raping a pre-pubescent child), I include it because the judicial response shows that many Utahns only saw that perpetrator and victim were male and focused solely on the issue of sodomy. As Gay theorist Daniel Shellabarger recently commented, "The homophobia of Utah territorial judicial system is exposed in this case. How odd that the molestation or rape of a child was not even the primary question. The issue of sodomy between two males blocked their vision of the *real* crime."[53]

Many Mormons felt little sorrow at the murder of Frederick Jones. Albert Carrington, editor of the *Deseret News* and future LDS apostle, editorialized that Jones's murder "should prove a warning to all workers of abominations, for there is always the chance that some one will be impatient of the law's delay in cases so outrageous and abominable."[54] As D. Michael Quinn has documented, even Brigham Young responded to the outcome of the Jones trial, writing in November 1864 that Utah lacked an anti-sodomy law at that time because "our legislators, never having contemplated the possibility of such a crime being committed in our borders[,] had made no provision for its punishment."[55] Jones, society's scapegoat, was not only a "sodomite" but a gentile as well. In essence, he represented everything Mormons feared: outside influences and challenges to their own sexual perversion. Carrington was unequivocal: Mormons could do nothing but murder Jones, first, to cleanse their community of God's judgment on sodomy, and second, to atone for their own feelings of guilt for deviating from Victorian socio-sexual mores.

Sodomy, or "the crime against nature," became illegal in Utah territory on 18 February 1876.[56] It was then obliquely defined as heterosexual and homosexual anal intercourse. As a felony it was punishable by imprisonment for not more than five years. In 1907, the punishment was changed to three to twenty years imprisonment.[57] In 1923 heterosexual and homosexual oral sex was added to the sodomy statutes, thus criminalizing most sex acts regardless of the sexual orientation or gender of the people involved.[58] Sodomy was reduced from a felony to a class B misdemeanor in 1953, while forcible sodomy (oral or anal rape) remained a felony.[59]

While Mormons reacted with various degress of intolerance when confronting sodomitical practices of both Mormon and non-Mormon men, there was still room in which many Mormon men could safely (and quite publicly) negotiate passionate relationships with other men without critical or punitive reactions from Mormon officials. In the 1850s Mormon converts Luke Carter and William Edwards constructed an intimate relationship without any apparent approbrium from church leaders. Carter, a forty-six-year-old convert, arrived in Liverpool in 1856 to emigrate to Utah with his daughter. He had been separated (probably divorced) from his wife for three years. While in Liverpool, he struck up a friendship with another recent convert, William Edwards, an unmarried man of thirty, who was emigrating with his younger sister.[60] Once this group had crossed the ocean and ridden the train to Iowa City, they found themselves at least two months behind schedule. The 576 Mormons left Iowa City in poorly constructed handcarts on 26 July 1856, having been promised by a Mormon apostle that God would keep winter at bay so they could arrive in Zion safely. Within days, the earliest winter on record set in. Fatigue, cold, malnutrition, snow, and poorly built handcarts took their toll. One of the first adults to die was William Edwards.

Josiah Rogerson, a fellow immigrant, later published an account of this disastrous event in which one third of the immigrants died. Rogerson describes the intimate friendship between Edwards and Carter when recounting Edwards's death: "About 10:30 this morning we passed Fort Keamey, and as one of the most singular deaths occurred on our journey at this time, I will give a brief and truthful narration of the incident.

"Two bachelors named Luke Carter, from the Clitheroe branch [of the church], Yorkshire, England, and William Edwards from

Manchester, England, each about 50 to 55 years of age, had pulled a covered cart together from Iowa City, Ia., to this point. They slept in the same tent, cooked and bunked together; but for several days previous unpleasant and cross words had passed between them.

"Edwards was a tall, loosely built and tender man physically, and Carter more stocky and sturdy. He had favored Edwards by letting the latter pull only what he could [walking between] the shafts [handles] for some time. This morning he grumbled and complained, still traveling, about being tired, and that he couldn't go any further. Carter retorted: 'Come on. Come on. You'll be all right again when we get a bit of dinner at noon.' But Edwards kept begging for him to stop the cart and let him lie down and 'dee' (die), Carter replying, 'Well, get out and die, then.'

"The cart was instantly stopped. Carter raised the shafts of the cart. Edwards walked from under and to the south of the road a couple of rods, laid his body down on the level prairie, and in ten minutes he was a corpse.

"We waited (a few carts of us) a few minutes longer till the captain came up and closed Edwards's eyes. A light-loaded open cart was unloaded. The body was put thereon, covered with a quilt, and the writer [Rogerson] pulled him to the noon camp, some five or six miles, where we dug his grave and buried him a short distance west of Fort Kearney, Neb."[61]

Several details in this story seem to signify what I have called "faggotry." Both Edwards and Carter were unmarried, which is especially significant in the context of polygamous Mormonism. Although sexual relations between men in England of that era were generally interclass affairs, this one was not, for both converts were from the lower class. However, their relationship was somewhat intergenerational—one was thirty years old, the other forty-six (not fifty to fifty-five, as Rogerson thought)—and that does have "class" overtones. And they not only shared a handcart and a tent, they cooked and "bunk[ed] together." Coincidentally Carter died a short time after Edwards, even though he was the sturdy one, perhaps in grief from the loss of his companion. Rogerson, despite these "clues," does not seem surprised by their intimate relationship. What is of note to him is that Edwards could will himself to die. Whether Edwards's and Carter's emotional and financial partnership extended to sexual attraction is ultimately unknown, but the image of two men pulling a handcart together, one nurturing the other, is fascinating, especially in juxtaposition to the traditional heterosexual scenes of Mormon iconography.

Edwards and Carter however were not the only Gay pioneers to migrate to Utah before the arrival of the train in 1869. Evan Stephens, Utah's most prominent musical composer as well as conductor of the Mormon Tabernacle Choir from 1890 to 1916, is consistently rumored to have been "Gay."[62] Beyond oral tradition, there is contemporary circumstantial evidence to support this claim. Stephens, born in Wales and in 1867 migrating with his family to Utah, never married, which in polygamous Utah was a difficult status to maintain, especially for someone as prominent as Stephens became. Instead of marrying, he filled his life with his two great passions: "love of friendship and music." Stephens's friendships always centered on passionate love and desire for other, usually younger, men.

Stephens went so far as to publish his autobiography (basically a lengthy account of the development of his desire to bond passionately with other men) in a periodical for Mormon children—without any apparent reprisal from the church. In this lengthy autobiography written in the third person and published in the 1919 *Children's Friend*, Stephens told Mormon children about his youth in Willard, Utah, where he discovered music through a local all-male ward choir (another instance of homosociality fostering same-sex desire). Stephens recounts that he "became the pet of the choir. The men among whom he sat seemed to take a delight in loving him. Timidly and blushingly he would be squeezed in between them, and kindly arms generally enfolded him much as if he had been a fair sweetheart of the big brawny young men. Oh, how he loved these men[;] too timid to be demonstrative in return he nevertheless enshrined in his inmost heart the forms and names of Tovey, Jardine, Williams, Jones and Ward."[63]

John J. Ward, the son of the last mentioned man, was the same age as Stephens, and the two became friends. However, Evan's and John's friendship developed into something more profound, as Stephens's autobiography attests. When the entire Mormon community in Willard (except for Ward's family) was called to move to Malad, Idaho, twenty-year-old Evan chose to remain with his "chum

John." In this same autobiography, Stephens calls Ward the first of his "life companions" with whom he shared his "home life."[64]

While criticism of polygamy became something of a national past-time during the Victorian era, what I find fascinating about this anti-polygamy rhetoric is how similar it is to anti-Gay and Lesbian rhetoric employed later by the Mormon church and society at large. For example, a non-Mormon living in Nauvoo in the 1840s claimed that polygamy is "a system which, if exposed in its naked deformity, would make the virtuous mind revolt with horror; a system in the exercise of which lays prostrate all the dearest ties in our social relations—the glorious fabric upon which human happiness is based—ministers to the worst passions of our nature and throws us back into the benighted regions of the dark ages." Again in an 1860 debate on the issue of polygamy, one Illinois congressman charged polygamy "to be a crying evil; sapping not only the physical constitution of the people practicing it, dwarfing their physical proportions and emasculating their energies, but at the same time perverting the social virtues, and vitiating the morals of its victims."[65] We need only substitute the word "sodomy" or "homosexuality" to see how Mormons and others took this rhetoric and in moments of heterosexual panic deflected it onto Lesbians and Gays.

During the 1860s and 1870s federal laws were passed outlawing polygamy. Believing this to be a violation of the separation of church and state, the First Presidency selected Mormon bigamist George Reynolds to be a test case. Reynolds was found guilty of polygamy, and the church appealed the decision to the U.S. Supreme Court. In January 1879, in the landmark *Reynolds v. the United States* case, the court ruled that anti-polygamy laws were not unconstitutional, for as the court wrote, "Laws are made for the government of actions and while they cannot interfere with mere religious beliefs and opinions, they may with practices."[66] This federal decision severely eroded not only the Mormon power base, but that of many other religions afterwards, as well. Ironically, this decision currently keeps pro-Gay religions (like Unitarian-Universalists, the Religious Society of Friends, and the Metropolitan Community Church) from *legally* performing same-sex marriages today (although many are performed illegally each year in the United States).

In the aftermath of *Reynolds v. United States,* Mormon polygamists were disenfranchised, children by polygamous wives were disinherited, female suffrage in Utah was abolished, the Corporation of the Church of Jesus Christ of Latter-day Saints was dissolved, and all church properties (including the Salt Lake temple) were confiscated. Bowing to such intense coercion, in 1890 church president Wilford Woodruff issued his "Manifesto," ostensibly ending the practice of polygamy in the Mormon church (although members of the hierarchy secretly sanctioned its continued practice for many years afterward).[67]

In the middle of this political strife England's most famous sodomite, Oscar Wilde, arrived in Salt Lake City to deliver a lecture at the Salt Lake Opera House on "Art Decoration: Being the Practical Application of the Aesthetic Theory to Every-Day Home Life and Art Ornamentation."[68] On 10 April 1882 Wilde arrived by train from Sacramento and was greeted by a large crowd of the curious. After greeting his well-wishers, he went to the Walker House on Second South and Main Street, where he and his servant scandalously disappeared through the Ladies' entrance. In honor of Wilde being known as the "Sunflower Apostle," his bellboy wore a sunflower in his buttonhole.[69] That afternoon Wilde visited LDS president John Taylor at Taylor's residence, one of the finest mansions in the valley.

That night, with the Opera House filled to standing room only, Wilde was visibly disconcerted when he walked out on stage and found an array of young men in the front row, all adorned with enormous sunflowers and lilies, in homage to the controversial British dandy. Obviously, he was not expecting such adoration from Utahns.[70] The *Deseret News* subsequently criticized his speech for being absurd and unoriginal, among other things. However, one historian believes that Mormons disapproved of his speech because of the "indecent morals" displayed in his writings.[71]

In 1895, five years after the Woodruff Manifesto "ended" polygamy, Wilde again entered the public eye in Utah, but this time because of his trial in England for sodomy. Wilde's story made front page headlines in twenty issues of the *Deseret News* as if to emphasize the dangers of such deviant practices.[72] Contemporary Gay historian Richard Dellamora has observed that in the late nineteenth century "masculine privilege was sustained by male friendships within institutions like the public schools, the older universities, the clubs, and the professions. Because, however, the continuing dominance of bourgeois males also required that they marry and produce offspring, the intensity and sufficiency of male bonding needed to be strictly controlled by homophobic mechanisms" such as public, anti-homosexual scandals—Wilde's trial being an example. Dellamora also states that these anti-homosexual scandals in England in the 1890s "provide a point at which gender roles are publicly, even spectacularly, encoded and enforced."[73] This applies as well to the willingness of the *Deseret News* to publicize the details of Wilde's trials. Because the United States placed so much negative attention on the sexual deviance of Mormon polygamy, Mormons returned the favor to Lesbian and Gay people with the assurance that their perversity was at least heterosexually (and procreatively) centered.

*Speaking the Unspeakable: The Later Development of Mormon Homophobic Discourse. Reynolds v. United States* dealt a serious blow to the Mormon hierarchy. An 1885 article in the *Salt Lake Tribune* explored "a more basic opposition" to polygamy: "The essential principle of Mormonism is not polygamy at all, but the ambition of an ecclesiastical hierarchy to wield sovereignty to rule the souls and lives of its subjects with absolute authority."[74] In other words, what had separated Mormons as a distinct people—the sexual politics of polygamy—had collapsed, severely weakening male religious prerogative. In order to reconstruct its power, the hierarchy created a power-consolidating institution called "Priesthood Correlation" in 1908. Following the end of polygamy, the "gifts of the spirit" (speaking and singing in tongues, etc.) were frowned upon and eventually terminated. Women's organizations became auxiliary to the "priesthood." Women were commanded to stop performing healing and blessing rituals, which thereafter could only be performed by male priesthood holders. To set them off again as a "peculiar people," Mormons emphasized strict enforcement of the Mormon "health code" (the Word of Wisdom), the development and maintenance of the Welfare Program, and renewed emphasis on the monogamous heterosexual family as the basic unit of society.

During the early part of the twentieth century, as Mormonism steadily grew, problematic issues surrounding isolationism versus universalism arose. Confrontation with homosexuality (which was itself becoming more publicized) was inevitable. In 1946 it was discovered that Patriarch to the Church Joseph Fielding Smith III had had sexual relations with a young man. Church president George Albert Smith, after private conferences with those involved, their families, and the twelve apostles, decided to quietly release Smith from his calling.[75] That October, Smith's name was omitted from the roll of general authorities sustained in general conference. Later, when questioned why, the LDS First Presidency responded by having David O. McKay read a letter allegedly written by Smith himself, asking for his own release due to "an extended illness."[76] Interestingly the former patriarch was neither excommunicated nor disfellowshipped, although he was not allowed to perform any church duties.[77] He was exiled by church order to Hawaii, accompanied by his wife and children. Eleven years later, Smith was reinstated into full participation in the church after he "confessed to his wife and wrote a full confession to the First Presidency."[78]

In 1950 a music teacher at church-owned Ricks College in Rexburg, Idaho, was fired for sexual relations with several male students. When a Rexburg stake presidency counselor asked J. Reuben Clark of the First Presidency whether the former teacher should be tried in a church court for his membership, Clark said no, because "thus far we had done no more than drop them [homosexuals] from positions they held," indicating that church policy at that time did not consider homosexual activity an excommunicable offense.[79]

Two years later Clark became the first Mormon general authority to utter the words "homosexual" and "homosexuality" in public. In a 1952 address entitled "Home, and the Building of Home Life," which he delivered at the annual General Relief Society Conference, Clark pointed out that with regards to "the person who teaches or condones the crimes for which Sodom and Gomorrah were destroyed—we have coined a softer name for them than came from old; we now speak of homosexuality, which, it is tragic to say, is found among both sexes. . . . Not without foundation is the contention of some that the homosexuals are today exercising great influence in shaping our arts, literature, music, and drama."[80] This was during the "McCarthy era," in which anti-Gay rhetoric almost reached a national hysteria. As will be seen, Mormon attitudes concerning Gays and Lesbians typically came not by "revelation from God," but by revelation from the popular press.

In 1959 church president David O. McKay assigned apostles Spencer W. Kimball and Mark E. Peterson to help Mormon Lesbians and Gays overcome their "homosexual problems."[81] Apparently "quite a number of [Mormon] men were being arrested" for being "'peeping toms', exhibitionists, homosexuals, and perverts in other areas."[82] That same year Kimball decided that the church needed "an extensive treatise on repentance" and began "jotting down scriptures for people to study . . . [and] developed some lists for recurring problems," including homosexuality.[83] These notes on homosexuality resulted in three major works (as well as numerous minor works or statements): *A Counselling Problem in the Church* (1964), "The Crime Against Nature" chapter in his *The Miracle of Forgiveness* (1969), and *New Hope for Transgressors* (1970), which was revised and published as both *New Horizons for Homosexuals* (1971) and *A Letter to a Friend* (1978).[84]

The earliest of these three homophobic texts was originally a speech Kimball gave to a group of LDS psychiatrists. A few months later, on 10 July 1964, he delivered a similar speech to a conference of the LDS church's seminary and Institute teachers assembled at Brigham Young University. Although dealing with various problems in Mormon society, the largest portion of *A Counselling Problem in the Church* dealt with homosexuality and became the basis for all subsequent homophobic discourse in the Mormon church.[85]

Kimball culled most of his information from popular tabloids and magazines, such as *Life* and *Medical World News.* Anti-Gay articles had appeared in both these magazines during the month before Kimball's speech.[86] As John D'Emilio documents, "The notion of homosexuality as mental illness was receiving greater dissemination during the early 1960s," and for Gay radicals in larger cities like New York, this negative "medical model of homosexuality hung like a millstone around the [homosexual] movement's neck."[87] Both Irving Bieber's 1962 psychoanalytic study *Homosexuality* and the New York Academy of Medicine's 1964 report which argued that "homosexuality was an acquired illness susceptible to cure" received extensive publicity in the press, which in turn influenced Kimball's teachings on homosexuality. (Kimball, for example, echoes the medical model when he writes that "we know such a disease is curable," and briefly quotes from the statement made by the New York Academy of

Medicine.[88]) While these reports promulgated views built on "loose reasoning . . . poor research . . . [and] an examination of nonrepresentative samplings," it broke the media's and church's silence on homosexual issues.[89] Kimball's ideas went on to influence fellow church leaders and hundreds of thousands of followers. Thus Kimball, like Mormon leaders before and since, was affected by mainstream homophobic views, which he then intensified through his ecclesiastical authority. It was also in this speech that Kimball first used the phrase which serves as title for this essay: "We are told that as far back as Henry the VIII, this vice was referred to as 'THE ABOMINABLE AND DETESTABLE CRIME AGAINST NATURE,' and some of our own statues [sic] have followed that wording."[90]

On 5 January 1965 Kimball again spoke at BYU, this time to students, and condemned homosexuality in "Love versus Lust," later published in *BYU Speeches of the Year*. This talk drew heavily from his speech of the previous year. The following is a brief quote from the address:

"Good men, wise men, God-fearing men everywhere . . . denounce the practice as being unworthy of sons of God; and Christ's Church denounces it and condemns it so long as men have bodies which can be defiled. This heinous homosexual sin is of the ages. Many cities and civilizations have gone out of existence because of it. It was present in Israel's wandering days, tolerated by the Greeks, and found in the baths of corrupt Rome. In Exodus, the law required death for the culprit who committed incest, or the depraved one who had homosexual or other vicious practices.

"This is a most unpleasant subject to dwell upon, but I am pressed to speak it boldly so that no student in this University, nor youth in the Church, will ever have any question in his mind as to the illicit and diabolical nature of this perverse program. Again, Lucifer deceives and prompts logic and rationalization which will destroy men and make them servants of Satan forever. . . . Let it never be said that the Church avoided condemning this obnoxious practice nor that it has winked at this abominable sin. And I feel certain that this University will never knowingly enroll an unrepentant person who follows these practices nor tolerate on its campus anyone with these tendencies who fails to repent and put his or her life in order."[91]

After ten years of preparation Kimball finally published in 1969 his classic treatise on sin and repentance: *The Miracle of Forgiveness.* In the chapter "The Crime Against Nature," he detailed his theory that masturbation caused homosexuality, which in turn often led to bestiality. He also claimed that "the sin of homosexuality is equal to or greater than that of fornication or adultery," effectively placing homosexuality next to murder in the Mormon hierarchy of sins. Ironically, this "definitive" statement against homosexuality came out just as the "Gay liberation movement" gained national attention with the watershed "Stonewall Riots" in New York City beginning on 27 June 1969.

In 1970 the First Presidency sent a letter to the church-at-large, stating that "homosexuals can be assured that in spite of all they may have heard from other sources, they can overcome and can return to normal, happy living."[92] This was but a precursor to the more official (and ecclesiastically binding) First Presidency statement of 1973 which declared that "homosexuality in men and women runs counter to . . . divine objectives and, therefore, is to be avoided and forsaken." Gays and Lesbians who refused to find their sexuality evil were promised "prompt Church court action."[93] Excommunication to faithful Mormons means eternal exclusion from the "celestial kingdom"—a hell in and of itself.

That same year LDS psychologist Allen E. Bergin of Brigham Young University and Victor L. Brown, Jr., of LDS Social Services wrote the twenty-page *Homosexuality: Welfare Services Packet I* for use in counseling Lesbians and Gay men. The packet indicated that "an essential part of repentance" was to disclose to church authorities the names of other homosexuals in order to "help save others." It also stated that the Lesbian "needs to learn feminine behavior" while the Gay man "needs to learn . . . what a manly Priesthood leader and father does." It also explained that "excommunication cleanses the Church. . . . There is no place in God's Church for those who persist in vile behavior."[94] Ironically, church leaders concluded that the *Packet* was so "weakly" written that it could only be used on a limited basis.[95]

During the priesthood session of October LDS general conference in 1976 Apostle Boyd K. Packer gave a speech entitled "To Young Men Only" that discussed situations in which young men are "tempted to handle one another, to have contact with one another in unusual ways." He commented that "such practices are perversion. . . . Physical mischief with another man is forbidden." Packer also essentially advocated anti-Gay violence when he recounted the story of a male missionary who "floored" his mission companion apparently for making sexual advances. Packer told the missionary, "Well, thanks. Somebody had to do it and it wouldn't be well for a General Authority to solve the problem that way." "I am not recommending that course [of violence] to you," Packer told his all-male audience, "but I am not omitting it. You must protect yourself."[96] This speech was later made into a pamphlet and distributed worldwide for use in counseling young men.

In the late 1970s "born-again Christians" and Mormons, usually vociferous enemies, found themselves temporarily on friendly terms. National attention was turning toward Gay rights legislation in Florida in 1977, and Anita Bryant's subsequent anti-Gay Christian crusade, "Save Our Children." Barbara B. Smith, general president of the LDS Relief Society, sent a telegram to Bryant, saying, "On behalf of the one million members of the Relief Society . . . we commend you, for your courageous and effective efforts in combatting homosexuality and laws which would legitimize this insidious life style."[97] A month later Apostle Mark E. Peterson claimed that "every right-thinking person will sustain Miss Bryant, a prayerful, upright citizen, for her stand," which Peterson hoped would "keep this evil from spreading, by legal acceptance, through our society."[98] That same year Spencer Kimball, now church president, told reporters that Bryant was "doing a great service" because church leaders felt that "the homosexual program is not a natural and normal way of life."[99]

Also in 1977 Gay Mormons in Los Angeles founded a support group. Originally called the Gay Mormon Underground (GMU), it soon changed its name to Affirmation. Other GMU chapters were organized in both Salt Lake City and San Francisco within a year.

From July 1977 to July 1979 Apostle Peterson wrote six editorials for the Mormon *Church News* attacking the national Gay rights movement. For Peterson, homosexuality was "a menace to the population at large." Also, according to Peterson, Lesbian and Gay pleas for tolerance and legal recourse for discrimination "should disgust every thinking person."[100] Peterson, like Kimball, drew "expert evidence" from popular media sources such as *Newsweek, Time,* and the *Sacramento Bee.*

Also in 1978 the First Presidency issued a lengthy statement opposing the Equal Rights Amendment (ERA). In part, the statement claimed that passage of the ERA would bring about an "encouragement of those who seek a unisex society, an increase in the practice of homosexual and lesbian activities, and other concepts which could alter the natural, God-given relationship of men and women." These and other anti-Gay phobias were reiterated in subsequent anti-ERA propaganda published by the church in 1979 and 1980.[101]

This fear of a "unisex society" lies at the core of Mormon homophobia, for the hierarchy has a vested interest in keeping gender lines firmly drawn. Any blurring of those lines, any weakening of gendered activities, places Mormon men in a locus where they can only lose power. As the First Presidency wrote in 1991, "a correct understanding of the *divinely appointed* roles of men and women will fortify all against sinful practices" such as "homosexual and lesbian behavior."[102]

Mormon men also fear the "homosexual within." If church leaders believe that the world can "convert" to homosexuality as easily as to Mormonism, then they must include themselves in that conversion. Spencer Kimball, in *New Horizons for Homosexuals,* asked readers to "imagine, if you can, the total race skidding down in this practice . . . just one generation of gratification of lusts and the end." Furthermore, "where would the world go if such a practice became general? The answer: To the same place other unbridled civilizations have gone."[103] Earlier, Kimball proclaimed that "if the abominable practice became universal it would depopulate the earth in a single generation."[104] Mormon bishop T. Eugene Shoemaker ironically denied that homosexuality is a "crime against nature," going so far as to argue that "homosexuality is wrong, not because it is unnatural, but rather because it is *too* natural, and unless the human species changes utterly, men and women will continue to choose freely to do evil."[105]

At the same time Mormon leaders are aware that homosociality is closely aligned to homosexuality. LDS therapist Victor L. Brown, Jr., told in 1977 of a "recent case of a man who with his wife came to Utah to get help in overcoming his homosexuality: there were times when he felt so good, so fond of other men that he wanted to hug them to express it. He was repulsed by any suggestion of *sexual* involvement, however!" Brown explained that the general authorities of the church "so hugged each other at [general] conference, sometimes for rather long periods of time, that this was not homosexuality at all!! The man left, and his wife [was] very relieved and enlightened. Six months later [Brown] got a letter from them saying what a tremendous difference it had made to him to realize that these feelings of genuine love and rapport were normal and *not* homosexual! The man's guilt burden had been totally lifted."[106]

Brown, also addressing the church's awareness of female homosociality, said that "it is fairly common to find women who are turned off by the male society, and who find friendship and companionship from another female, but between the pair there is absolutely no sexual situation at all, just companionship. The Church is aware and sensitive to this; the [definition] of homosexuality has been 'carefully reworded' to try to steer around this, the word 'relations' was changed to 'relationships' for this reason." Brown indicated that the "gospel ideal" of the male gender role actually "has many feminine qualities" because a Mormon man "should be tender, loving, gentle, etc., [which] implies femininity." Brown believed that a "male does *not* give up his masculinity when he behaves this way," and society "must get rid of the idea that to be male, a male must be aggressive, brutal, pugnacious, possessive."[107]

*Private and Public Anti-Homosexual Policies at Brigham Young University, 1959-80.* Meanwhile, problems had been brewing at Mormon-owned Brigham Young University because private policies developed during the late 1950s through the 1970s began to receive public criticism from both students and the national press, influenced in part by the rise of the national Lesbian and Gay liberation movement. BYU's response to homosexuality is important for several reasons: its large (and surprisingly open) Gay and Lesbian population; its semi-open bureaucracy which has allowed selected important documents concerning homosexuality to surface; and the tension created by religion and academics which provides interesting (and recently traumatic) dilemmas for the people who work, teach, and study there. Close examination of policies, practices, and attitudes regarding homosexuality at BYU reveals the homophobic mechanisms which were created, reproduced, modified, and sustained (even when unethical and/or illegal) by church and university leaders, sometimes even at the expense of great criticism from external sources. BYU and church administrations have operated behind closed doors, carefully and deliberately attempting to eradicate "the Queer experience" without even once challenging the supposition that homosexuality (desire and/or practice) is an illness, abnormality, sin, or crime. Because Mormon apostles comprise BYU's board of trustees (with only one or two exceptions), the attitudes of the church hierarchy have directly affected BYU's policies. However, because BYU is also an academic institution where free inquiry is encouraged, at least in principle, the school's policies on homosexuality have changed over time. Thus BYU has in turn influenced the church's position on homosexuality like no other "outside" institution.

On 21 May 1959 BYU president Ernest L. Wilkinson met with the executive committee of the board of trustees. He asked the committee "whether the Dean of Students should send questionnaires to bishops asking whether students had a propensity for stealing or immorality or anything of that kind," effectively violating the confidentiality of the confessional; and wondered about "the growing problem in our society of homosexuality."[108] Wilkinson recorded that "these two problems interested the Brethren very, very much," and that church president David O. McKay had recently voiced "his view [that] homosexuality was worse than immorality; that it is a filthy and unnatural habit." Wilkinson was instructed that unless the homosexual student was "really repentant and immediately working out their problems," the school "should suspend them." Administrators then wondered if they should record on transcripts that the student had been expelled for homosexuality. The executive committee recommended avoiding the possibility of law suits. Wilkinson was also told to come up with a "better plan to find out from bishops the information requested by the Dean of Students." Although progress on Wilkinson's questionnaire was temporarily halted, he would eventually receive permission to implement it.

On 12 September 1962 Wilkinson met with the school's general counsel, Clyde Sandgren, the new Dean of Students, Elliott Cameron, and apostles Spencer Kimball and Mark Peterson "on the question of homosexuals who might possibly be a part of our student body."

They decided that the number of homosexuals on campus was "a very small percentage of the whole" and therefore administrators "ought not to dignify it by meeting with the men or women of the university [in a public setting] but handle each case on its own." They then worked out a cooperative plan whereby Mormon general authorities and other church administrators would give BYU information they obtained about homosexuality on campus, and BYU would give church administrators information. They decided "as a general policy that no one will be admitted as a student at the B.Y.U. whom we have convincing evidence is a homosexual."[109]

Apparently BYU found more homosexuals than initially anticipated. First, Apostle Kimball felt compelled to condemn homosexuality in his "Love versus Lust" address to the assembled student body on 5 January 1965. Then in the fall of that year Wilkinson went public with anti-Gay policies during an address to the student body. As part of the speech, Wilkinson indicated that BYU did not intend "to admit to our campus any homosexuals. If any of you have this tendency and have not completely abandoned it may I suggest that you leave the university immediately after this assembly and if you will be honest enough to let us know the reason, we will voluntarily refund your tuition. We do not want others on this campus to be contaminated by your presence."[110] By resorting to the metaphor of viral contagion, Wilkinson voiced his own—and presumably others'—fear of the "homosexual within."

Finally in 1967 Wilkinson received permission to ask Mormon bishops at BYU to provide the BYU Standards Office with lists of students who were "inactive in the church" or who had confessed to "not living the standards of the church." The number of students visiting the Standards Office subsequently rose dramatically. The first year of the new policy, Standards counselled seventy-two students who were "suspected of homosexual activity."[111] The discovery spurred the university into action in which security files were kept on suspected Gay students, student spying was encouraged,[112] and suspensions/expulsions increased significantly. One student, suspended from the university on suspicion of homosexuality, was taken to court by BYU for trespassing when he was spotted on campus after his suspension.[113] Even prospective teachers at the Language Training Mission on BYU campus had to be interviewed by a general authority, because a "homosexual ring" had seemingly infiltrated the campus. Church leaders wanted to be assured that no Lesbians or Gay men were teaching missionaries at the language school.[114]

In 1969 the board of trustees ruled that Lesbian, Gay, and Bisexual students "would not be admitted or retained at BYU without approval from the General Authorities."[115] Three years later Apostle Marvin J. Ashton was asked by trustees to help further define a policy on homosexuals at BYU because the new president of the university, Dallin Oaks, was concerned about what to do with students or school personnel who were not overtly homosexual.[116] Six months later trustees ruled that those who were not "overt and active homosexuals" could remain at the university's discretion and upon recommendation by the "ecclesiastical leader having jurisdiction over the case." However, those who were "overt and active" would still be automatically expelled unless a general authority recommended otherwise.[117] In early 1978, Gerald Dye, the chair of University Standards reported what the "set process" was for "homosexual students referred to Standards" for counseling:

> *They are asked to a personal interview with Standards . . . to determine the depth or extent of involvement; previous involvement, if any, of offender; does the student understand the seriousness of the matter; if the branch president or bishop [is] aware.
>
> *The individual's branch president or home bishop is contacted.
>
> *Standards is to determine if the offense is serious or not.
>
> *serious: repetition; anal/oral intercourse.
>
> *less serious: experimential [sic]; mutual masturbation.
>
> *Action taken.
>
> *If determined to be serious the student is expelled.
>
> *If less serious, the student may remain at BYU on a probationary basis.
>
> *Standards also acts as an intermediary between the student who remains and a counseling service. Students who remain are required to undergo therapy.[118]

Although therapy was required, Dye promised that "no student working through Standards will ever undergo aversion therapy." Electroshock and vomiting aversion therapies were nonetheless used in special cases.[119]

Gay and Lesbian rights rhetoric finally reached BYU by the 1970s, inducing some students to come out of the closet. In January 1975 administrators sent campus security officers to quash a "homosexual ring" on campus. Security officers descended *en masse* on the Harris Fine Arts Center and took all male drama and ballet students out of class to interrogate them in hallways.[120] Some drama students involved in the "Purge of '75'" had T-shirts printed which read sarcastically, "I'm on the list–are you?"

Not all Lesbian and Gay students could respond to this situation with humor. As the purge continued into 1976, BYU security sent officers and volunteers to Gay bars in Salt Lake City to record license plate numbers of cars with BYU parking stickers on them. One student attempted suicide. When taken to the hospital, medical personnel reported him to BYU security who in turn informed his bishop and his wife of his situation. In a joint effort between Utah County sheriff's officers and BYU security during March 1976, fourteen men were arraigned in Pleasant Grove (near BYU) on charges of "lewdness and sodomy" at two freeway rest stops. One of these men shot himself two days after his arrest. During surveillance of these rest stops, officers documented more than 100 men, many of whom were from BYU, who were "believed to engage in homosexual activity" there.[121] Gay journalist and former LDS missionary Robert McQueen recounted the stories of five Gay men he had known at BYU who were caught in this "purge," coerced into aversive therapies, expelled from BYU, exposed by church officials, and excommunicated. Each one of the five killed himself rather than face the oppression and bigotry of family, church, and society.[122]

BYU and church officials grew so alarmed that in 1976 they established an Institute for Studies in Values and Human Behavior on campus, with psychology professor Allen Bergin as director.[123] The institute was to produce a manuscript "which would set forth significant empirical evidence in support of the Church's position on homosexuality."[124] A book, funded by the church, would be written for a "*New York Times* type of audience" by Bergin and Victor L. Brown, Jr., approved of by at least one general authority, published by a popular eastern press, and made to appear as though it had no tie to the church. The resulting book would then be available as "secular evidence" to back up the church's anti-Gay stance.[125]

Other institute goals included: (1) reviewing "the means by which the [homosexual] 'opposition' attempts to indoctrinate our people," (2) explaining "the developmental pattern of sexual deviance," (3) creating "an LDS book on human behavior after the manner of the Articles of Faith," (4) creating "a political action kit for use of member-Citizens in local [anti-Gay] legislative efforts," (5) preparing other kinds of anti-Gay papers and rebuttals, (6) supporting academic and scientific research that would vindicate the church's homophobic position, and (7) recommending to the First Presidency "specific steps the Church might take in combating homosexuality and other sexual misconduct."[126] Anti-Gay papers and research conducted, sponsored, or supported by the institute included Elizabeth C. James's 1976 Ph.D. dissertation, "Treatment of Homosexuality: A Reanalysis and Synthesis Outcome Studies," Bergin's 1979 paper, "Bringing the Restoration to the Academic World: Clinical Psychology as a Test Case," Ed D. Lauritzen's 1979 paper, "The Role of the Father in Male Homosexuality," and possibly Max Ford McBride's 1976 dissertation at BYU, "Effect of Visual Stimuli in Electric Aversion Therapy." McBride used fourteen Gay male subjects to determine if using photographs of nude men and women from *Playgirl*- and *Playboy*-type magazines was helpful in electroshock therapy.

Ultimately, the institute's greatest challenge came from an unexpected quarter: BYU student Cloy Jenkins. About June 1977, after attending an anti-Gay lecture by BYU psychology professor I. Reed Payne (a member of the institute), Jenkins, a Gay student, prepared a thoughtful anonymous response to Payne's lecture, calling for a "well-reasoned dialogue on these issues." After getting help from two friends in editing his response (now published as *Prologue*) Jenkins had copies of it mailed to various church officials.[127] The paper was soon circulating among faculty and administration at both BYU and Ricks College, as well as television and radio stations, and newspapers throughout Utah and Idaho.[128]

The church's reaction was immediate. According to a social services counselor at BYU, Jenkins's paper caused "a real stir at BYU and in the Church—officials in both places are very touchy over it."[129] Allen Bergin was directed by LDS Social Services and the BYU Comprehensive Clinic to prepare a rebuttal. This proved to be difficult, however, because Jenkins had made several "really good and undisputable points," his figures on the numbers of Gays at BYU were accurate, and, according to BYU's executive committee, he had used a "rather sophisticated pro-homosexuality platform."[130] Bergin finished his response on 22 August 1977 and titled it "A Reply to Unfounded Assertions Regarding Homosexuality." BYU's executive committee hailed it as "an excellent piece refuting [Jenkins's] major claims."[131] Despite this initial optimism, one BYU professor said it was so poorly written that "it was an embarrassment to all involved."[132] Word went out that "all copies be returned [to Bergin] as he hopes to rewrite his reply"[133] Apparently, Bergin tried to rework his response, without much success. Bergin's colleague, Victor L. Brown, Jr., also tried to rebut *Prologue,* but his response was never released to the public.[134]

When it became apparent that no authoritative response was forthcoming from the Values Institute, the church hierarchy decided to intervene personally. President Spencer Kimball asked Apostle Boyd K. Packer to "specifically address the local problem of homosexuality and to offer solutions" to BYU students. Packer at first declined, but when pressed again by Kimball decided to speak to students in early March 1978. At the same time a national Gay magazine was also preparing to publish excerpts from Jenkins's paper. About three weeks prior to its 22 February publication, the magazine sent out press packets to newspaper agencies across the United States. The religion editor of a newspaper in Oregon sent a copy of the release to a Mormon friend, who forwarded it to Dallin Oaks. Oaks then drafted a letter to Packer, warning that "in view of this national publication, and the accusations it makes . . . your [upcoming] remarks are likely to get wide newspaper coverage and to be viewed by many against the background of this article and these charges."[135]

On 5 March 1978 Packer went ahead and delivered his now-famous "To the One" speech during a twelve-stake fireside at BYU. Although the entire speech dealt with homosexuality, Packer used the word "homosexual" only once because he felt that "We can very foolishly cause things we are trying to prevent by talking too much about them." This was not Packer's only theory about the causes of homosexuality—and causation was vital, because, for Packer, finding the cause was an "essential step in developing a cure." Packer theorized that the cause "will turn out to be a very typical form of selfishness."[136] Two weeks after Packer's speech, a BYU counselor commented that Packer's "spiritual" approach to homosexulaity had actually originated with the director of LDS Social Services who "was in charge of working with homosexuals."[137]

Response to Packer by members of the Utah Gay community was quick. Bob Waldrop, the Gay pastor of the Metropolitan Community Church in Salt Lake City (and an ex-Mormon), termed the speech "very offensive and highly inaccurate" and demanded that the PBS television station KBYU, which had broadcast Packer's sermon, give him equal air time. Bruce Christensen, KBYU general manager, denied Waldrop's request and told the media that KBYU recognizes its "responsibility to cover all aspects of the Gay rights issue and we believe we have done that with fairness."[138]

A BYU student in attendance at Packer's speech quickly wrote a rebuttal, which was published anonymously in the local Gay newspaper, *Salt Lake Open Door.* The student criticized Packer's approach as "some kind of pseudo-psycho-spiritual counsel which close analysis will prove to be a substantial assemblage of a profound lack of reason and education." However, he warned that Packer "is clever. Packer's treatise on 'selfishness' zeros right in on the desperate attempt many have made in trying to attribute their sexuality to some personality characteristic or quality which is causing their homosexuality. If this quality can be changed (and it is usually some malleable trait—like selfishness), then the homosexuality will disappear. This approach also has the therapeutic return of displacing guilt (a burden of guilt encouraged by the heterosexual moralist-theologian). The homosexual is thereby informed that he should be feeling guilty for being selfish—not for being homosexual. This helps ease his anguish and he experiences an instantaneous relief. He is well on his way to escaping into health, to optimistically denying his authentic nature, to psychological swindle. Even when he fails (which is inevitable), he comes back to focusing on his selfishness and not on his sexuality. It is much easier warring against an attribute like selfishness than challenging one's sexuality."

Packer's assertion that "the cure" is something which "finally has to take place in the spiritual realm" was the most serious flaw in his theory, this student felt, because then "we don't have to talk about the realities here of sexual impulses when we can focus on the transcendent sacred dimension out there. When the [Gay] subject fails, then [Packer] simply declares . . . that the subject is somewhere in transgression of spiritual matters." In conclusion, he reiterated that "as appalling as [Packer's] talk was, I am encouraged by it. It is miles ahead of President Kimball. . . . At least the subject [of homosexuality] seems to have finally come out of the closet—too bad Packer has dressed it in rags."[139]

In the meantime, church and BYU administrators were trying to locate the anonymous author of *Prologue* to bring suit against him for "the misleading representations in this publication [as] a violation of the postal laws and regulations." In a November 1978 report to LDS church commissioner of education Jeffrey R. Holland, Oaks summarized BYU's unsuccessful attempts to track down the author and recommended that "it would be best for us now to let this matter drop" because "any direct action by the University against the publishers would be counterproductive, arousing greater public attention and resentment [than] any benefit to be gained."[140]

By late 1979 the Institute for Studies in Values and Human Behavior had not succeeded in achieving its goals. Bergin and Brown had not rebutted Jenkins's paper; Bergin's "scholarly objectivity" was challenged during professional conferences and his professional standing was being questioned; and President Oaks was annoyed at what he perceived to be an undermining of his own authority. On 13 September 1979 Oaks wrote to Apostle Thomas Monson to explain the problems associated with the "Bergin-Brown Book on Values" and to inform church officials that school administrators had become persuaded "that we cannot achieve the original objectives to the extent hoped" by having the book appear through an "independent popular publisher."[141]

By 1980 the institute had spent almost $150,000 in church funds trying to produce an anti-Gay manuscript. According to Oaks, general authorities were getting "squeamish" about the project. Pressure on the institute became too great for Bergin, who resigned as chair. Soon the manuscript project was scrapped and the institute was disbanded.[142]

*Mormonism and Homosexuality Today.* I have not dealt with the period after 1980 because AIDS, which first appeared in the United States around that year, has radically changed the face of Gay and

Lesbian issues nationally. The juxtaposition of sex, death, morality, and politics (embodied in AIDS) has been such a complex and painful landscape for both the Gay community and the Mormon church to negotiate that it requires its own analysis.

Suffice it to say that Mormon homophobic discourse has currently "softened," resorting to the cliched epigram of "love the sinner, hate the sin." But I find this as difficult to believe as if I were to say that I love all Mormons, while hating Mormonism. Personally I cannot divorce who a person is from what a person believes or does. Despite attempts at "compassionate" response, anti-Gay rhetoric abounds in Mormonism as never before. The church unofficially supports the Evergreen Foundation and its claim of success in "reorientation therapy."[143] In 1992 the church published the homophobic *Understanding and Helping Those Who Have Homosexual Problems*, without realizing that homophobia and heterosexism are the *only* "homosexual problems."[144] The following year Apostle Boyd Packer made it clear that the three greatest "dangers" to the modern church are "the gay-lesbian movement, the feminist movement, and the ever present challenge from the so-called scholars."[145] Purges of Lesbians, Gays, and Bisexuals at BYU and elsewhere in the church continue unabated. These are not acts of love, but of fear.

For unmarried heterosexual Mormons and for Gays and Lesbians who choose celibacy to remain in the Mormon church, heterogamy is still compulsory. In 1993 an unmarried Mormon over thirty from Minnesota wrote to the church, questioning its current policy of not allowing older single people to "serve as ordinance workers" in Mormon temples. Apostle Russell M. Ballard replied, "It is not a policy set forth because of concern for improper sexual behavior by those over age thirty." Ballard counseled that rather than desiring to officiate in the temple, "perhaps it would be more wise that those who have not married and over the age of thirty, should seek to establish for themselves the full blessings of the atonement of Jesus Christ" by getting married. Ballard continued that heterogamy "is so paramount in the life of each individual member of the Church that every effort should be made by individuals to appropriately and according to their own wisdom find a companion wherewith they may receive the joys and blessings of an eternal family unit."[146]

While emphasizing the importance of marriage and family, Mormon leaders can only sanction heterogamy and a family unit with a heterosexual couple as parents (following the paradigm of the divine, heterosexual couple whom Mormons view as the Father and Mother in Heaven). This places Gay and Lesbian Mormons in a no-win situation where they are commanded to marry for eternal salvation but are unable to marry the person of their choice. Furthermore, Mormon leaders move beyond the realm of theology and into the political by mandating that any alternative to the heterosexist family structure requires immediate societal and legal condemnation. A First Presidency statement issued to the church in 1994 explained that "the principles of the gospel and the sacred responsibilities given" to Mormons require that the church "oppose any efforts to give legal authorization to marriage between persons of the same gender." The First Presidency further encouraged "members to appeal to legislators, judges, and other government officials to preserve the purposes and sanctity of marriage between a man and a woman, and to reject all efforts to give legal authorization or other official approval or support to marriages between persons of the same gender."[147]

Consequently Lesbian, Gay, and Bisexual Mormons have responded to their religion's teachings on sexuality in three ways: (1) remain "closeted" to conform to Mormon demands in appearance; (2) come out of the closet while remaining loyal to Mormonism in order to struggle for a voice in the church; or (3) leave the church. For those who are closeted and trying to remain in Mormonism, their path is fraught with profound isolation and guilt—especially if they have started families which further causes them to assume roles for which they were not meant.

For Lesbian, Gay, and Bisexual Mormons who continue to struggle for a voice in the church, there are several organizations available for support. Affirmation now has an international network of some twenty chapters. There are also organizations for Gay BYU alumni and Gay returned missionaries which allow members to explore and find consolation in common experiences. Periodicals, pamphlets, books, and symposia are also media through which the views of these people have recently been expressed. Others, like me, find Mormonism too rigid, too oppressive to remain in its structures and continue their journey elsewhere. However, the common bond all Lesbian and

Gay Mormons share is the questioning of our lives in Mormonism—the values we learned from and the time and energy we devoted to it. We all struggle to make meaning out of the pain we feel at the realization that because of the intensity and authenticity of our desire to love and be loved by someone of our own sex, to "multiply and replenish" heterosexually is not a realistic imperative for us. Our bruised and battered bodies, lying at the feet of the church, demand at least a thoughtful, inclusive, and loving response.

*NOTES*

1. Throughout this essay, unless quoting others, I capitalize Lesbian, Gay, and Bisexual as a way of affirming my belief that we have constructed an ethnic identity: a social and cultural system which includes but is not limited to a history, a language, and a political sensibility, and which drastically differs in many ways from the identity of the Straight (heterosexual) community.

2. Homophobia is an irrational, unfounded fear of homosexuals and homosexuality. Heterosexism is the assumption that all people are heterosexuals or should be. Both engender such practices as anti-Gay legislation, "reorientation" therapies, or passive, but debilitating, silence.

3. By homosocial, I mean the dynamic of groups of people of the same gender who socialize together. "Male bonding" is a form of homosociality. Other aspects of this "homo-continuum" include the homopolitical, homospiritual, homointellectual, homophysical, homoemotional, homophilic, homoerotic, and ultimately homosexual.

4. T. Eugene Shoemaker, "Human Sexuality in Mormonism: Reflections from the Bishop's Couch; an Essay on Understanding," no date, in Sunstone Papers, Special Collections, Marriott Library, University of Utah, Salt Lake City.

5. Richard Van Wagoner, *Mormon Polygamy: A History,* 2d ed. (Salt Lake City: Signature Books, 1989), 56.

6. In 1991 the Mormon church deleted the embrace at the veil. However, this deletion is minor and the metaphor is still appropriate.

7. Adrienne Rich, "Compulsory Heterosexuality and Lesbian Existence," reprinted in *Lesbian and Gay Studies Reader* (New York: Routledge, 1993), 239, 242.

8. The term "sister-wife" combines two intensely sensual, emotional, and personal concepts: conjugality and sorority.

9. Gail Farr Casterline, "Ellis R. Shipp," in Vicky Burgess-Olson, ed., *Sister Saints* (Provo, UT: Brigham Young University Press, 1978), 371.

10. Casterline, 369-70.

11. Ibid., 371, italics in original.

12. Carol Lasser, "'Let Us Be Sisters Forever': The Sororal Model of Nineteenth Century Female Friendship," *Signs: Journal of Women in Culture and Society* 1 (1988), 1:161.

13. "Louie B. Felt," *Children's Friend,* 18 (18 Dec. 1919): 410.

14. Ibid., 411.

15. "Mary and May," *Children's Friend,* 18 (18 Dec. 1919): 421.

16. While Aurelia Spencer Rogers actually founded the first Primary organization, Louie Felt organized the second branch a month later in September 1879. On 19 June 1880 Felt became the first general president of the Primary and in 1890 called May Anderson to be general secretary. Anderson first suggested in 1893 that the Primary have its own church-sponsored publication, and in 1901 the Primary General Board received permission to begin publishing the *Children's Friend,* with Anderson as editor. Felt and Anderson together conceived of the idea for the Primary Children's Hospital after seeing a disabled boy on the streets of Salt Lake City. In 1925, when Felt was released as the Primary general president, Anderson succeeded her. For further details on the relationship and accomplishments of these two women, see their biographies in the following issues of the *Children's Friend:* "Louie B. Felt," 18 (18 Dec. 1919): 404-17; "Mary and May," 18 (18 Dec. 1919): 418-22; "The New Presidency," 24 (Nov. 1925): 21-23; "Louie B. Felt: A Tribute," 24 (Nov. 1925): 422-25; and "A Friend of the Children," 39 (Apr. 1940): 146-52; as well as Susan Staker Oman, "Nurturing LDS Primaries: Louie Felt and May Anderson, 1880-1940," *Utah Historical Quarterly,* 49, 3:262-75.

17. "Mary and May," 420-1.

18. See 1 Sam. 18:1-4; 2 Sam. 2:25-27. For discussions of David and Jonathan as historical signifiers of male-male desire, see John Boswell, *Christianity, Social Tolerance, and Homosexuality* (Chicago: University of Chicago Press, 1980), 105, 238-39, 252, and 299; and Richard Dellamora, *Masculine Desire: The Sexual Politics of Victorian Aestheticism* (Chapel Hill, NC: University of North Carolina Press, 1990), 221.

19. Sarah E. Pearson, "Sister to Sister," see loose sheet in Kate Thomas Papers, Utah State Historical Society, Salt Lake City.

20. "Veteran Worker in Primary Recalls History for Jubilee," *Deseret News,* 21 Apr. 1928.

21. For biographical information on Thomas, see "Biographical Notes" accompanying the register for the Thomas Papers, donated to the Utah State Historical Society by her brother, U.S. senator Elbert Thomas (D-Utah). Included in the Thomas Papers is another biography written by LeNae Peavey entitled "Kate Thomas (1871-1950)."

22. "To ________," Record Journal of Love Poems, Kate Thomas Papers.

23. "A Scarlet West," 36, Thomas Papers.

24. See commentary on the 1868 song, "Gay Young Clerk in the Dry Goods Store," in Jonathan Katz, *Gay/Lesbian Almanac* (Cambridge, MA: Harper and Row, 1983), 315. Male dry goods clerks were considered by Victorian America to be effeminate and suspected of being homosexual.

25. Katz, *Almanac,* 405-407.

26. "Narcissus," 80.

27. "A Gay Musician," 79.

28. "Biographical Notes," Kate Thomas Papers.

29. See *Polk's Directory* for Salt Lake City, 1923 and 1927, and for Ogden, Utah, 1919 and 1925.

30. Interview with L. H. on 8 Aug. 1988, and interview with J. B. B. on 7 Jan. 1990.

31. For biographical information on Cora Kasius, see "Utah Woman to Join Dutch Welfare Group," *Deseret News,* 8 Mar. 1945.

32. D. Michael Quinn, basing his information in part on Maxine Hanks, has identified Fanny Fern as non-Mormon feminist Grata P. Willis Eldredge Parton and claims that her brief essay was originally published in the *New York Ledger* (see D. Michael Quinn, "Same-sex Dynamics among Nineteenth-century Mormons: A Social Context," circulated by a prospective publisher to a limited group of readers, 29 and n81). Coincidentally, "Fern" is an archaic, somewhat derogatory word for a Gay man, similar to "pansy" or "fairy."

33. See the 31 December 1877 letter from Alice Blackwell to her sister-in-law Kitty Blackwell for an almost identical description of the painfulness of manipulative "smashing" at an eastern women's college, in Katz, *Almanac,* 176. For another description of "smashing," see Yale University student newspaper of 1873, quoted in Nancy Salhi, "Smashing: Women's Relationships Before the Fall," *Chrysalis* 8 (1979): 21.

34. "Women Lovers," *Women's Exponent,* 15 Apr. 1873, 175.

35. Quinn, "Same-sex Dynamics," 29.

36. For information on John C. Bennett, see John Taylor Family Papers, Special Collections, Marriott Library.

37. Samuel Taylor Papers, handwritten notes on typed page of rough draft of *Nightfall at Nauvoo,* unnumbered first page of Chapter VII, "Every Species of Abomination," Taylor Family Papers.

38. Sam Taylor to T. Edgar Lyon, Feb. 1969.

39. T. Edgar Lyon to Sam Taylor, 4 Feb. 1969, 2, Taylor Family Papers.

40. "Bennettiana: or the Microscope with Double Diamond Lenses," *The Wasp,* 27 July 1842, emphasis in original.

41. Sam Taylor to T. Edgar Lyon, 31 Jan. 1969, Taylor Family Papers.

42. William H. Holyoak to John Taylor, 9 Oct. 1886, quoted in correspondence of Raymond W. Taylor to Samuel W. Taylor, 7 June 1972, 2-3, Taylor Family Papers.

43. *Salt Lake Tribune,* 2 Aug. 1886.

44. For Taylor's "excommunication" notice, see *Deseret News,* 28 Aug. 1886. For rumors published in the newspaper, see "City and Neighborhood" column of the *Salt Lake Tribune,* 22, 24, 29 Aug., 2 Sept. 1886.

45. Thomas Taylor to John Taylor, 22 Sept. 1886, 5, Taylor Family Papers.

46. Rudger Clawson Journal, 30 Jan. 1894, Special Collections, Marriott Library.

47. Ibid.

48. Ibid.

49. Ibid.

50. *Salt Lake Tribune,* 24 Dec. 1886, 4.

51. Taylor had three wives, and Hunsaker had two. Both lost plural wives in divorce proceedings immediately following revelations of their sexual contact with other men. Christopher Cramer, Salt Lake's "Pioneer Florist," was another homosexual polygamist, or "queer," as one informant called him in an interview I conducted with C. E. B. As mentioned, while rumors of Taylor's excommunication were published in the papers, they appeared only in the anti-Mormon *Salt Lake Tribune,* which even then merely referred to Taylor's "sexual vice."

52. For accounts of the Jones trial and aftermath, see *Salt Lake Daily Telegraph,* "A Heavy Case," 27 Oct. 1864; "That Case," 28 Oct. 1864; "The Death of a Sodomite," 31 Oct. 1864; *Daily Union Vedette,* 1 Nov. 1864; and *Deseret News,* 2 Nov. 1864.

53. Daniel Shellabarger, written comments on the Frederck Jones trial, 23 Apr. 1994, in my possession.

54. *Deseret News,* 2 Nov. 1864. Ironically, Carrington would later be excommunicated for sexual relations with his female secretary.

55. Brigham Young to Daniel H. Wells and Brigham Young, Jr., 18 Nov. 1864, in "Correspondence," *Latter-day Saints Millennial Star* 27 (7 Jan. 1865): 14, as quoted in Quinn, "Same-sex Dynamics," 92 and note.

56. "The Crime Against Nature," *Compiled Laws of Utah,* 1876, p. 598.

57. "The Crime Against Nature," *Compiled Laws of the State of Utah,* 1907, c.28.

58. "The Crime Against Nature," *Laws of the State of Utah,* 1923, c. 13.

59. "Sodomy " *Utah Code Annotated,* 1953, 8B, title 76 (76-5-403).

60. For biographical information, see passenger lists for the Mormon emigrant ship *Horizon* (microfilm no. 025,691), International Genealogical Index entries for Lancashire, England (for Carter), and Sussex, England (for

Edwards), and Family Group Sheets for their families, all at Family History Library, Salt Lake City.

61. Josiah Rogerson memoirs, *Salt Lake Tribune,* 4 Jan. 1914.

62. Prior to beginning any research on Stephens, I had been told from four unrelated sources that this famous Mormon was Gay.

63. "Evan Bach: A True Story for Little Folk, by a pioneer," *Children's Friend* 18 (Oct. 1919: 387.

64. Ibid., 389. See the accompanying intimate photograph of the two young men, ca. 1875, when both were about twenty-one years old, on page 388.

65. Both are quoted in Van Wagoner, *Mormon Polygamy,* 67 and 106, respectively.

66. *United States Reports, Supreme Court, 98,* pp. 166-68, as quoted in Van Wagoner, *Mormon Polygamy,* 110.

67. Van Wagoner, *Mormon Polygamy,* 133-39.

68. See advertisement in *Deseret News,* 5, 6 Apr. 1882.

69. "Art Decoration: Oscar Wilde Enlightens a Large Audience on the Subject," *Salt Lake Tribune,* 11 Apr. 1882.

70. Alfred Lambourne, *A Play-House* (Salt Lake City: n.p., n.d.), 28.

71. Helen L. Warner, "Oscar Wilde's Visit to Salt Lake City," *Utah Historical Quarterly* 55 (Fall 1987): 333-34.

72. *Deseret News,* 3, 4, 5, 6, 8, 11, 19, 24, 26, 30 Apr.; 1, 3, 4, 7, 20, 22, 23, 24, 25, 27 May 1895.

73. Dellamora, *Masculine Desire,* 301-302.

74. *Tribune,* 15 Feb. 1885, quoted in Van Wagoner, *Mormon Polygamy,* 133.

75. George Albert Smith diary, 10 July and 16 Sept. 1946; Joseph F. Smith diary, 10 July 1946; J. Reuben Clark office diary, 30 July, 16 Sept. 1946; typescripts in my possession. George Albert Smith's journal indicates that Joseph F. Smith's partner may have been A******** R***** B*******, who was Gay and a neighbor of Joseph F. Smith for several years. On the other hand, records dating from the 1950s in the First Presidency files indicate that the young man was B**** D** B*******, who was still alive at the time of this essay. To complicate matters further, Eldred G. Smith, who replaced Joseph F. Smith as Patriarch to the Church, claimed that the young man was named N******* S******.

76. See conference report in the *Improvement Era,* Nov. 1946, 685 and 708.

77. George F. Richards diary, 6 Dec. 1947, typescript in my possession.

78. David O. McKay office diary, 10 Apr., 9 May, and 10 July 1957; First Presidency files, 1959; typescripts in my possession.

79. J. Reuben Clark diary, 11 Sept. 1950.

80. Clark, "Home and the Building of Family Life," *Relief Society Magazine,* 39 (Dec. 1952): 793-94.

81. Edward L. Kimball and Andrew E. Kimball, Jr., *Spencer W. Kimball: Twelfth President of the Church of Jesus Christ of Latter-day Saints* (Salt Lake City: Bookcraft, 1977), 381.

82. Spencer W. Kimball, "A Counselling Problem in the Church," 10 July 1964, archives, historical department, Church of Jesus Christ of Latter-day Saints, Salt Lake City (hereafter LDS archives). For arrests of homosexuals published in newspapers at that time, see "Suspect Held in Boys Morals Ring," *Salt Lake Tribune,* 13 Feb. 1958, and "Police Nab 23 in 27-Day Morals Drive," *Salt Lake Tribune,* 29 May 1958.

83. Kimball and Kimball, pp. 383-84.

84. Spencer W. Kimball, "A Counselling Problem in the Church"; *The Miracle of Forgiveness* (Salt Lake City: Bookcraft, Inc., 1969), Chapter Six, "The Crime Against Nature"; *New Hope for Transgressors* (1970); *New Horizons for Homosexuals* (1971); and *A Letter to a Friend* (1978), all published by the Church of Jesus Christ of Latter-day Saints. Minor works and speeches include "Love versus Lust," 5 Jan. 1965, LDS archives; "Voices of the Past, of the Present, of the Future," *Ensign* 1 (June 1971); "God Will Not Be Mocked," *Ensign* 4 (Nov. 1974); "The Foundations of Righteousness," *Ensign* 7 (Nov. 1977); and "President Kimball Speaks Out on Morality," *Ensign* 10 (Nov. 1980).

85. Kimball, "Counselling," 12.

86. *Life,* 26 June 1964, and *Medical World News,* 5 June 1964.

87. John D'Emilio, *Sexual Politics, Sexual Communities* (Chicago: University of Chicago Press, 1983), 162.

88. Kimball, "Counselling," 13.

89. D'Emilio, *Sexual Politics,* 164.

90. Kimball, "Counselling," 13.

91. Spencer W. Kimball, "Love versus Lust," *BYU Speeches of the Year, 1964-1965* (Provo, UT: Brigham Young University Press, 1965), 1-30, esp. 24.

92. First Presidency Circular Letter, 19 Mar. 1970, LDS archives.

93. *Priesthood Bulletin,* Feb. 1973.

94. *Homosexuality: Welfare Services Packet I* (Salt Lake City: Corporation of the Church of Jesus Christ of Latter-day Saints, 1973), n.p.

95. Interview with Bill Marshall, 22 Mar. 1978, copy of notes in my possession.

96. Boyd K. Packer, *To Young Men Only* (Salt Lake City: Corporation of the Church of Jesus Christ of Latter-day Saints, 1976), n.p.

97. "Relief Society Leader Hails Anita Bryant's Homosexual Stand," *Salt Lake Tribune,* 11 June 1977.

98. "Unnatural, without excuse," *Church News* supplement of the *Deseret News,* 9 July 1977.

99. "LDS Leader Hails Anti-Gay Stand," *Salt Lake Tribune,* 5 Nov. 1977.

100. "Unnatural, without excuse," 9 July 1977; "The strong delusions," 14 Jan. 1978; "On the safe side," 4 Feb. 1978; "Calling the kettle clean," 18 Mar. 1978; "Is it a menace?" 29 July 1978; and "Sin is not excuse," 16 Dec. 1978, all in "Church News" section of *Deseret News.*

101. *Why Mormon Women Oppose the ERA* (Salt Lake City: Relief Society, 1979), n.p.; and *The Church and the Proposed Equal Rights Amendment: A Moral Issue* (Salt Lake City: *Ensign Magazine,* 1980), 9 and 22.

102. "Standards of Morality and Fidelity," First Presidency to All Members of the Church of Jesus Christ of Latter-day Saints, 14 Nov. 1991.

103. Spencer W. Kimball, *New Horizons for Homosexuals* (Salt Lake City: Church of Jesus Christ of Latter-day Saints, 1971).

104. Kimball, *Miracle of Forgiveness,* 80-81.

105. Shoemaker, "Sexuality in Mormonism," 5-6.

106. Interview with Victor L. Brown, Jr., 21 Dec. 1977, copy of notes in my possession.

107. Ibid., 2.

108. Wilkinson private journal, 21 May 1959, photocopy in Wilkinson Collection, Marriott Library, University of Utah.

109. Ibid., 12 Sept. 1962.

110. *Deseret News,* "Church News" supplement, 13 Nov. 1965, 11.

111. "Annual Report Summary of Cases," 1 Sept. 1967 to 31 Aug. 1968, copy in my possession.

112. *Brigham Young University Bulletin: Catalog of Courses,* 1968/70, 39-40.

113. K. A. Lauritzen to E. L. Wilkinson, 18 June 1969, copy in my possession.

114. Interview with E. M., 14 Aug. 1991.

115. Minutes, BYU Board of Trustees, 2 May 1973, copy in my possession.

116. Ibid., 6 Dec. 1972.

117. Ibid., 2 May 1973.

118. Interview with Gerald Dye, 1 Feb. 1978, copy of notes in my possession.

119. Ibid., 2.

120. Dean Huffaker, "Homosexuality at BYU," *Seventh East Press,* Apr. 1982; and Jerald and Sandra Tanner to the *New York Times,* Feb. 1975.

121. Interview with Sgt. Kal O. Farr, 3 Feb. 1978, copy of notes in my possession; *Provo Daily Herald,* 22 Mar. 1976.

122. Robert I. McQueen, *The Advocate,* 13 Aug. 1975; and *The Vanguard* (student newspaper at Portland State University), 28 Oct. 1975.

123. Minutes, Combined Boards' Meeting, 1 Sept. 1976, copy in my possession.

124. Dallin Oaks to Thomas S. Monson, 13 Sept. 1979, copy in my possession.

125. Oaks to Monson, 13 Sept. 1979; Victor L. Brown, Jr., to Robert K. Thomas, 14 Nov. 1978; Dallin H. Oaks to J. Richard Clarke, 7 Mar. 1979; and Victor L. Brown, Jr., to Robert K. Thomas, 11 Sept. 1979; copies of all in my possession.

126. Brown to Thomas, 14 Nov. 1978.

127. Minutes, BYU Executive Committee, 15 Sept. 1977, copy in my possession; *Prologue: An Examination of Mormon Attitudes Towards Homosexuality,* (n.c.: Prometheus Enterprises, 1978), reprinted by Affirmation: Gay and Lesbian Mormons.

128. *The Open Door,* Sept. 1977, Marriott Library.

129. Marshall interview.

130. Ibid.; Dean Huffaker, "Homosexuality at BYU," 12; Minutes, BYU Executive Committee, 15 Sept. 1977.

131. Minutes, BYU Executive Committee, 15 Sept. 1977.

132. Huffaker, "Homosexuality at BYU," 12.

133. Anonymous, handwritten statement on frontispiece of one copy of Bergin's "Reply" in my possession.

134. Marshall interview.

135. Dallin H. Oaks to Boyd K. Packer, 14 Feb. 1978, copy in my possession; *The Advocate,* 22 Feb. 1978.

136. Boyd K. Packer, *To the One* (Salt Lake City: Church of Jesus Christ of Latter-day Saints, 1978), 5 Mar. 1978. Ironically, Plato took an opposite point of view, theorizing that selfishness causes homophobia, not homosexuality: "Thus whenever it is accepted that it is shameful to value same-sex lovers, this is due to malice in the legislators, selfishness in the rulers, and cowardice in the governed" (Plato, *Symposium,* 182-D, my translation).

137. Marshall interview.

138. *Salt Lake Open Door,* Apr. 1978, 5.

139. Anonymous letter, *Salt Lake Open Door,* Apr. 1978, 11.

140. Dallin H. Oaks to Jeffrey R. Holland, 9 Nov. 1978, copy in my possession.

141. Oaks to Monson, 13 Sept. 1979.

142. See Gary James Bergera and Ronald Priddis, *Brigham Young University: A House of Faith* (Salt Lake City: Signature Books, 1985), 83-84.

143. *Evergreen International's Principles and Programs* (n.c.: n.p., 1993).

144. *Understanding and Helping Those Who Have Homosexual Problems: Suggestions for Ecclesiastical Leaders* (Salt Lake City: Church of Jesus Christ of Latter-day Saints, 1992).

145. "Apostle Packer Says 'So-Called' Scholars, Gays, Feminists Are Leading LDS Astray,"*Salt Lake Tribune,* 24 July 1993, B1.

146. M. Russell Ballard to M. T., 10 Aug. 1993, copy in my possession.

147. First Presidency statement, 13 Feb. 1994, copy in my possession.

# 8.
# Gender and Spirit

*Jeffrey E. Keller*

THERE HAS NEVER BEEN A CONSENSUS AMONG MORMON THEOLOGIANS as to when we acquire our premortal individual characteristics, including sexual identity.[1] Church founder Joseph Smith's original teaching on the subject stated only that "the Spirit of Man is not a created being; it existed from eternity."[2] Though the prophet never explicitly mentioned gender, and indeed used a neuter pronoun to describe one's eternal spirit, some of his contemporaries inferred preearthly gender. Joseph Lee Robinson, for example, wrote, "As we understand, [our spirits] are organized upon the principle of male and female."[3]

Though later church president Brigham Young and several key apostles were never as direct in elucidating a doctrine of spiritual gender as Robinson, they assumed that "the spirit is in the likeness and shape of the body which it inhabits."[4] Apostles John Taylor and Orson Pratt referred to "male and female spirits,"[5] and Taylor further proclaimed that courtship between spirits led to sexual covenants in a preearthly life. According to Taylor, women in a preearth life "chose a kindred spirit whom [they] loved in the spirit world . . . to be [their] head-stay, husband and protection on earth."[6]

Decades later Elder B. H. Roberts became the first church theologian formally to postulate gender before spiritual birth: "There is in that complex thing we call man, an intelligent entity, uncreated, self-existent, indestructible, . . . possessed of powers that go with personality only, hence that entity is he, not it, . . ."[7] Apostle James Talmage similarly proclaimed six years later, "The Church of Jesus Christ of Latter-day Saints affirms as reasonable, scriptural, and true, the doctrine of the eternity of sex [i.e. gender] among the children of God." Talmage unintentionally anticipated future questions when he also declared: "There is no accident of chance, due to purely physical conditions, by which the sex of the unborn is determined; the body takes form as male or female according to the sex of the spirit whose appointment it is to tenant that body."[8]

The issue of assigned gender resurfaced most recently as a response to questions regarding homosexuality and the role of women in the church. Addressing the latter topic in a sermon to the 1983 October Women's Conference, President Gordon B. Hinckley stated, "I know of no doctrine which states that we made a choice when we came to earth as to whether we wished to be male or female. That choice was made by our Father in Heaven in his infinite wisdom."[9]

Seven years earlier in the October 1976 priesthood session of general conference, Apostle Boyd K. Packer had tackled the issue of homosexuality. In this talk he addressed a concern of transsexuals (i.e. people who feel trapped in the body of the opposite gender). Echoing Talmage's 1914 sentiments, Packer stated, "From our premortal life we were directed into a physical body. There is no mismatching of bodies and spirits."[10]

Modern sexual issues present more theological questions than simply a mismatching of spirits, however. As intuitively obvious as gender may seem, it is difficult to define precisely.[11] Briefly, all human embryos initially have the complete cellular apparatus for making male as well as female sexual organs. The sex of the end product is determined by the embryo's particular genetic make-up as reflected in its paired sexual chromosomes, designated X and Y. If an embryo has two X chromosomes, its potentially male system degenerates and the female system develops. If the embryo has one X and one Y chromosome, the reverse happens and a male develops.

In the real world, however, every conceivable variation on this idealized system occurs. Depending on the physical location of each type of cell line, some individuals may develop into true hermaphrodites, having one testicle and one ovary, or both types of tissue on a single gonad. Further, since sexual development also depends on genes found in non-sexual chromosomes, malfunction of these other critical genes can cause a variety of sexual misdevelopment: infertile but normal appearing females, infertile but normal appearing males, and many varieties of pseudohermaphrodism wherein it is impossible to say by looking at the genitals of a newborn whether the child is male or female. Whether to raise these children as male or female is often an arbitrary decision made by doctors and parents. Both decisions usually require reconstructive surgery and lifelong hormonal therapy. One would expect that with respect to the indwelling spirit, the choice of gender made by these parents is incorrect 50 percent of the time. There are also cases of male children who have been raised as psychologically normal females (albeit infertile) following accidental amputation of the penis.

These cases, as a whole, are not as uncommon as one might think. They are problematic to Mormon theology because they suggest that many people who were, say, males in the preexistence have in this life a female body and a female self-image; they marry and are sealed as females and raise adopted children as females. The theological issue of their eternal sexual status is understandably of vital interest to them.

One possible way to explain these cases would be to invoke the omniscience of God: God knew that the surgeon would slip during the circumcision and amputate the penis and as a result the child would be raised as a female. Therefore, God inserted a female spirit originally. However, such a solution may invoke an inordinate amount of predestination for Mormon theology.

The case of transsexuals is even more problematic. The transsexual male sincerely feels that he is a female inside a male body, typically from his earliest childhood memories. Despite public assurances by church authorities that God never makes mistakes assigning gender, and despite the fact that participation in a sex-change operation may be grounds for excommunication, the church has been surprisingly lenient in dealing with individual cases of transsexualism and sexual misdevelopment.

If spirits before earth life are male or female, it follows that sexual identity will persist after the resurrection. This is also implied by the Mormon concept of (1) a heavenly father and mother who have begotten our spirits in their image,[12] and (2) our capacity to become like them after resurrection. Indeed, the epitome of exaltation to

Mormons is "eternal lives," meaning that after resurrection some will create eternal spiritual offspring.[13]

According to this theology, sexual gender after the resurrection is essential because "[God] created man, as we create our children; for there is no other process of creation in heaven, in the earth, or under the earth or in all eternities."[14] Indeed, Orson Pratt went so far as to assign post-resurrection sexual reproduction to all living things: "the spirits of both vegetables and animals are the offspring of male and female parents which have been raised from the dead."[15] Apostle Heber C. Kimball went further, assigning spiritual gender and sexual reproduction to inanimate objects like the earth: "The earth has a spirit as much as any body has a spirit," and added, "Where did the earth come from? From its parent earths." Kimball understood the interaction in this life between a farmer and the soil to be a type of sexual congress resulting in the "conception" of plants: "Does this earth conceive? it does, and it brings forth. If it did not, why do you go and put your wheat into the ground? Does it not conceive it? But it does not conceive except that you put it there. It conceives and brings forth, and you and I live."[16] In the twentieth century Apostle John Widtsoe was more reserved: "Sex is an eternal quality which has its equivalent everywhere. It is indestructible. The relationship between men and women is eternal and must continue eternally."[17]

However, Apostle Joseph Fielding Smith qualified this by noting that "only resurrected and glorified beings can become parents of spirit offspring."[18] When questioned as to how resurrected beings in the lower kingdoms would be kept from cohabitation, he responded that "the privileges of increase or cohabitation between men and women in these kingdoms would be impossible because of peculiar conditions pertaining to these glories."[19] Smith based this interpretation on Orson Pratt's teaching in *The Seer*[20] that "there will be several classes of resurrected bodies: . . . each of these classes will differ from others by prominent and marked distinctions." Smith interpreted Pratt's "marked distinctions" to be the absence of sex organs and sexual gender in the lower kingdoms: "I take it that men and women will, in [the Terrestrial and Telestial Kingdoms], be just what the so-called Christian world expects us to be—neither man nor woman, merely immortal beings having received the resurrection."[21]

The Mormon doctrine of sexual gender encompasses several seemingly inconsistent beliefs. First, Mormon theologians agree that gender has existed from the beginning, but they disagree as to when this beginning was. Nevertheless, men and women created in the image of divine heavenly parents procreate spirits via sexual union; our mortal bodies look like these spirits. Second, the blurring and overlapping of sexual identity in this life do not necessarily negate the concept of eternal gender if the omniscience of God can always be invoked to explain them. Finally, gender and procreation may continue after the resurrection in the celestial kingdom but not necessarily in the lower kingdoms.

A related question was addressed on a national level early in 1981 when the U.S. Senate tried to determine when "human life" begins. At issue was a statement in an anti-abortion bill sponsored by Senator Jesse Helms which read, "Present day scientific evidence indicates a significant likelihood that actual human life exists from conception."

Although several distinguished scientists, philosophers, and theologians spoke on both sides of the issue, the Senate committee was unable to substantiate Helms's claims. The National Academy of Sciences subsequently declared that Helms's bill dealt "with a question to which science can provide no answer." Leon E. Rosenburg of the Yale Medical School added, "I believe that the notion embodied in the phrase 'actual human life' is not a scientific one, but rather a religious, metaphysical one."[22]

The religious, metaphysical issue of "human life" in Mormon theology boils down to the question of when the spirit enters the body. If, as Mormons believe, physical death is that moment when the spirit leaves the body, it follows that a fetus is not yet alive in the fullest sense until it unites with a spirit to form a living soul.

There are basically three periods when a fetus could acquire its spirit: (1) at conception, (2) at "quickening" (the first movements of life felt by the mother, usually in the fourth month of pregnancy), or (3) at birth. Interestingly, each of these three periods has had its supporters among LDS church leaders.

The idea that the spirit enters the embryo at the moment of conception logically entails the corollary that abortion is murder. While never directly addressing the issue of the spirit-body, many church leaders in the mid- to late 1800s equated prenatal killing with infanticide. Church president John Taylor, speaking of abortionists, wrote, "They are murderers and murderesses of their infants. . . . and you that want them, take them, and you that do will go with them, and go to perdition with them and I tell you that in the name of the Lord."[23] In 1884 Apostle George Q. Cannon stated, "They [abortionists] will be damned with the deepest damnation: because it is the damnation of shedding innocent blood, for which there is no forgiveness."[24] As late as 1916 Joseph Fielding Smith wrote, "It is just as much murder to destroy life before as it is after birth, although man-made laws may not so consider it: but there's One who does take notice and his justice and judgment is sure."[25] Seven months later the First Presidency gave its "unqualified endorsement" of Smith's writing.[26]

However, unlike other anti-abortion groups such as the Catholic church which recognized a fixed period of "ensoulment," the Mormon position has never been derived explicitly from an assumed time when the spirit enters the body. Brigham Young also associated abortion with infanticide, although not as explicitly as John Taylor and George Q. Cannon[27]; still, Young did not believe the spirit enters the body until the time of quickening, though he did not differentiate between abortion before and after quickening.[28] As quoted by Joseph Fielding Smith in *Doctrines of Salvation*, Young stated, "When the spirit leaves them [mortal bodies] they are lifeless: and *when the mother feels life come to her infant, it is the spirit entering the body prepatory to the immortal existence*."[29] The First Presidency was likely referring to Young when it wrote, "True it is that the body of man enters upon its career as a tiny germ embryo, which becomes an infant, quickened at a certain stage by the spirit whose tabernacle it is, and the child, after being born, develops into a man."[30] A scriptural precedent for this view may be inferred from Luke 1:41, "when Elizabeth heard the salutation of Mary, the babe [John] leaped in her womb; and Elizabeth was filled with the Holy Ghost," although this scripture has not been explicitly quoted for this purpose.

Unfortunately, although "quickening" has been a popular concept, there is no scientific phenomenon recognizable as quickening. The fetus begins to move as soon as the biochemical contractile proteins actin and myosin come together, and the mother does not feel this movement until months later. Perhaps in part because of this, modern church authorities have not publicly supported Young's hypothesis.

Interestingly, since Joseph F. Smith's 1917 statement, the Mormon church has also rejected the notion that abortion is murder. When asked if abortion was murder, Apostle David O. McKay wrote in 1934, "To this question the Church has not made an authoritative answer. It does, however, condemn abortion as a very sinful act."[31] Nearly forty years later the First Presidency affirmed this position: "As the matter stands, no definitive statement has been made by the Lord one way or another regarding the crime of abortion. So far as is known, he has not listed it alongside the crime of the unpardonable sin and shedding innocent blood. That he has not done so would suggest that it is not in that class of crime and therefore it will be amenable to the laws of repentance and forgiveness."[32]

One possible reason why abortion is not defined as murder is the possibility that the spirit has not yet entered the body. Not surprisingly, McKay believed that the spirit enters the body at birth. In the same letter quoted above, he wrote: "Undoubtedly the nearest approach we have to definite knowledge on this subject is the statement made by the Savior, 3 Nephi 1:13, wherein he said: 'Tomorrow come I into the world.' This indicates that the spirit takes possession of the body at birth. Life manifest in the body before that time would seem to be dependent on the mother."[33]

President J. Reuben Clark, citing the same scripture, similarly stated, "But it seems possible that the *spirit* may not be present in the embryo till at least shortly before birth, whether the birth be regular or premature."[34] Another scripture that may refer to the spirit's inhabitation of the body at birth is Moses 6:59: "Ye were born into the world by water, and blood, and the spirit which I have made, and so became of dust a living soul, . . ."

A second reason why abortion is viewed differently from murder is an idea propounded by Brigham Young—that the union of body and spirit prior to birth, or even shortly after birth, is reversible. As recorded in Wilford Woodruff's journal, 15 October 1867, Young said: "When some people have little children born of 6 & 7 months pregnancy & they live but a few hours then die they bless them &c. but I dont do it for I think that such a spirit has not a fair chance for

I think that such a spirit will have a chance of occupying another Tabernacle and developing itself."[35]

Whether intentionally or not, Elder McConkie refuted Young's sentiments as well as indirectly supported the notion of spirit-body association at birth when he wrote, "Mortality is fully upon us when we first breathe the breath of life."[36]

Despite the various opinions voiced by church authorities on when the spirit enters the body, or perhaps because of them, the First Presidency of Joseph Fielding Smith's era concluded in 1970: "We may say that there is no direct revelation upon the subject of when the spirit enters the body; it has always been a moot question. That there is life in the child before birth is an undoubted fact, but whether that life is the result of the affinity of the child in embryo with the life of its mother, or because the spirit has entered it remains a mystery."[37]

This admission, however, in no way diminished the church's abhorrence of abortion. Indeed, although the LDS church did not directly address the Senate Hearing on Human Life in 1981, previous editorials in the *Church News* indicated that the church would support the proposition that human life exists from conception. A *Church News* editorial from 3 August 1974 approvingly quoted Senator James Buckley of New York: "Anyone with the biological facts knows that a fetus, from the moment of conception, is a living human."[38] Elder James E. Faust supported this view in an April 1975 general conference address, while at the same time explicitly disassociating the concept of "human life" from dependence on a spirit-body doctrine: "Some say, as did the Supreme Court of the United States, that it is only a theory that human life is present from conception. This is contrary to insurmountable medical evidence. . . . Because she feels it, every mother knows there is sacred life in the body of her unborn babe. There is also life in the spirit, and sometime before birth, the body and spirit are united. When they do come together we have a human soul."[39]

Three years later Patriarch Eldred G. Smith intimated for the first time since 1916 that abortion may be murder, although he was probably speaking of the concept of "human life" rather than spirit-body and did not intend his remarks to represent a change in church policy. After quoting Doctrine and Covenants 132:19 ("And if ye abide in my covenant, and commit no murder whereby to shed innocent blood"), Smith stated, "What do you think He's talking about? Is it possible that He was referring to abortion? Think about it! Is there more innocent life than that of the unborn child? And why is murder referred to when the Lord is talking about marriage?"[40]

It should be noted that despite the sentiments expressed above, the fetus has never been accepted as having full individual rights by society in general or the church in particular. For example, if human life truly begins at conception, the embryo, from the moment of conception, would enjoy all of the rights any individual has in our society, such as inclusion in the National Census and Social Security payments under Aid to Families with Dependent Children. In the case of a miscarriage, birth and death records should be filed and the fetus buried in a cemetery as is customary for other, older, individuals. In the church such a miscarried fetus would be entitled to a name, a blessing, and a burial, none of which is currently given.

From the perspective of the medical profession, the concept of human life from conception is also fraught with difficulties. First, there is no consensus about when conception (the beginning of pregnancy) actually occurs. The dictionary definition of "conception," which presumably most of the commentators quoted above had in mind, usually refers to the moment when an egg is fertilized by a sperm. However, the medical profession does not recognize the beginning of pregnancy until the dividing, developing egg implants itself in the uterus six days after fertilization. This is the earliest point at which pregnancy can be detected clinically. Thus, the Food and Drug Administration labels the I.U.D., which works by preventing implantation of the fertilized egg, as a contraceptive (preventing pregnancy) rather that as an abortifacient (inducing abortion). (To date the LDS church has not singled out the I.U.D. as being less acceptable than other forms of contraception.) Other points when "conception" may occur are (1) at two weeks, when the possibility of twinning is past (no "individual" exists until then), or (2) when the fetus demonstrates awareness of or responsiveness to external stimuli, spontaneous muscular movement, reflexive action, or a positive brain scan (EEG). The presence of any one of these criteria negates a clinical finding of "death," according to the report of the Ad Hoc Committee of Harvard Medical School.[41]

No matter which definition of conception is used, once a decision by society or church is made to recognize human life from conception, any medical procedure which increases the rate of miscarriage could be viewed as involuntary manslaughter. This would include amniocentesis, x-rays, cancer chemotherapy, and medications for the mother. An interesting case along these lines involves the hydatidiform mole, which is a potentially cancerous cluster of cells sometimes found in a woman's uterus. Removal of this mole theoretically could be murder, as it is nothing more than a fertilized egg gone awry.

In conclusion, the LDS church's stand against abortion does not derive from a doctrine fixing the time when the spirit enters the body. Further, although church authorities have held various opinions about the subject of the spirit entering the body, no "orthodox" view exists in the church; it is a "moot question." An interesting corollary doctrinal point developed in the process is that life can exist without direct spiritual inhabitation, through "affinity" with another spirit, in this case the mother's. Finally, although the fetus does not enjoy all of the rights of other individuals, the LDS church has generally affirmed its right to live.

*NOTES*

1. See Blake Ostler, "The Idea of Pre-existence in the Development of Mormon Thought," *Dialogue: A Journal of Mormon Thought* 15 (Spring 1982): 59-78.

2. Andrew F. Ehat and Lyndon Cook, eds., *The Words of Joseph Smith* (Provo, UT: BYU Religious Studies Center, 1980), 60.

3. Hyrum L. Andrus, *God, Man and the Universe* (Salt Lake City: Bookcraft, 1966), 20.

4. Charles W. Penrose, *Journal of Discourses*, 26 vols. (Liverpool: Latter-day Saints' Booksellers Depot, 1854-86), 26:21 (hereafter JD); see also JD 15:242; 26:216; Parley P. Pratt, *Key to Theology* (Salt Lake City, 1943), 50, 124.

5. JD 13:333; in *Origin and Destiny of Women* (N.p., n.d.), 4.

6. Ibid.

7. B. H. Roberts, *The Seventy's Course in Theology: Second Year, Outline History of the Dispensations of the Gospel* (Salt Lake City: Skelton Publishing Co., 1908), 8.

8. *Young Women's Journal* 25 (1914): 600.

9. Gordon B. Hinckley, in *Ensign* 13 (Nov. 1983).

10. *October 1976 Conference Reports* (Salt Lake City: Church of Jesus Christ of Latter-day Saints, 1976), 101.

11. Duane Jeffery has treated this issue in some detail in "Intersexes," *Dialogue: A Journal of Mormon Thought* 12 (1979): 107-13.

12. James R. Clark, ed., *Messages of the First Presidency* (Salt Lake City: Bookcraft, 1970), 4:203; Linda P. Wilcox, *Sunstone* 5 (1980): 9-15.

13. Bruce R. McConkie, *Mormon Doctrine* (Salt Lake City: Bookcraft, 1958), 220.

14. Brigham Young, JD 11:15; see also JD 6:101; 16:376.

15. Orson Pratt, *The Seer*, 274.

16. JD 5:172, 6:36.

17. John A. Widtsoe, *A Rational Theology* (Salt Lake City: General Priesthood Committee, 1915), 69.

18. "The Father and the Son: A Doctrinal Exposition by the First Presidency and the Twelve," in Joseph Fielding Smith, *Man: His Origin and Destiny* (Salt Lake City: Deseret Book Co., 1954), 129.

19. Joseph Fielding Smith, *Answers to Gospel Questions* (Salt Lake City: Deseret Book Co., 1963), 4:64-67.

20. *The Seer*, 274.

21. Joseph Fielding Smith, *Doctrines of Salvation* (Salt Lake City: Bookcraft, 1955, 2:287-88.

22. *Science News*, 9 May 1981, 293.

23. JD 22:320.

24. JD 26:14-15.

25. In *Relief Society Magazine* 3 (1916): 367-68.

26. Ibid., 4:68.

27. JD 12:120-21.

28. See Lester Bush, "Birth Control Among the Mormons," *Dialogue: A Journal of Mormon Thought* (Autumn 1976): 12-44, for a complete discussion of early attitudes towards abortion.

29. Smith, *Doctrines of Salvation*, 2:280-81, emphasis in original. See also JD 18:258.

30. "The Origin of Man," in Clark, *Messages of the First Presidency*, 4:205.

31. David O. McKay to Tiena Nate, copy in my possession.

32. *Church News*, 27 Jan. 1973, 7.

33. McKay to Nate.

34. J. Reuben Clark, "Man: God's Greatest Miracle," BYU address 21 June 1954, reprinted in pamphlet form.

35. Wilford Woodruff journal, under date, archives, historical department, Church of Jesus Christ of Latter-day Saints, Salt Lake City, Utah.

36. Bruce R. McConkie, in *Ensign* 7 (Apr. 1977): 3.

37. Joseph Fielding Smith to W. Dean Belnap, 22 Feb. 1970, copy in my possession.

38. *Church News*, 1 Jan. 1975.

39. James E. Faust, in *Ensign* 5 (May 1975): 27-29.

40. Eldred G. Smith, in *Ensign* 8 (May 1978): 29-30.

41. See *A Lawyer Looks at Abortion* (Provo, UT: Brigham Young University Press, 1982), chap. 2.

# 9. Ethical Issues in Reproductive Medicine: A Mormon Perspective

*Lester E. Bush*

THIS ESSAY—ORIGINALLY DELIVERED AT THE UNIVERSITY OF UTAH'S Fifth Annual Birth Defects, Mental Retardation, and Medical Genetics Symposium in 1983—bears on four emerging medical ethical issues: the termination of pregnancies with fetal abnormalities which will not cause serious impairment until well after birth, genetic engineering, *in utero* surgery, and *in vitro* fertilization. It does not represent *the* Mormon perspective but the point of view of *a* Mormon. *The* Mormon point of view does not exist on the subjects under discussion. Certainly many hold strong views, and some argue their views reflect those of the LDS church.[1] But if one wrote, as I did, to ask the First Presidency—which is solely entrusted with the authority to establish official church policy—if it has "a position, or a doctrine . . . relating to the subject" of any of the four medical processes this essay addresses, one would be informed that there is not "an official position with respect to the issues raised by the scenarios." Surprised that this should be so regarding abortion, I wrote again and was referred without elaboration to the "current official policy of the Church with respect to [abortion]" and advised that "the scenarios . . . should be viewed in light of this policy."[2]

With this in mind, let us review the Mormon view of medicine in general, then examine the Mormon record on birth control (the most closely related issue on which much doctrinal history exists), abortion, and other related subjects. To the extent that generalizations emerge from this review, I will hazard a guess as to what they might portend for the future.

Although not prominent on the agenda of early Mormonism, medical ethical questions were an early and persistent concern in the church. The first and most conspicuous of these involved what was then termed the heroic medical practice of orthodox physicians. Joseph Smith and his colleagues regularly condemned what they viewed as dangerous heroics in the treatment of disease.

Given the state of the medical art at that time, this view was pragmatic; but the justification went well beyond what otherwise might have been labelled common sense. As biblical literalists, Mormon leaders felt doctrinally bound to the advice of New Testament apostle James who counseled the sick to "call for the elders of the church; and let them pray over him, anointing him with oil in the name of the Lord" (5:14). Should an additional step be necessary, according to a revelation announced in 1831, sick believers who "[had] not faith to be healed [by priesthood administration] . . . shall be nourished with tenderness, with herbs and mild food" (D&C 42:43)—guidelines again in harmony with biblical precedents.

Authoritative counsel reinforced these implicitly anti-heroic guidelines in unequivocal terms. During the Mormon trek west, for example, Brigham Young, acting as president of the church after Joseph Smith's death, advised members of the Mormon Battalion: "If you are sick, live by faith, and let the surgeon's medicine alone if you want to live, using only such herbs and mild food as are at your disposal."[3]

At least at the theoretical level, this anti-heroic ethic extended to severe cases such as that of Elizabeth Morgan, a fifty-five-year-old convert living in London in 1842. She had a "spasmodic affection" which one day developed into an inflammation of the bowel. Despite a rapid deterioration in her condition, treatment was limited to anointing "with oil in the name of the Lord, . . . sage tea with Cayenne pepper, [and] leeches." All efforts failed and the "beloved sister" died.

The lessons drawn from these developments were revealing. The coroner feeling the "remedy . . . worse than the disease," and shocked that no "medical gentleman" or "surgeon" was called in, "had his doubts whether [the case was] not one of manslaughter." A jury was convened to investigate but "after some deliberation returned a verdict of 'natural death,' with a hope 'that the present inquiry would act as a caution to [the Mormons] how they acted in such cases for the future.'" Mormons reprinted a *London Despatch* article on the story in their own official journal and added a hyperbolic editorial observing that "what gives deep interest to the fact [of Sister Morgan's death] and adds solemnity to the scene is that she died a *natural death!!!!!"* rather than be allowed "the privilege of being killed through the administration of the learned medical faculty."[4]

With the passage of time, orthodox medicine became more "scientific," herbalism fell into disrepute, and LDS opposition to regular medical doctors began to erode. Late in life, Brigham Young sent young Mormons back east to be educated in leading orthodox medical schools and hospitals. Under the influence of this growing cadre of well-educated physicians and a few regular physician emigres, "scientific medicine" came to dominate the Utah medical scene. By the turn of the century, the LDS church had fully embraced modern medicine. The increasingly "state-of-the-art" practice espoused at this time was judged not so much by a doctrinal yardstick as by—in the words of Apostle James Talmage—the "intelligent exercise of common sense."[5] In the words of a *Deseret News* editorial accompanying the opening of a well-equipped church-sponsored hospital in 1902, "Remedies are provided by the Great Physician or by nature as some prefer to view them and we should not close our eyes to their virtues or ignore the skill and learning of the trained doctor."[6]

While herbalism was discarded during the general accommodation, orthodox therapy and priesthood blessings came to be seen as adjuncts to each other, especially when a serious illness was involved. Again, the words of Apostle Talmage, "We must do all we can, and then ask the Lord to do the rest, such as we cannot do. Hence we hold the medical and surgical profession in high regard. . . . When we have done all we can then the Divine Power will be directly applicable and operative." This symbiotic relationship has continued to the present. On 19 February 1977, in the face of a resurgence of nineteenth-century anti-medical "fundamentalist" theology, the LDS *Church News* repeated editorially that "our belief in the divine power of healing should in no way preclude seeking competent medical assistance."

Looking back on this, many would say that God had commended to the early Saints the most effective and safest treatments of the day. While the case for herbalism, even in 1830, is debatable, for our purposes the important point is that general medical judgments were demonstrably pragmatic, even though they were couched in a doctrinal vernacular. This is the same standard against which the church today seems to evaluate even the most heroic medical measures. It is no longer, as it once was, *a priori*, a matter of doctrine. Rather—to paraphrase Talmage—it is a question of common sense and technical feasibility.

While a sympathetic relationship now exists between medicine and Mormonism, there are a few points of discordance. Most typically, they are issues involving human reproduction.[7]

The early-twentieth-century birth-control controversy provides an instructive parallel to the current national ferment over abortion. It was during a time of radical reform, when artificial contraception was illegal, that the first formal statements by the Mormon hierarchy were made on the subject. Joseph F. Smith, the first LDS church president to address in any detail what was then termed "prevention," had heard as early as 1900 that "steps were being taken" among Latter-day Saints "to prevent . . . spirits being tabernacled." He spoke regularly on the subject for nearly two decades.[8]

One of Smith's earlier statements was in response to a physician's inquiry in 1908 as to whether it was ever right "intentionally to prevent, by any means whatever, the spirits . . . from obtaining earthly tabernacles?" Smith's answer was that "in a general way, and as a rule, the answer to this question is an emphatic negative. I do not hesitate to say that prevention is wrong." In addition to promoting selfishness and a "host of social evils," it would also "disregard or annul the great commandment of God to man, multiply and replenish the earth.'"[9]

While the tone and substance of the statement derived from a nineteenth-century perspective, he also added a caveat reminiscent of the new pragmatism with which Mormons viewed medicine in general: "I am now speaking of the normally healthy man and woman. But that there are weak and sickly people who in wisdom, discretion and common sense should be counted as exceptions, only strengthens the general rule." His thinking was less liberal than this might suggest: Smith concluded that in such exceptional cases the only legitimate preventive was "absolute abstinence."

While Smith held to the same basic view throughout his presidency, which ended with his death in 1918, his last extensive counsel on the subject introduced another exception to his general condemnation: "I think that [curtailing the birth of children] is a crime whenever it occurs," he advised the women's Relief Society in 1917, "where husband and wife are in possession of health and vigor and are *free from impurities* that would be entailed upon their posterity." Without elaborating such disorders, Smith continued: "I believe that where people undertake to curtail or prevent the birth of their children that they are going to reap disappointment by and by. I have no hesitancy in saying that I believe this is one of the greatest crimes in the world today."[10]

Smith's successor, Heber J. Grant, presided over the church during Utah's depression years, which began in the early 1920s, a decade earlier than for the nation. During these years, the birth rate among Mormons dropped to levels not again reached until the advent of "modern" contraceptives in the 1960s. However, senior church authorities said relatively little in response to this unprecedented family limitation; even then, advice was generally given only in personal correspondence.

J. Reuben Clark, a member of the First Presidency, wrote privately in 1933 that the LDS church did not have an official position on birth control.[11] Several years later, in 1939, a similar letter from Grant set forth his views. He first invoked the counsel of his predecessor, then added, "Married couples who, by inheritance and proper living, have themselves been blessed with mental and physical vigor are recreant in their duty if they refuse to meet the natural and rightful responsibility of parenthood. Of course, in every ideal home the health of the mother, as well as the intelligence and health of the children should receive careful consideration."[12]

In 1942, the influential apostle John A. Widtsoe advised a personal correspondent that "as far as I know the Church has not expressed itself as to birth control."[13] Later that year he published an important essay in the *Improvement Era* entitled "Should Birth Control Be Practiced?" It was a remarkably even-handed treatment of the subject, clearly reflecting another phase in the evolution of the leadership's view. Instead of rejecting economic arguments out of hand, he found them "seldom convincing." Equally interesting, he rejected total abstinence as the sole recourse open to those with legitimate grounds for controlling fertility. His advice was that "a careful recognition of the fertile and sterile periods of woman would prove effective in the great majority of cases."[14]

Four years later, Apostle David O. McKay[15] in private correspondence carried this position a step farther in advising that "when the health of the mother demands it, the proper spacing of children may be determined by seeking medical counsel, by compliance with the processes of nature, or by continence." While some leaders were—and still are—willing to label birth control "gross wickedness"[16], McKay's more tolerant view was the dominant perspective after he became president in 1951. The high-water mark in this direction can be found in the writings of his counselor Hugh B. Brown who wrote in 1960 that "the Latter-day Saints believe in large families wherever it is possible to provide for the necessities of life, for the health and education of their children, and when the physical and mental health of the mother permits."[17]

Ultimately, probably at Brown's prompting, the First Presidency issued a formal statement on 1 April 1969—the first and only formal statement specifically dealing with birth control. In this McKay, Brown, and N. Eldon Tanner wrote:

> "The First Presidency is being asked from time to time as to what the attitude of the Church is regarding birth control. . . .
>
> "We seriously regret that there should exist a sentiment or feeling among any members of the Church to curtail the birth of their children. We have been commanded to multiply and replenish the earth that we may have joy and rejoicing in our posterity.
>
> "Where husband and wife enjoy health and vigor and are free from impurities that would be entailed upon their posterity, it is contrary to the teachings of the Church artificially to curtail or prevent the birth of children. We believe those who practice birth control will reap disappointment by and by.
>
> "However, we feel that men must be considerate of their wives who bear the greater responsibility not only of bearing children, but of caring for them through childhood. To this end the mother's health and strength should be conserved and the husband's consideration for his

wife is his first duty, and self-control a dominant factor in all their relationships.

"It is our further feeling that married couples should seek inspiration and wisdom from the Lord that they may exercise discretion in solving their marital problems, and that they may be permitted to rear their children in accordance with the teachings of the gospel."[18]

This masterpiece of diplomacy effectively combined the essence, and often the exact wording, of guidance issued throughout the twentieth century into one ultimately ambiguous statement which transferred responsibility from the church to the individual. Their success is indicated by the fact that Mormons across the entire spectrum of possible attitudes cited it in defense of their beliefs. Beyond reiterating the strong pro-family tradition which has sustained nearly all commentary on the subject, the statement placed individual decisions above ecclesiastical review.

In a larger sense, perhaps, church leadership also ratified the collective judgment of rank-and-file Mormons. For years surveys of active Mormons found that a large majority either used or planned to use contraceptives; and by the late 1960s, when the First Presidency statement was issued, Mormon birth rates were at historic lows, ranging between 26 and 28 births per thousand.

The point to be made is not that the church capitulated on the issue of birth control, but rather that a change in societal perspective was accompanied, eventually, by a similar change in religious belief. In fact, the LDS church did not really capitulate on its more fundamental concern—that procreation and family life lie at the heart of human existence. While this is now interpreted in the context of a broadly defined medical concern for the well-being of the total family, there still has been no formal sanction of arbitrary spacing of births because of educational or economic goals.

The positive injunction given to Adam and Eve to multiply and replenish the earth was really the foundation of all Mormon commentary on birth control. And Mormons at large have responded to this ideal. While unmistakably influenced by changing socioeconomic circumstances, Mormon families still collectively average 1.5 additional children per family than their non-Mormon contemporaries—a distinction held throughout the twentieth century.

Those who followed McKay to the presidency of the church have been both more outspoken and more conservative in their commentary on birth control. However, they have chosen not to revise the formal guidance already issued on the subject. While the new emphasis may have created a brief rise in the birth rate of Mormons in Utah in the late 1970s, it seems not to have influenced the overall use of contraceptives in the church (which by the end of childbearing seems ultimately to approach 90 percent). A recent study based on a small sample from the 1975 National Fertility Studies found that 96 percent of reporting Mormons had used birth control.[19] Though this is somewhat higher than previous reports, surveys since 1935 have found the majority of Mormon respondents either endorsing or using birth control.[20] Indeed, the most recent guidance on the subject of birth control in official church forums is essentially indistinguishable in tone and substance from that which appeared in the 1960s. One of the most extensive commentaries appeared in the *Ensign's* "I Have a Question" column in August 1979. In a thoughtful response to the question, "Is there not any kind of 'gospel family-planning,' for lack of a better way to say it?", Mormon obstetrician Homer Ellsworth first noted "our spiritual obligation, to bear children and to have a family," then lamented family limitation for "selfish" reasons. But, on the other hand, he continued (in part), "we need not be afraid of studying the question from important angles—the physical and mental health of the mother and father, the parents' capacity to provide basic necessities, and so on. If for certain personal reasons a couple prayerfully decides that having another child immediately is unwise, the method of spacing children—discounting possible medical or physical effects—makes little difference. Abstinence, of course, is also a form of contraception, and like any other method it has side effects, some of which are harmful to the marriage relationship."[21]

Although there was no formal statement of church policy on abortion until recently, the views of early church leaders on the subject were clear: abortion was synonymous with murder. Polemically, at least, no distinction was made between "foeticide," the abortion of an embryo, and "infant murder." John Taylor, for example, spoke with some regularity of "pre-natal murders," or "murders . . . committed while the children are pre-natal"; of infants killed "either before or after they are born"; and of murdering children "either before or after they come into the world." Similar language can be found in the related sermons of nearly all late nineteenth-century Mormon leaders.[22]

Given this perspective, it is not surprising that those involved in such "hellish" practices were condemned. George Q. Cannon of the First Presidency in 1884 was perhaps the most graphic: "They will be damned with deepest damnation; because it is the damnation of shedding innocent blood, for which there is no forgiveness. . . . They are outside the pale of salvation. They are in a position that nothing can be done for them. They cut themselves off by such acts from all hopes of salvation." John Taylor had given the same message in 1881: "They are murderers and murderesses of their infants . . . and you that want them, take them, and you that do will go along with them, and go to perdition with them, and I tell you that in the name of the Lord."[23]

Despite this seemingly categorical stance, the condemnation of abortion was not absolute. A few years earlier, in 1876, amid the national anti-abortion crusade which fueled much of the Mormon commentary, Utah passed an anti-abortion statute. The criminal penalties were not as severe as one might have expected: one to five years for mothers, two to ten for doctors. More importantly, there also was an explicit exemption in cases where abortion was necessary "to preserve [the] life [of the mother]."[24]

In practice, abortion seems to have been uncommon. After the intense national agitation ended, the subject largely disappeared from church commentary for nearly a century. When it reemerged, the social and medical context was radically different from that faced by John Taylor and associates.

The twentieth century brought an unprecedented public acceptance of active intervention in the reproductive processes. Infant mortality had declined precipitously, so there no longer was a need to have extra children as "insurance" to guarantee a "full" family surviving into adulthood. Society became increasingly mobile and urbanized. Those with large families encountered emotional and economic challenges from which their parents and grandparents seemingly were spared. And family limitation through birth control, despite a controversial entry into the national arena, became increasingly acceptable—even in the Mormon community.

To a growing number of participants in this social revolution, particularly since 1960, a logical next step was to make therapeutic abortions available in cases other than those threatening the mother's life. Some Mormons have seen this as yet another symptom of sweeping moral decay. Others find convincing the statistical evidence that, although illegal "abortionists" operated with high mortality, therapeutic abortions in legal medical settings result in substantially less maternal morbidity and mortality than does childbirth itself.

Both medical and popular sentiment on abortion had moved substantially away from the categorical abhorrence of earlier decades. Accordingly many states had revised their abortion laws. In 1969, Utah Senate Bill 121 was introduced to revise Utah's century-old statute, proposing to allow abortions where the mother's mental or physical health was at stake, where pregnancy resulted from rape or incest, or if the child was likely to have "grave or permanent physical disability or mental retardation." As a member of LDS Hospital's house staff in 1968-69, I recall numerous conversations among the hospital's physicians. Many felt that the church would not oppose the proposed legislation—an indication of how far sentiment within the LDS community had shifted. As startling as this view may seem in retrospect, there are several reasons why it might have been true.

First, there was the practical consideration that a somewhat liberalized policy was already tacitly in effect in most major hospitals in Salt Lake City, including the LDS Hospital itself. Only Holy Cross Hospital reported no therapeutic abortions between 1954 and 1964. Although far from routine, abortions were being performed occasionally, including 9 percent for fetal deformities and 18 percent for psychiatric reasons. Perhaps as many as 73 percent of abortions labelled "medical" were, in fact, performed for other reasons.[25]

Second, in the 1960s there was a relatively tolerant attitude toward birth control on the part of the current church leadership. The use of contraceptives was largely viewed in actual practice as principally a medical judgment.

Third, there were theoretical reasons why abortion laws might have been ecclesiastically acceptable. The LDS church had never taken an official stand on abortion. Given nineteenth-century rhetoric, this may seem a technicality, but it is not. Notwithstanding its authoritarian image, Mormonism in fact has few authoritative doctrines. Its canon, the standard works, rarely bears unequivocally on twentieth-century issues. Principles continue to be extracted and applied, but there is always a strong subjective or "inspired" interpretive element in these applications.[26] Moreover, unless these interpretations are publicly issued by the First Presidency—which is rarely the case—they do not attain the status of formal doctrines of the church. Even those so issued are subject to later revision, though an effort is made to avoid explicit rejection of a previously published view. The record on birth control illustrates both these points. What often passes for "doctrine" in Mormon society is in reality a widely held consensus, perhaps espoused in sermon or print by Mormon general authorities, but ultimately without formal sanction by the First Presidency. In theory, such a consensus is not binding on church members. In practice, it is not unlikely to change.

Despite the level of nineteenth-century church rhetoric, mid-twentieth-century Mormon leaders did not view abortion in entirely the same doctrinal light as their predecessors. While nothing definitive had been stated publicly, as early as 1934 Apostle David O. McKay privately expressed his opinion that the church had not made an "authoritative answer" to the question of whether abortion should be "termed murder or not." [27] Later, as church president, McKay and the First Presidency affirmed that "as the matter stands, no definitive statement has been made by the Lord one way or another regarding the crime of abortion. So far as is known, he has not listed it alongside the crime of the unpardonable sin and shedding innocent blood. That he has not done so would suggest that it is not in that class of crime."[28] In 1958 J. Reuben Clark, though generally opposed to abortion, was willing to advise a pregnant woman who had contracted German measles that on the question of terminating the pregnancy "she should seek the advice of her physicians . . . and also seek the Lord in prayer."[29]

That abortion should not be viewed as murder resulted in optimism that there might be no official objection to some modest liberalization in state laws. The church also had no formal stand on another theologically relevant subject: the relationship between a noncorporeal spirit and the physical body of flesh and blood with which it is associated. Assumptions about this relationship are central to some frequently heard condemnations of abortion.

Mortal existence, as we know it, was represented by Joseph Smith as the union of a spirit with its earthly body to form what was termed a "soul." At death, the spirit and body again separated, to be permanently reunited at the time of resurrection. Ultimately this resurrected soul accounts before God for his or her conduct on earth.

The essence of this theology is not unique to Mormonism. Among other common themes, it shares the popular notion—of some medical interest—that the spirit animates the body and that death coincides with the departure of the spirit. As biblical literalists, early Mormons have assumed, as did many of their contemporaries, that the spirit was prenatally present, using as proof-text the familiar passage in Luke 1:44 in which Elizabeth's child "leaped in [her] womb for joy" at the news of Mary's pregnancy. The problem with this as a firm Mormon scriptural guide was a Book of Mormon episode in which the adult Jesus appeared—presumably in spirit form—the day prior to his birth.

With these paradoxical precedents, it is understandable that leading Mormons held a variety of views over the years about timing of ensoulment—and that none of these views attained the status of formal doctrine. Brigham Young assumed the spirit arrived at the time of quickening.[30] This view, the conventional Protestant wisdom of the day, was easier to maintain before modern science demonstrated that fetal motion was present almost from the outset of pregnancy, long before it could be detected by the mother. President McKay felt that the spirit joined the body at the time of birth. "Life manifest in the body before that time would seem to be dependent upon the mother."[31] To the best of my knowledge, no leading Mormon ever asserted the third obvious alternative—that the spirit arrived at the time of conception.

Although McKay's position would seem intrinsically more flexible than Young's, this was not necessarily so. Young also believed, as quoted by successor Wilford Woodruff, that "when some people have little children born at 6 & 7 months from pregnancy & they live a few hours then die . . . I think that such a spirit will have a Chance of occupiying [sic] another Tabernacle and develop itself."[32] While it is not clear where he would draw the line, he periodically ridiculed the notion that babies who die are "resurrected" into new, mortal infant bodies.[33] Ultimately the First Presidency wrote—though it did not formally publish—that "there is no direct revelation upon the subject [of when the spirit takes possession of the body] . . . it has always been a moot question. That there is life in the child before birth is undoubted fact, but whether that life is the result of the affinity of the child in embryo with the life of its mother, or because the spirit has entered it remains an unsolved mystery."[34] So far as I am aware, nothing further has been said on the subject.

In practice, Mormon ritual has always distinguished between miscarriages or stillborn deliveries and neonatal deaths. The former are not formally recorded in church records; the latter are. Vicarious ordinance work, deemed essential for all humankind in Mormon theology, is never performed in the case of a miscarriage or stillborn delivery. It is for a deceased infant. In essence then whatever the doctrinal uncertainties, church practice treats birth as the time when the spirit-body bond takes place. (It also should be noted that the church follows the variable legal definitions current in different jurisdictions as to what constitutes a live birth.)

Returning to 1969, the church did issue a short statement on the proposed abortion reform bill, about a week after it was introduced in the Utah legislature. In this, the First Presidency stated that after "careful consideration," they were opposed "to any modification, expansion, or liberalization of laws on these vital subjects."[35] The bill was not enacted.

Some flexibility in this official opinion became evident just a few weeks later in a private letter from Joseph Anderson, secretary to the First Presidency, on their behalf. The letter stated: "Nevertheless there may be conditions where abortion is justified, but such conditions must be determined acting under the advice of competent, reliable physicians, preferably members of the Church, and in accordance with the laws pertaining thereto."[36] Two years later this private counsel was given much wider circulation when a new First Presidency published an identically worded statement in the official *Priesthood Bulletin.* The following June 1972 the presidency's views were more fully elaborated in another bulletin. Their statement at that time remains the most comprehensive official Mormon response to the question of abortion. Because of its importance to the present discussion, I will quote it in full:

"The church opposes abortion and counsels its members not to submit to or perform an abortion except in the rare cases where, in the opinion of competent medical counsel, the life or good health of the mother is seriously endangered or where the pregnancy was caused by rape and produces serious emotional trauma in the mother. Even then it should be done only after counseling with the local presiding authority and after receiving divine confirmation through prayer.

"As the matter stands today, no definite statement has been made by the Lord one way or another regarding the crime of abortion. So far as is known, he has not listed it alongside the crime of the unpardonable sin and shedding of innocent human blood. That he has not done so would suggest that it is not in that class of crime and therefore that it will be amenable to the laws of repentance and forgiveness.

"These observations must not be interpreted to mean that acts of abortion, except under circumstances explained in the preceding paragraph, are not of a serious nature. To tamper or interfere with any of the processes in the procreation of offspring is to violate one of the most sacred of God's commandments—to multiply and replenish the earth. Abortion must be considered one of the most revolting and sinful practices in this day, when we are witnessing the frightening evidences of permissiveness leading to sexual immorality.

"Members of the Church guilty of being parties to the sin of abortion must be subjected to the disciplinary action of the councils of the Church as circumstances warrant. In dealing with this serious matter it would be well to keep in mind the word of the Lord stated in the 59th section of the Doctrine and Covenants, verse 6: 'Thou shalt not steal; neither commit adultery, nor kill *nor do anything* like unto it.'"

This statement stops short of defining abortion as murder, finding it rather "like unto it"—possibly in the sense that some might consider a fetus not to be identical with human life in the normal usage, but like unto it. Although a "most revolting and sinful practice" when unwarranted, abortion is defined more liberally than, for example, in Utah laws of the time and, excepting only the cases of fetal abnormalities and incest-related pregnancy, was compatible with the unsuccessful legislative reform introduced three years earlier.

While a panel of federal judges held in 1971 that Utah's abortion law was constitutional, the statute did not withstand the 1973 Supreme Court ruling which in essence struck down all state laws on the subject. In the wake of this development, the LDS church reissued its 1972 guideline; and over the past decades, it has periodically republished essentially identical official statements.

With the advent of the Spencer W. Kimball presidency in late 1973, abortion regained the prominence in sermon and print it had been given a century before in Mormon circles. Abortion was again a national issue, as well, and Kimball regularly cited it in a litany of grave sins besetting society. Although the characteristically hyperbolic *Church News* editorials which accompanied this renewed focus (for example, that of 17 May 1975) occasionally suggested that spirits assigned to aborted fetuses would lose their chance for an earthly experience, I believe this view was generally assumed to be without official basis.[37] It was more the tone than the substance of church discourse that changed during these years.

One quasi-official departure from the 1972 statement was evident in 1976, when the church distributed to all Mormon congregations a graphic filmstrip reinforcing its opposition to abortion. In addition to the proscriptions already outlined in the official statement, the following new counsel was included as part of an accompanying discourse by Kimball entitled "A Visit With The Prophet" which was reprinted in the *Church News,* 27 March 1976, page 6: "Occasionally the question of pregnancy by rape will be asked. Medical evidence indicates that this is an extremely rare situation. But regardless of how the pregnancy was caused, abortion would greatly compound the wrong. An unborn baby must not be punished for the sins of his father. Letting the baby be born and placing him in an adoptive home would surely be a better solution for an unfortunate situation."

Despite the extensive distribution of the filmstrip and explicit guidance of the accompanying talk, the LDS church did not officially depart from its former stand—a paradox which illustrates some of the problems in assessing an authoritative or authoritarian religion with few formal doctrines. That there had been no binding departure from previous guidance was clear within just a few weeks when the First Presidency reaffirmed its previous policy on abortion in an "official statement." Circumstances which allowed for abortion included "pregnancy . . . caused by forcible rape and producing serious emotional trauma in the victim."[38]

Despite ongoing debate, this is where things generally stand at present.39 Interestingly enough, the First Presidency never has condemned the termination of pregnancies involving seriously defective fetuses. Rather, they chose the indirect condemnation of not exempting such cases from a general indictment of abortion. In his remarks accompanying the 1976 filmstrip, Kimball did assert that "no one, save the Lord himself, has the right to decide if a baby should or should not be permitted to live." One can presume therefore that he personally would counsel against intervening in such cases. Nonetheless, the First Presidency appears to have intentionally avoided singling out this difficult issue for unequivocal condemnation, despite periodic inquiries from concerned physicians on this specific subject or on the related use of amniocentesis.

My impression is that this quasi-silence on the part of the church coincides with a continuing evolution in perspective among both Mormon physicians and patients, an evolution of just the sort previously seen under similar circumstances on the question of birth control. While I do not foresee any wholesale endorsement for terminating abnormal pregnancies, there nonetheless already has been some change in attitude. At the anecdotal level, for example, I am aware of local church leaders who have availed themselves of amniocentesis for high-risk pregnancies within their own families. They argue that this option promotes larger families, for without it they would not risk further pregnancies. For Mormon physicians there is a growing ethical and legal obligation to at least discuss amniocentesis, as an option in high-risk pregnancies.

One LDS obstetrician, not in Utah, estimated that in the general area where his practice is located, about half of the LDS women pregnant after age forty requested amniocentesis. This figure seems generally consistent with a Centers for Disease Control study which found that about 10 percent of Utah women pregnant after age thirty-five sought amniocentesis—a figure about half the national average.[40] It is compatible with figures given by Dr. Robert Fineman that nationally about 80 percent of pregnancies found to have genetic abnormalities were terminated, and in Utah about 66 percent. While proportionately few amniocenteses reveal abnormalities, it apparently is not rare for LDS women discovering significant fetal abnormalities to have these pregnancies terminated.

Despite church guidelines encouraging disciplinary action against those involved in abortions, I have yet to learn of church courts held when known fetal abnormalities were involved. On the contrary, I understand that inquiries about such cases as anencephaly have received unofficial, tacit endorsement. Outside of Utah, one suspects such agonizing personal problems are not infrequently dealt with, or more accurately not dealt with, entirely by local leaders who counsel the family involved, but indicate that the final moral judgment must reside within the family.

A counter-theme which runs through much of the material on birth control relates to the question of genetic "impurities." As early as 1917, Joseph F. Smith sanctioned marital abstinence when the husband or wife was not "free from impurities which would be entailed upon their posterity." This same caveat can be readily traced throughout the twentieth century, right up to the First Presidency statement of 1969 which quotes Smith verbatim on this point.

This concern can be identified in early church history. Apostle Parley P. Pratt, for example, wrote in *Key to the Science of Theology*—a study second only to the standard works in defining church doctrine for nineteenth-century Mormons—that "a wise legislation, or the law of God . . . would not suffer the idiot, the confirmed, irreclaimable drunkard, the man of hereditary disease, or of vicious habits, to possess or retain a wife."[41] Although Utah's territorial legislature did not enact such legislation, the state of Utah eventually did so in 1925. A statute passed that year, in the wake of a national enthusiasm over eugenics, provided for the sterilization of institutionalized individuals (including infants) who were "habitually sexually criminal, . . . insane, mentally deficient, epileptic, or . . . afflicted with degenerate sexual tendencies," if "by the laws of heredity [they were] the probable potential parent of socially inadequate offspring likewise afflicted."[42]

While such "a taint in the blood"—to use John Widtsoe's phraseology—if "known to be capable of transmission, should be hemmed in and not allowed further propagation," the historical Mormon solution to this issue always has been to encourage healthy people to have more children. It was this sort of positive eugenic which justified Mormon polygamy. Or as Brigham Young said in 1856 in terms not infrequently heard even today, "I have told you many times that there are multitudes of pure and holy spirits waiting to take tabernacles, now what is our duty?–to prepare tabernacles for them; to take a course that will not tend to drive those spirits into the families of the wicked, where they will be trained in wickedness, debauchery, and every species of crime. It is the duty of every righteous man and woman to prepare tabernacles for all the spirits they can."[43]

There is thus a eugenics heritage in Mormonism which may be relevant to the scenarios to be addressed. First, there is a clear precedent for taking otherwise unacceptable measures to avoid encumbering awaiting spirits with predictable defective "tabernacles." Second, there is a strong tradition which seeks to provide the best possible chance for "good" people to become parents.[44]

Aside from the narrowly-defined exemptions for eugenic reasons, until recently Mormon Utah rejected all grounds for sterilization. Even the tolerant David O. McKay administration opposed an effort to liberalize a state law which as late as 1969 was interpreted as allowing only eugenic sterilizations. This presidency statement also opposed a bill which would have authorized voluntary sterilizations "where medically necessary to preserve the life or prevent a serious impairment of the mental or physical health of the patient or spouse."[45] However, while this legislative initiative failed, judicial review later determined that no prohibition against such sterilizations existed in Utah law. Unlike the case of abortion, this did not bring about a formal statement of guidance from the church.

In 1976 the Church Commissioner of Health prepared a short statement on sterilization, obviously patterned after the guidance on birth control–and taken almost verbatim from privately issued First Presidency guidance, which stated, "The Lord's commandment imposed upon all Latter-day Saints is to multiply and replenish the earth. Nevertheless there may be medical conditions related to the health of the mother where sterilization could be justified. But such conditions, rare as they may be, must be determined by competent medical judgment and in accordance with laws pertaining thereto."[46] Although one Mormon authority warned two years later that those submitting to vasectomy might be ineligible for participation in temple ordinances, this guidance was never formally implemented. Nor have temple-recommend interviews ever officially included questions relating to sterilization (or birth control). Among other reasons, sterilization, like birth control, can be seen as medically justifiable in most cases. The increasing frequency with which procedures such as hysterectomy are performed for non-pregnancy-related complications (e.g., uterine prolapse, fibroids, etc.) has contributed coincidentally toward making the question of birth control moot for many women in their later childbearing years.[47]

One might suppose that Mormons would look favorably on almost any technique which would lead to successful pregnancies in otherwise infertile marriages. And this may be true, as long as the semen is the husband's. Of relevance is the biblical and nineteenth-century Mormon precedent for "raising up seed" to a dead husband whereby a woman sealed to the deceased man would marry another man for time but not eternity. Still, when the question of artificial insemination was first officially addressed by the LDS church in 1974, it was made clear that "the Church does not approve of artificial insemination with semen other than that of the husband" because donor semen "may produce problems related to family harmony." At the prompting of the Church Commissioner of Health, this condemnation was softened by the addition of an acknowledgment that "the Church recognizes that this is a personal matter which must ultimately be left to the determination of the husband and wife with the responsibility for the decision resting solely upon them."[48]

In view of the record on birth control, it is not surprising to learn that there has been some additional development in the church position on this subject. Two years later "the Church does not approve" was recast into the more positive counsel that "the Church approves of artificial insemination only in cases where the semen of the husband is used." Then in 1977 the First Presidency softened the wording even further in counseling that "the Church discourages artificial insemination with other than the semen of the husband." This formal statement clearly implied, moreover, that births through artificial insemination were to be viewed in the same ecclesiastical light regardless of the semen's origin.[49]

After this historical tour, it is clear that attempts to project a specific Mormon perspective on emerging ethical issues must be tentative. Still, some useful generalizations emerge from the record to date.

First, contrary to its media image, the LDS church—and specifically the First Presidency—often chooses not to express itself on issues with obvious ethical or theological overtones. This is especially true when the issues are complex or when important scientific questions remain unanswered. A corollary to this is that there are relatively few fixed doctrines. For example, in a 7 September 1968 statement on citizen obligations and contemporary social and political conditions, the First Presidency wrote: "The growing worldwide responsibilities of the Church make it inadvisable for the Church to seek to respond to all the various and complex issues involved in the mounting problems of the many cities and communities in which members live. But this complexity does not absolve members as individuals from filling their responsibility as citizens in their own community."[50] The large number of statements issued in recent years affirming that the church has no position on organic evolution is a parallel case. David O. McKay on 3 February 1959 wrote cogently, "While scientific people themselves differ in their interpretations and views of the theory, any conflicts which may seem to exist between the theory and revealed religion can well be dealt with by suspending judgment as long as may be necessary to arrive at facts and at a complete understanding of the truth."[51]

Second, when the First Presidency does comment on complex issues, the initial guidance is usually given privately, in response to questions from those most directly involved.

Third, formal public statements by the First Presidency on medical ethical issues—those which effectively establish church policy—generally do not appear until relatively late in the public discussion. At this point, it is not unusual for individual members and local leaders to have reached independent judgments on the questions involved. While inevitably leading to some confusion, this general process is not necessarily viewed as bad. More disruptive are the rare occasions when the first-issued public guidance contradicts that previously given in private. An example is the issue of sex-change surgery, the most recent medical ethical issue to be dealt with. Within recent years, such surgery was privately ruled not to disqualify one from participation in temple marriage and other ordinances. Subsequent public guidance not only reversed this, but imposed on offenders (patient or physician) severe ecclesiastical sanctions. In October 1980 ecclesiastical leaders received a replacement for Chapter 8, "The

Church Judicial System" for the *General Handbook of Instructions* (1976) which stated: "In cases of . . . transsexual operations, either received or performed, [excommunication is mandatory and] . . . no readmission to the Church is possible." Prospective converts who had such surgery were to be baptized only "on condition that an appropriate notation be made on the membership record so as to preclude [them] from either receiving the priesthood or temple recommends." Though having or performing an abortion was also potential grounds for excommunication, local leaders were allowed discretion in bringing offenders to trial. Nor were there any prescribed restrictions on readmission.

A fourth generalization to emerge is that the passage of time almost always sees an evolution in church guidance on specific medical ethical issues. The public phase of this evolution invariably has been in the direction of greater conformity to the general medical/social consensus on the subject. We have seen this on the issues of birth control, sterilization, artificial insemination, abortion, and medicine in general. Note that this generalization applies to the public record only. As the instance of sex change surgery indicates, there may be a decided hardening of the official view during the pre-public phase.[52]

Fifth, to some extent this evolution is accompanied by the emergence of what in retrospect might be termed the core of ethical concern which motivated the guidance from the outset. This core is generally expressed in terms unambiguously tied to central tenets of the faith: the centrality of marriage and children; the overriding importance of maintaining family harmony and stability, and protecting the health and well-being of mother, children, and "tabernacles-to-be"; the preservation of free agency and personal accountability; and the total unacceptability of decisions based on "selfish" rationales.

Sixth, guidance which eventually is discarded in this evolutionary process in retrospect generally falls into one of two categories. The first is policy by fiat, with no effort at doctrinal rationale. Church guidance on sex change surgery specifies sanctions without offering any rationale whatever. To some extent, this situation also describes the case with sterilization and abortion.

In the second type of case, a particular view may have been

justified with socio-cultural (often emotion-laden) rationales readily identifiable with former societal values. This position is most explicit in the guidance on artificial insemination but is implicit in many other statements as well. At one point in late 1976, the guidance on artificial insemination noted that "the legitimacy of offspring of artificial insemination from semen other than that of the husband is open to question."

Seventh, core beliefs themselves can be modified in accommodating new knowledge which is simply unreconcilable with the previous view. This development does not pose as much a challenge to church authority as might be supposed. It is in fact a tenet of the Mormon faith that this sort of refinement periodically will take place.

With these generalities as a backdrop and in the context of the history just covered, let us now turn to some developing ethical issues yet to be dealt with by the LDS church. The first scenario involves known genetic defects which will not be manifest until later in life. Although the First Presidency has not granted exemptions from their general condemnation of abortion, there is substantial historical precedent for modification in their stance. One can readily see several theological or theoretical reasons why this might eventually take place.

Mormon values would seem to favor interdicting demonstrably abnormal pregnancies. Some measures intended—as John Widtsoe put it—to "[hem] in and not allow further propagation" of "taints in the blood" would insure more healthy "tabernacles" for the pure spirits beginning their earthly experience. This is, after all, just the other side to counsel already given that expectant parents take no action which might cause infants to be born with defects. An example is the counsel of nineteenth-century church leaders that coitus be continued during pregnancy lest through abstinence "they might . . . entail on their offspring unholy desires and appetites."[53] Expectant mothers were also warned against wishing for such harmful things as tobacco, tea, coffee, and liquor.[54] Moreover, if couples afraid to risk pregnancy because of a history of genetic disorders in the family or advanced age were enabled safely to attempt to bear healthy children, yet another Mormon ideal would be achieved.

Objections to abortion that outweigh such benefits must of necessity be substantial. Abortion has been officially labelled as a grave sin which intrudes in the most violent way possible into the sacred processes of reproduction. In so doing, it brings about the death of a human embryo or fetus, an act once labelled murder and now interpreted as "like unto it." Even the most cautious step toward liberalizing the grounds for abortion is viewed as potentially leading to the abandonment of ethical restrictions on its use. It is feared that the legacy of such a development could be an increasing and grossly self-serving irreverence for the sanctity of human life. In the Mormon mind, this would strike at the heart of the entire purpose of humankind's mortal existence.

As insurmountable as these obstacles seem, it is arresting to recall that virtually identical arguments could have been made—indeed, were made many times—on the subject of birth control. It seems that neither the vigor with which such statements have been expressed nor the length of time over which they were espoused have proven infallible guides to their ultimate fate. To some extent, this situation is due to the difficulty of separating culturally mediated perspectives from those based on underlying theological absolutes, especially when emotional (or aesthetic) motives are strong. While the distinction between culture and eternal principle is difficult to make, technological advances have a curious way of clarifying things. When new, aesthetically less traumatic techniques are developed, emotional considerations disappear. For example, as unlikely as the idea may currently seem, the development of a monthly pill or intra-uterine implant which insured the viability of only defect-free conceptions (normal menstruation otherwise occurring) might well be acceptable to individuals who had "ethical" reservations to a d&c at ten weeks.

But doesn't Mormonism have some truly fundamental, theological objection to abortion? Unquestionably the LDS church will always view a decision to terminate fetal life as a step with profound moral overtones. A selfish or callous decision of this sort will, I expect, always be considered a serious sin. But when it comes to a broader condemnation or even to a fixed definition of what should be considered an "abortion," the doctrinal record suggests some flexibility. In addition to a tradition which has accommodated a surprising degree of ethical readjustment, Mormonism has never taken a stand categorically barring all abortion. Right from the outset, it has recognized legitimate reasons for terminating pregnancy. The question never has been *if* there were such grounds, but always *which* grounds were legitimate. And the answers have varied with differing times and differing circumstances.

In particular, Mormons have important doctrinal latitude on the question of the nature of the embryonic or fetal life potentially jeopardized. Since this issue may alone distinguish selective abortion theologically from birth control, it is worth considering a little further.

The nineteenth-century equation of infant murder with abortion must have derived some intuitive support from the idea that infant deaths were about as common as grossly evident spontaneous abortions. Both seemed to kill perhaps 20 to 25 percent of fetuses or infants at risk. Recent research shows that 70 to 75 percent of conceptions actually fail to survive to term, and the dramatic decline in infant mortality to near 1 percent has changed this subjective equation markedly.[55] In terms of relative risk nine months before or nine months after birth, there is no longer much epidemiological similarity between prenatal and infant life. In a sense, the prenatal period is no longer viewed as only the process whereby human life comes into being. It now also appears to be a process designed by nature to insure–albeit imperfectly–that only the most viable conceptions are carried to term. Thus pre- and postnatal survival rates are inherently of an entirely different order of magnitude.

New developments in medical sciences have undermined other aspects of our traditional understanding. An animating role for a maternal spirit can not readily be argued when an ova is fertilized in a petri dish, even less when the ova, semen, or early embryo remains frozen but viable well after the death of the original donors. It is similarly awkward to invoke an essential role for maternal spirit in a brain-dead "mother" sustained on life-support systems until the fetus can be delivered with some chance of surviving. Assumptions about an obligatory role for an "embryonal spirit" also are difficult when it is realized that twins may develop from what was for a number of days a single individual; or, conversely, that more than one embryonal animal may fuse into a single individual (chimera) of normal appearance. A mandatory role for any discrete spirit presence at all can be argued only with great difficulty in the case of living cell cultures, perhaps fetal in origin, alive and well in a petri dish. Most problematic of all is to impute a mandatory spirit presence in the cloning process whereby entirely normal animals are "created" through the bio-physical manipulation of individual cells (cells which, in theory—to underscore the point—could have been obtained from cell cultures, and need not have originated in the reproductive system).

Conceptually at least medical science is increasingly committed to the notion that early prenatal life may be entirely understood in bio-physical terms applicable to a cell culture. The record to date suggests that the LDS church may eventually take advantage of its open theology in this area and acknowledge the medical consensus: the church may no longer at some point assume that either a maternal or a fetal spirit is essential to prenatal viability. This would not be a concession to secularism, but rather a recognition that medical facts cannot easily be reconciled otherwise. Should this more naturalistic view become commonplace—a development which surely will be facilitated by the widespread use of *in vitro* fertilization techniques—the Mormon perspective on elected therapeutic abortions for known, serious defects could change.

If in fact the official Mormon view follows such a path, it most likely will not be initially manifest through detailed new guidance on abortion. More likely, there will be acquiescence to the judgment of "competent physicians," whose judgment in turn will reflect this emerging perspective. While I cannot foresee a theological distinction ultimately being made between serious embryonal defects which will manifest at birth and grave defects which will not become evident until somewhat later, it is possible that during a transitional period such a distinction would be made. I would expect that only the most grotesquely abnormal defects—such as anencephaly or serious glycogen storage diseases—would initially be considered grounds for intercession. Even these may well be justified ostensibly by the imputed risk to the mother of continuing the pregnancy. While I expect no public change in the immediate future, a continuation of the general societal approval of such selected abortions[56] and the inevitable development of earlier and less emotionally traumatic means for accomplishing this may well change things eventually.

The next scenario to be considered, involving genetic engineering, is the sort of thing which in the past has been labelled by the LDS church a purely medical question. To the extent that its use is limited to the treatment of disease, I cannot conceive of a predictable rationale for Mormon objections to this amazing new tool. Certainly church leaders do not presently view deoxyribonucleic acid (DNA) as theologically any more sacrosanct than any other component of the human body. If a disease can be traced to some defect repairable through such engineering, this would certainly be hailed by leaders as yet another scientific miracle. That it might be subject to abuse at some future time would probably not distinguish it in their minds from drugs or other treatments also subject to abuse. To judge from the past, they would still defer to responsible medical expertise as to whether the potential benefits justified the perceived risks.

I would guess that much the same would prevail for *in utero* surgery. Aside from the hope it might offer as an alternative to abortion, it does not strike me as having major ethical overtones– at least in the Mormon context. One obviously must consider again James Talmage's standard that such heroic intervention be moderated by the "intelligent application of common sense"; but if such procedures proved to be successful and relatively safe, church leaders would probably view them as just another extraordinary technological development. I doubt that any guidance would be issued, even privately, on the question of prioritizing who should be treated. So far as I am aware Mormon leaders have never considered this type of question within their official domain. If they were pressed, I would expect them to defer to the prayerful consideration of those more directly involved.

The final scenario, in the case of *in vitro* fertilization is a more interesting one to assess from a Mormon perspective. It both poses a dilemma and illustrates some of the points of convergence with church doctrine. It is at once a technique which enhances the chances of a couple's having children of their own, yet simultaneously raises– in some minds–the specter of abortion.

So far as the official record is concerned, the church has not offered an opinion on the question of *in vitro* fertilization. If the public communications arm is asked, they sometimes reply that the church views the subject as a matter to be decided by the individuals concerned. Though both Mormon physicians and patients are apparently now availing themselves of this technology, neither counsel nor sanctions have been publicly forthcoming. While the recent record on sex-change surgery shows this to be no sure indicator of even near-term events, the overall record on reproductive questions suggests that the LDS church will continue its present neutrality.[57]

The over-reaching Mormon concern that members "multiply and replenish the earth" could hardly be more applicable than to a technique specifically designed to make this possible. A rationale for the church's support of *in vitro* fertilization therefore requires no imagination. Are the potential objections efficient to nullify this benefit?

Among the ethical arguments put forth against *in vitro* fertilization, one of the most common is that early embryos are aborted. One also hears that it is "unnatural" and that it poses unusual risks to the children so conceived. Of the various reservations I have seen expressed, only those relating to abortion seem to relate directly to contemporary theological concerns. Certainly the question of acceptable risk would be considered by the church as purely in the realm of medical and personal judgment. Nor does the church normally distinguish between "natural" and "unnatural" medical intervention. On these two counts, the Mormon tradition is by and large fully aligned with the medical mainstream.

What of the abortion question? It is evident that this is not a simple question. While it could be assumed that discarding an embryo or a fertilized egg was abortion, it has thus far not been seen in this light. Discarding a four-cell blastocyst (that is, a very early "embryo") created by *in vitro* techniques is much closer emotionally to preventing the implantation of a fertilized egg through the use of an IUD than it is to surgically terminating a multi-week embryo or fetus. The church never has equated use of an IUD with abortion, and it seems likely to me that *in vitro* fertilization will be viewed in a comparable, if uneasy, limbo. With the passage of time, and increasing use of these techniques, a *de facto* if not *ex cathedra* judgment will be affirmed that this is not a proscribed form of abortion. In addition, this may well become a stepping stone to allowing interdiction of somewhat older embryos taking nutrients from the uterine wall rather than from a petri dish. It is just this type of progression which has marked the evolution of Mormon medical ethical thinking in the past.

In conclusion, my impression is that on science-related issues, scientists shape theology as much as theologians do. This is not so much through confrontation or default on the part of theologians, but rather through new discoveries which directly or indirectly force modifications in the old ways of thinking. New facts have to be accommodated. Dated but inapparent sociocultural assumptions are exposed and eroded.

This phenomenon is surely evident in the Mormon record. That is a strength of the Mormon point of view rather than a weakness—because Mormons view scientific and religious truth ultimately as one and the same. The acquisition of knowledge, whether through secular or religious means, is held to be a divinely mediated accomplishment. There are, of course, some practical problems with this position; but in the final analysis, the Mormon point of view is healthy because it is designed to incorporate progress. I would suggest that in theory—and sometimes even in practice—"Mormonism" typically sees frontiers in medicine as opportunities for expanding its perspective rather than occasions for limiting personal choices.

*NOTES*

1. The complex subject of what constitutes official "doctrine" in the Mormon church is beyond the scope of this essay. In general I use statements issued by either the president of the church or the First Presidency as my guide. A conspicuous article in an official church journal is also used occasionally to indicate at least the range of acceptable beliefs. Some useful criteria are given in J. Reuben Clark, Jr., "When Are the Writings and Sermons of Church Leaders Entitled to the Claim of Scripture?," reprinted in *Dialogue: A Journal of Mormon Thought* 12 (Summer 1979).

2. Francis M. Gibbons (secretary to the First Presidency) to Lester E. Bush, 17 Dec. 1982 and 13 Jan. 1983.

3. Daniel Tyler, *A Concise History of the Mormon Battalion in the Mexican War, 1846-47* (1881); reprint ed. (Glorieta, NM: Rio Grande Press, 1969), 146.

4. "She Died a Natural Death," *Times and Seasons,* 1 Mar. 1842; reprinted in *Dialogue: A Journal of Mormon Thought* 12 (Winter 1979): 86-89.

5. James E. Talmage, "Dr. James E. Talmage Urges Vaccination Against Smallpox," *Utah Public Health Journal* 2 (Jan.-Feb. 1922): 3.

6. N. Lee Smith, "Herbal Remedies: God's Medicine?" *Dialogue: A Journal of Mormon Thought* 12 (Autumn 1979): 50.

7. The most significant other problem to bring the church into conflict with the received medical view came in 1900. It involved the issue of "free

choice," and grew out of a Utah Board of Health initiative to require all school-aged children to have smallpox vaccinations. Although the First Presidency accepted the merits and wisdom of vaccination, other prominent Mormons, notably Charles E. Penrose, the influential editor of the church's *Deseret News,* felt the procedure was dangerous and unwarranted. (In a sense, this is a vestige of the old anti-heroic philosophy.) Penrose, who not long thereafter became a member of the Quorum of the Twelve, led a vigorous crusade against the initiative, and ultimately the Mormon-dominated state legislature banned (over the governor's veto) a compulsory vaccination program. Despite their support of vaccination *per se,* the First Presidency chose not to exert its influence in support of an involuntary program. This same ingrained aversion to mandatory programs later created popular opposition to such public health programs as quarantines and fluoridation of water supplies.

8. Cf. *Conference Reports of the Church of Jesus Christ of Latter-Day Saints,* 70 A (Annual), (1 Apr. 1900): 39-40. Lester Bush, Jr., "Birth Control Among the Mormons: Introduction to an Insistent Question," *Dialogue: A Journal of Mormon Thought* 10 (Autumn 1976): 12-44.

9. Joseph F. Smith, "A Vital Question," *Improvement Era* 11 (Oct. 1908): 959-61.

10. Joseph F. Smith, Excerpt of conference talk published as "President Joseph F. Smith," *Relief Society Magazine* 4 (June 1917): 317-18.

11. D. Michael Quinn, *J. Reuben Clark: The Church Years* (Provo, UT: Brigham Young University Press, 1983), 158.

12. Heber J. Grant to Arnold Haymore, 1 May 1939, copy in my possession.

13. John A. Widtsoe to Cardon Klinger, 15 Apr. 1942, copy in my possession.

14. John A. Widtsoe, "Should Birth Control Be Practiced?" *Improvement Era* 45 (Dec. 1942): 801, 803.

15. David O. McKay to unidentified correspondent, 27 May 1946, from the "files of LaMar Berrett, Professor of Religion, Brigham Young University," in "Statements of the General Authorities on Birth Control," Department of Religion, Brigham Young University, n.d., photocopy of typescript.

16. Bruce R. McConkie, *Mormon Doctrine* [1st ed.] (Salt Lake City: Bookcraft, 1958), 81; Joseph Fielding Smith, *Doctrines of Salvation,* 2 vols. (Salt Lake City: Bookcraft, 1955), 2:86-89.

17. Hugh B. Brown, *You and Your Marriage* (Salt Lake City: Bookcraft, 1960), 135-36.

18. First Presidency to Presidents of Stakes, Bishops of Wards and Presidents of Missions, 14 Apr. 1969, copy in my possession.

19. Tim B. Heaton and Sandra Calkins, "Contraceptive Use Among

Mormons: 1965-1975," *Dialogue: A Journal of Mormon Thought* 16 (Fall 1983), 106-109.

20. Bush, "Birth Control Among the Mormons," 32.

21. Homer Ellsworth, "I Have a Question," *Ensign* 9 (Aug. 1979): 23-24. Since this essay was first published, a new edition of the authoritative *General Handbook of Instructions* (Salt Lake City: Church of Jesus Christ of Latter-day Saints, 1989), has been issued, including the most open-ended statement on "birth control" yet published by the church: "Husbands must be considerate of their wives, who have a great responsibility not only for bearing children but for caring for them through childhood. Husbands should help their wives conserve their health and strength. Married couples should seek inspiration from the Lord in meeting their marital challenges and rearing their children according to the teachings of the gospel" (11-4).

Five years earlier, Elder Gordon B. Hinckley's 29 January 1984 address on "Cornerstones of a Happy Home," which subsequently was published as a brochure and delivered by home teachers to every LDS family, had contained similar counsel. Hinckley had added, "[The Lord] did not designate the number [of children], nor has the Church. That is a sacred matter left to the couple and the Lord." Paradoxically, as with the relatively liberal guidance of 1969, this statement follows the decline of the Mormon birthrate to the lowest level to date, 24.5 births per thousand for 1983.

22. Bush, "Birth Control Among the Mormons," 14-16, 42n104.

23. *Journal of Discourses*, 26 vols. (Liverpool, Eng.: Latter-day Saints' Booksellers Depot, 1855-86), 22:320 (hereafter JD).

24. *Utah Code Annotated,* sec. 1972, 1876; sec. 76-7-301 et seq. 1973.

25. Richard W. Lohner, "Therapeutic Abortion in Salt Lake City, 1954-64," *Selected Writings by the Staff of Latter-day Saints Hospital* 6 (Spring 1967): 9-19.

26. An instructive contrast is the distinctly different approach taken to medical ethical issues by the Reorganized Church of Jesus Christ of Latter Day Saints, which, with access essentially to the same body of scripture, rarely makes categorical statements. Decisions on abortion, for example, are considered to be individual decisions. Such decisions may not be lightly made, but church leadership also "recognizes that there may be *rare* occasions which might make necessary, because of the conditions of the conception or the pregnancy, to terminate a particular pregnancy" (First Presidency [RLDS church], *Handbook of Church Organization and Administrative Policies and Procedures* [Independence, MO: Herald House, 1974]).

27. David O. McKay to Tiena Nate, 31 Oct. 1934, copy in my possession.

28. First Presidency, "Statement on Abortion," *Ensign* 3 (Mar. 1973): 64.

29. Quinn, *J. Reuben Clark,* 158.

30. JD 17:143.

31. David O. McKay to A. Kent Christensen, 3 Feb. 1959, copy in my possession.

32. *Wilford Woodruff's Journal, 1833-1898,* Typescript, ed. Scott G. Kenney, 9 vols. (Midvale, UT: Signature Books, 1984), 5:109.

33. Ibid., 6:361; JD 12:66.

34. First Presidency to Presidents of Stakes, Bishops of Wards and Presidents of Missions, 12 Feb. 1970, copy in my possession.

35. *Deseret News,* 23 Jan. 1969.

36. Joseph Anderson (secretary to the First Presidency) to unidentified correspondent, 16 May 1969, copy in my possession.

37. There is an inherent tension between the Mormon belief that we will be punished only for our own sins and the idea that we can deprive a person of an opportunity to grow through an earthly experience by killing or otherwise harming him or her. The problem posed by the death of young children was handled early by assuming that all who died before "the age of accountability" (eight years) were assured exaltation. That historically this could amount to perhaps 40 percent of all births makes the attempted analogy to abortion a little more intelligible. But our present medical understanding that as many as 85-90 percent of all conceptions fail to reach eight again undermines the whole proposition.

38. *Church News,* 5 June 1976, 3.

39. The 1983 *General Handbook* statement added pregnancy from incest to the published list of exceptional cases in which abortion might be justified. The other exceptions remained pregnancy resulting from rape, and circumstances where the "life or health of the woman is in jeopardy" (77-78). The 1989 *General Handbook* added a severely deformed fetus that will not survive beyond birth as another justification (11-4).

40. See *Centers for Disease Control,* Sept. 1982.

41. Parley P. Pratt, *Key to the Science of Theology* (Liverpool: Franklin D. Richards, 1855), 167.

42. *Utah Code Annotated,* Sec. 89-0-1, 1925; Sec.64-10-1 after 1953).

43. JD 4:56

44. Beyond the physically redeeming merits of adherence to its Word of Wisdom and otherwise living righteously, nineteenth-century Mormons were taught that they were literally part of a "chosen lineage." In a sense, this identification was just another aspect of the effort to create or restore the biblical ideal. It also promoted a sense of unity and served as an emotional shield during many trying years. Though now perhaps anachronistic, this notion of being elect still appears in popular Mormon lore. Indeed, at least symbolically it is an essential part of the Mormon tradition of patriarchal blessings. In its most fully developed form, this idea extended beyond this-worldly bonds of kinship to the belief that these bonds somehow existed in the pre-earthly spirit world. Certain spirits were said to be destined to be

born into specific Mormon families. While not a formal doctrine of the LDS church, this idea nonetheless in part shapes the way Mormons view, for example, such things as the number of children "destined" for their families.

45. *Deseret News*, 23 Jan. 1969.

46. Lester Bush, ed., "Mormon Medical Ethical Guidelines," *Dialogue: A Journal of Mormon Thought* 12 (Autumn 1979): 100, 106.

47. The 1983 *General Handbook* combined Utah's legal proviso with church counsel into what was the first statement on sterilization to be published by the church: "Sterilization may possibly be justified in a case where (1) medical conditions jeopardize the health of a mother, or (2) a person is born with defects or has suffered severe trauma that renders him mentally incompetent and not responsible for his actions. Such conditions, rare as they may be, must be determined by competent medical judgment and in accordance with the law" (77). This, of course, endorsed the exemption that the church opposed in 1969. The 1989 *General Handbook* retained the same advice (11-5).

48. Bush, "Mormon Medical Ethical Guidelines," 97.

49. Ibid., 101.

50. *Deseret News*, 7, 11 Sept. 1968.

51. McKay to Christensen, 3 Feb. 1959.

52. A subtle shift also has begun in the case of sex-change surgery as well. The 1983 *General Handbook* advised that "a change in a member's sex ordinarily justifies excommunication" (53), and exceptions under this proviso were known to have been made. Formerly the officially published guidance stated flatly, "Members who have undergone transsexual operations must be excommunicated," with the added penalties detailed in the October 1980 version of Chapter 8 (2). By 1989 the *General Handbook* read, "Church leaders counsel against elective transsexual operations. A bishop should inform a member contemplating such an operation of this counsel and should advise the member that the operation may be cause for formal Church discipline. In questionable cases, a bishop should obtain the counsel of the First Presidency" (10-4). Public counsel on such surgery will surely continue to evolve. Some provision is no doubt made for children whose sex is "changed" as the only solution to ambiguous genitalia or some other purely medical miscue. As the church encounters (or fails to detect prior to conversion, etc.) well-adjusted adults who have undergone elective sex-change surgery, even further moderation will probably come about.

Another parallel is also apparent in recent counsel on oral sex in marriage. This crystallized from ambivalent or non-existent counsel to a First Presidency directive in January 1982 that married couples involved in such practices be denied access to temple ordinances, which in turn was rescinded in a follow-up directive in October 1982 that instructed local leaders to avoid inquiring into "personal intimate matters involving marital relations between a man and his wife."

53. A. Karl Larson and Katharine Miles Larson, eds., *Diary of Charles Lowell Walker*, 2 vols. (Logan, UT: Utah State University Press, 1980), 2:621.

54. JD 13:3

55. Daniel R. Mishell, Jr., "State of the Art—What Can We Offer Patients?" *Contemporary Ob/Gyn* 20 (Nov. 1982): 219-23.

56. LeRoy Walters (June 1982) reports that according to national surveys taken in 1972-80 by the National Opinion Research Center at the University of Chicago, "a substantial majority of the adult population (range, 79 percent to 92 percent) finds abortion ethically acceptable in cases involving the so-called hard reasons for abortion (serious danger to the woman's health, rape, serious fetal defect)." As noted above, the 1989 *General Handbook* did in fact make the first move in this direction, in approving abortion in cases of fetuses with such severe defects that they would not survive beyond birth.

57. Following the original publication of this essay, the 1989 *General Handbook* finally did address IVF, with guidance very similar to that given on artificial insemination: "*In vitro* fertilization using semen other than that of the husband or an egg other than the wife's is strongly discouraged. However, this is a personal matter that ultimately must be left to the judgment of the husband and wife."

# 10.

# Single Cursedness: An Overview of LDS Authorities' Statements about Unmarried People

*Marybeth Raynes and Erin Parsons*

Being married is one of the most important ideas in Mormon culture, emphasized almost to the exclusion of other states of being. Much like the moon that is visible only when reflecting the sun's light, mention of singleness occurs most frequently in articles and talks about marriage, most frequently coupled with exhortations to marry. Not only does this condition hold true in official statements but it also seems to be a fact in personal lives. According to one single woman, "To be determined not to be determined by marriage is to be determined by marriage."[1]

Our research focused only on never-married people. Numerous statements about divorced and widowed persons merit additional discussion on their own. We found no mention of separated, deserted, or prisoner-of-war spouses or out-of-wedlock parents. So, though we do not mention these categories, we are aware of them and suspect they experience many of the same conditions as never-married people within the LDS church.

Overall, statements about singleness in official LDS settings take the form of both blessings and cursing with little nonjudgmental material. We found the earliest statement about singleness recorded in 1831 and concluded our survey with statements from 1982. The remarkable thing about this time-span is that the major message for singles developed very early and, except for an occasional variation, never changed. That message can be summarized briefly: (1) God's plan is marriage. Singleness violates that plan, and therefore has at least overtones of unrighteousness or abnormality. (2) If you marry outside the temple or outside the church, unhappiness will follow.

These views began in 1831 when a revelation to Leman Copley, a former celibate Shaker and missionary to the same, announced that "whoso forbiddeth to marry is not ordained of God, for marriage is ordained of God and man" (D&C 49:15). After 1850 when polygamy was openly espoused, Apostle Orson Hyde warned reluctant bachelors that "better men would step forward to do the job" if they did not marry and he also denounced Paul's statement as "false doctrine": "It is better to remain unmarried even as I."[2]

Even after the cessation of plural marriage, the pressure on man was not relaxed. In 1914 Feramorz Y. Fox, president of LDS College, urged, "While counseling the women against marrying outside of the Church, we must use every means to overcome the tendency among Mormon men to delay marriage."[3] In 1924 Apostle George F. Richards was "appalled" to learn that 27,104 members of the church over twenty-one were single the previous year. "Why," he demanded, "when we believe in marriage? Forbidding to marry is the doctrine of devils."[4]

Even though singleness is equally "wrong" for men and women, there are clear gender differences in the attitude of authoritative statements: Women are gentle victims of man's selfishness. Thus unmarried men need to "repent" of singleness as they would any other sin, and the chief means of persuasion is threats. From the speeches, four reasons emerge for men's refusal to marry:

1. It is their nature to avoid marriage. Brigham Young believed that "not one man in a 1000 would have wife or children except for religious reasons."[5] In years as widely separated as 1874, 1958, and 1981, a "growing indifference" to marriage throughout the nation is cited as a reason why increasingly large numbers of Mormon men choose not to marry.[6]

2. Single men are less righteous. Those who do not choose a wife

are "unwilling" to accept God's commands, don't "understand" gospel principles, and are "not living their religion."[7]

3. As a result single men are worldly and materialistic, "too niggardly to support a wife" because "a wife in this day is too expensive an article to keep." It is "unfortunate when comfort, social position, desire to travel or professional or political ambitions stand in the way of rearing a family."[8]

4. Single men are defective or disabled in some way. Perhaps out of false charity, most of the speculation about continuing singleness fell in this category. In chronological order, men are purported to suffer from: disability (1892), inability to support a wife (1913), incompetence (1974), "lacking in guts . . . [or] suffering a chemical imbalance" (1979), "inadequate to meet the demands of personal involvement" (1981), and "battered and scarred" (1981).[9] A bishop in a singles ward explained this last statement: "Life is a test. Some who are especially battered and scarred inside have not been asked to face the Celestial challenge of marriage. It is enough for them to simply make it through, pointing to two ward members—a nymphomaniac and a homosexual—who fought their battles daily. Perhaps winning the *not* doing battle is just as important as winning the doing something battle. Those who may be mentally or severely physically handicapped are not compelled to marry during earth life."[10]

Only one article reflected single men's perspective on singlehood and many of those interviewed mentioned their sensitivity to the labeling they felt occurred from other members of the church: These labels included homosexuality, too "picky," "immaturity," "lack of self-knowledge," and "lack of interpersonal skills."[11] None of the sources searched revealed any positive reasons or acceptable reasons why men do not marry.

The reasons why women do not marry are less stringently negative but still less than positive.

1. Men may not be available due to war disability, or disinterest.[12]

2. Career or education decisions may preclude marriage. This reason is not, however considered acceptable. Remarked Helen Rowland in the 1917 *Relief Society Magazine,* "Don't accept substitutes: don't accept a career instead of marrying the right man. Art is thrilling but you can't run your fingers through its hair. A career is absorbing, but you can't tie pink ribbons in the curls of your brain

children. Work is beautiful and enobling, but it never calls you sweetly foolish names, takes you out to dinner, admires your latest hat, or tells you how different you are from all the other women. In short, the most radical, self-ordained bachelor girl will admit that she is making no great human sacrifice when she wants to give up her freedom, her wild ways, and dances, in order to make herself worthy of a pure, sweet man."

3. The woman may be undesirable marriage material. No church discussions of singleness stated personal undesirability as a reason directly, but the implication is there. For example, when women are exhorted to stay sweet, well-groomed, skilled at homemaking, and of service to mankind to be "more ready" when marriage comes along,[14] the implication is that one may be undesirable or unmarriageable without these qualities.

4. Other reasons include the fear that men cannot support them, while some women may be responsible for dependent members of their immediate families or be repelled by sex. These last two reasons are mentioned once only in *Alone but Not Lonely,* a 1973 book by a Mormon who was not a church authority. The author, Wayne J. Anderson, also provided the sole positive reasons for women remaining unmarried: wider career opportunity and greater service to all of humanity.[16]

Although these reasons lack the directly threatening tone common when addressing single men, they still assign blame in a quiet way. Staying "sweet" and being careful about too much career involvement are enjoinders to wait in an appropriate way to be available for marriage, with the implication that it will result. No advice was ever given on direct steps single women might take to get married.

Another frequent theme of official statements—again a form of negative persuasion—is warnings about the unhappy fate of the unmarried. First, a single child is a reproach to his/her parents who "will receive condemnation on their heads if their children do not learn the correct . . . principle of eternal marriage."[17] Unmarried women are warned that they will be forced to work in the field or in the mines, and are left, in Brigham Young's phrase, as "female outcasts and marriageable outlaws."[18] Without marriage women are "unprotected," and in 1892 Samuel W. Richard, president of the European Mission, asserted, "By men remaining single, women are denied their right to marry—no wonder they are demanding the franchise so that they may protect their rights themselves."[19]

The most important costs, however, are personal and spiritual. Single men "will not have a principality in the hereafter" and will have to face the Lord empty-handed when he asks "Where is your wife?"[20] Their presumed choice not to marry is "frustrating their own eternal progress," a theme church president Spencer W. Kimball spoke to at least twice in the mid-1970s. Quoting George Gilder's not always reliable research, he warned that single men live shorter lives, have poorer health, are emotionally less stable, and get fewer important posts.[21] Additionally, single people suffer discrimination in the church because they are often "viewed by other Church members as a failure or as incompetent" or as second-class citizens.[22] Seventy ElRay L. Christiansen predicted disappointment, regret, and remorse if people remain single.[23]

Furthermore, singleness also causes negative consequences for society. Orson Hyde warned that "men will gratify worldly desire out of wedlock, thereby increasing babies out of wedlock as well as prostitution." Consequently, God will send pestilence to lay waste to the cities and to "visit the guilty sensualist with dreadful punishment."[24] Later authorities maintained that the "bulwark" of society will be weakened because "all sorts of social problems are caused by singlehood, crime, immorality, divorce and poverty."[25]

Church officials, all of whom are male, consistently perceive the single man as selfish, sinful, and possibly suffering from chemical imbalance. A man who stubbornly retains bachelorhood is not worthy of his priesthood. In 1974 President Harold B. Lee sternly admonished: "All women have a desire for companionship. They want to be wives and mothers, and when men refuse the responsibility of marriage, for no good reason, they [the women] are unable to consummate marriage. Brethren, we are not doing our duty as holders of the priesthood when we go beyond the marriageable age and withhold ourselves from an honorable marriage to these lovely women."[26]

We found no positive statements about unmarried men, regardless of circumstance. As we might expect, at least one single male reported never having received any positive encouragement or understanding from church sources about his single state.[27] In contrast, worthy single women are consoled that, should they not be chosen for the "most choice career," they will yet receive all the blessings of matrimony in the hereafter.[28] Meanwhile, they should devote themselves to service and spiritual growth.

How do single people view their own experience? Women have spoken most openly. In 1839 Elizabeth Haven wrote to a friend: "Tell them [other women friends] not to be in a hurry about getting married, for I am not."[29] She married the next year. Later, Susa Young, a daughter of Brigham Young and divorced from Alma Dunford, her first husband, wrote to her mother, "Sometimes they tell me I must be saved by some good man. If that's all, I could be sealed to some one who has proved his integrity and has passed away. . . . I have no desire to be any man's wife. And doubt whether I ever shall." [30] She later married Jacob Gates and editorialized in the *Young Women's Journal* that a girl "really looks forward to marriage as the one desirable thing in her life."[31] Whether this statement was autobiographical or exhortatory we have no way of knowing.

Perhaps mirroring the social changes that have made singleness much more prevalent, personal writings of Latter-day Saints in the last two decades sound less defensive. The "single condition is not a trial or affliction, rather an opportunity for growth," said Carol Clark, a single Relief Society general board member.[32] "Don't judge yourself, find satisfaction in present joys and prepare for life, not just marriage," said another. A third asserted, "There is not just *one* acceptable life pattern for every woman in the Church, i.e. 'all Mormon women are . . . ,' 'all single people feel . . . ,' 'all mothers will . . . ,' etc."[34]

At least one person lamented, "I am perfectly content to remain single right now, but my bishop . . . has only one word for me: marriage. No one in my ward can believe that someone 'so far over the marrying age' . . . can be satisfied with a career."[35] The tension implied between personal acceptance and negative pressures identifies yet another source of negative feelings. Diane Higginson, writing in *Dialogue: A Journal of Mormon Thought* in 1971, identified the situation as "being in the right Church but in the wrong pew . . . neither a priesthood bearer nor a child bearer."[36] Other women specified some of their feelings: feeling "branded with a scarlet 'S'," depressed, impatient, feeling failure, lonely, discouraged, out of place, even though objectively things might be going well, unlovable with unattainable dreams, invisible and unrecognized by the church, and waiting.[37] They also mention feeling a double bind about marriage and education/career. If single women "don't get educated or adopt a career they will have to settle for a less stimulating, rewarding existence if they never marry; if they do get a rewarding career, they intimidate the men they might want to marry." Succinctly put, one woman entering graduate school was told, "You'll be sorry if you go to law school; no self-respecting missionary will marry you."[38] The dilemma is genuine: either course of action could be the "wrong decision" that might bring on a permanent single status for which one is fully responsible.[39]

Older single women mention their pain when "quips like 'I guess he died in the war in heaven' and 'some day my prince will come—in the Millennium' are no longer laughable."[40] One single woman confessed to new attitudes about men: "My right man has changed a lot since high school, and the range is narrowing: not just because the number of available men is decreasing . . . but because I find *myself* gradually becoming less flexible. I am no longer willing to date, but I find an increasing longing to have the experiences be meaningful. I also find myself struggling to be patient; patient with the 'relationship process' which takes time to enact."[41]

Single men have been largely silent, and no similar body of personal writings documents their feelings. From the informal survey in the only article on the topic, single men seem to feel chastised, lonely, labelled, left out, and often sexually frustrated. Additionally, they feel pressure from everywhere: parents, friends, bishops, and single women. One branch president expressed sympathy for a single counselor "literally backed against the wall after a fireside by five or six women—with no defense except a cookie and a glass of punch." In addition to labels like immature, immoral, selfish, and unrighteous, they are not seen as worthy of church callings that other men of commensurate age and activity are filling.

The church, lagging ten years behind society, discovered single people as a group in the 1970s and implemented singles wards and Young Special Interest programs. It recognized the different types of singleness (never-married, divorced, and widowed), dispensed alternative advice for singles: good grooming, reading a lot, performing compassionate service, and entertaining neighborhood children.

This program brought relief and relative enthusiasm from many singles and seemed to be partially successful in meeting some needs. Others point out that the labelling and stereotyping continued. "All that single saints have in common is that they're single," complained one. Another "pointed out the irony of participating in a program 'whose very existence advertises that you're failing. The only qualification you have to have to belong is being single. The only thing you have to do to get out is to get married.'"[45]

In an interview we conducted, one single man denied the "selfish single" label. Instead, he said, he and other men felt as trapped in their circumstances as women. No one seems available to point out patterns, give encouragement, or suggest positive changes that could lead to marriage.[46]

The church's efforts to solve singleness may have also created additional problems because its message is almost exclusively negative and because it contains a surprising number of double messages. The process of communication, if not the content of the message, is primarily characterized by a negative tone. Whether the content is gentle or harsh, overt or covert, the attitude of the speaker nearly always communicates that there is something wrong about being single. Two social scientists, William D. Payne and Merlin B. Brinkerhoff, pointed out in an insightful 1978 essay in *Dialogue* that labels create powerful social expectations. Thus: "It is difficult for a negatively labelled Church member to maintain a picture of himself inconsistent with the way in which others in the Church view him. Negative social labels with their accompanying expectations may lead someone to self-deprecating deviant behavior. The unconventional behavior conforms and reinforces the negative label. Within the Church, the role of the label, and its accompanying expectations in making the behavior come true is seldom considered."[47]

In addition, they note that "the possessor of a single stigmatizing characteristic is often seen as possessing several other discrediting characteristics which some member relates to the original label." The consequences of teaching Latter-day Saints that singleness is a "bad" state to be in undoubtedly has consequences for marriage, childraising, and larger issues of identity that deserve fuller exploration.

The double messages which coexist in talks, lessons, and general attitudes are:

1. Don't marry too young. Take your time. *But* don't marry too late or you will miss out. The "proper age" for marriage is definitely post-mission for men but otherwise remains undefined, although it is obviously a narrow slot. A recent example of a new attempt to define this optimum age is seen in a 1982 statement telling mission presidents not to offer advice about how soon missionaries should marry after their return home, which reverses decades of advice to marry within six months of returning home or be "a failure as a missionary."[48]

2. You can't reach exaltation on your own for you must be married, *but* your eternal exaltation is completely your own responsibility.

3. If you lead a good life even though not married you'll reap all the blessings in the eternities, *but* those who are not married will be ministering angels, and remain "separately and singly, without exaltation . . . to all eternity" (D&C 132:16-17). There are doctrinal provisions for those not married in this life to be married in the Millennium; however, not all church members may understand that doctrine and those who do may not be particularly comforted.

4. If you live the commandments while still single, you'll be rewarded by marriage; *but* those who don't marry are less righteous.[50]

5. Single women should develop their talents through career and service, *but* they should be prepared at any minute to marry and confine their efforts to family and church.

We also see a double message in the difference between the content and the form of the message: we care about you and you are important in the Lord's church, but we do not know how to talk positively to you or really recognize your existence in a positive way.

It is encouraging, however, to note that over half our sources about singleness have been printed since 1970, presumably because singleness has become more socially acceptable and because single people themselves have begun to make a place for themselves. Oscar McConkie, a former mission president, acknowledges that the single Mormon deserves a life as full and satisfying as a married person, even though there seems to be a tacit implication that "fulfillment" is really a substitute for marriage.[51]

Furthermore, research about church members is increasing. Statistics make people visible. When church authorities become aware that a substantial minority—some guess 30 percent—of the adults in the church are single, it is easier for them to address problems and programs. The recent emphasis in church talks and manuals about the importance of self-esteem and the ability to love has also somewhat mitigated the negative pressure on singles. Eleanor Knowles, at the time a single editor at the *Ensign*, observed in 1971: "From childhood women have been told that a woman's fulfillment comes with marriage and a family. Lessons at Church are often prefaced with 'when you marry.' Few persons warn that you may not marry, and therefore preparation for a full life must be made, regardless if it is within or without marriage."[52] "You're making a great contribution and the promises will be fulfilled in the eternities,"[53] President Kimball assured single *Ensign* readers in 1976. He also urged, "We should place emphasis on the person rather than the status. We should all be part of the mainstream . . . part of a big family in the Church. Part of the problem of the singles is that we are playing limits instead of realizing the limits of potential."[54] And speaking about the Special Interest program to church members in general, Elder James Faust, now an apostle, said, "What is proposed is a way to reach the singles and have each feel that someone cares and that each has a place in the Lord's Church. Too often we are insensitive to the feelings of the singles."[55]

In addition to shedding a more positive light on being single, a practical focus for solving issues is urged. In the *Guidelines for Single Adults* issued to regional, stake, and ward levels in 1980, policies and procedures were written in a positive, informative style. Unmarried persons were urged to participate in singles programs. Singles conferences have occasionally been reported in the *Ensign*. One single attender at a conference commented on the pleasure of "learning you're not alone. You can call on a fellow member of S.I. and get help. Someone who has been through your problem and survived shows you can too."[56] Counseling for all singles to discover "hangups" has been recommended as an acceptable course of action, though not by a general authority.[56] Service and spiritual growth have also been recommended. In short, if you "feel deprived by being single, expand your sphere of usefulness."[59]

This broader vision of the last two decades is still double vision, however. Although some church authorities speak of singleness with sympathy and insight, a member of the First Quorum of the Seventy reportedly said, during a singles conference at BYU in 1982, that a single person is not a whole person, and being single—particularly divorced singleness—was described as being unacceptable to the Lord.[60] The continuing themes have not changed fundamentally but are simply supplemented with new positive statements backed up and encouraged by programs tailored for single people.

*NOTES*

1. Diane Higginson, "Single Voices," *Dialogue: A Journal of Mormon Thought* 6 (Summer 1971): 79.

2. Orson Hyde, 6 Oct. 1854, in *Journal of Discourses*, 26 vols. (Liverpool: F. D. Richards, 1855-86), 2:84.

3. Feramorz Y. Fox, "Comments on June Editorial," *Young Woman's Journal* 15 (Sept. 1914): 559.

4. George F. Richards, *Conference Reports*, 4 Apr. 1924, 30-31.

5. Brigham Young, 9 Aug. 1868, *Journal of Discourses* 2:90.

6. "Better One than Two," *Juvenile Instructor* 9 (July 1874): 163; ElRay L. Christiansen, "Whom and Where Will You Marry?" *Relief Society Magazine* 45 (Oct. 1958): 644-48; Jan Thompson, "Prepare for Life, Not Just Marriage" (interview with Susan Memmot), *Church News*, 18 July 1981, 7.

7. Samuel W. Richards, "The Duty of Marriage," *The Contributor* 13 (1892): 92. Hyrum M. Smith, *Conference Reports*, 4 Apr. 1913, 115. Oscar W. McConkie, *She Shall Be Called Woman* (Salt Lake City: Bookcraft, 1979), 112. "An Everlasting Covenant" (Lesson Department), *Young Woman's Journal* 33 (Feb. 1922): 116.

8. Hyde, *Journal of Discourses*, 2:84-85; Blanche Beechwood [Emmeline B. Wells], *Women's Exponent*, July 1876; "Marriage as a Religious and Moral Obligation" (Social Service Lesson), *Relief Society Magazine* 10 (May 1923): 155-58.

9. Richards, "The Duty of Marriage," 90; Hyrum M. Smith, *Conference Reports*, 114-15; Paul E. Dahl, "Some Factors Which Differ Between Married and Never Married L.D.S. Males and Females Who Attended 1969 Summer School at Brigham Young University in Relationship to Their Families of Orientation," Ph.D. diss., Brigham Young University, 1971, 29; McConkie, *Woman*, 109; Thompson, "Prepare for Life," 7; Kay Senzee, "Single Survival," *Exponent II* 8 (Winter 1981): 11.

10. Senzee, "Single Survival," 11.

11. Lavina Fielding Anderson and Jeffrey O. Johnson, "Endangered Species: Single Men in the Church," *Sunstone* 2 (Summer 1979): 5.

12. Brigham Young, *Journal of Discourses,* 12:262; Henry Bowman, "Are Girls Become Pursuers?" *Improvement Era* 48 (July 1945): 7; Richards, "The Duty of Marriage," 90.

13. Helen Rowland, "Making a Husband out of a Man," *Relief Society Magazine* 4 (Nov. 1917): 612.

14. McConkie, *Woman,* 108.

15. Hyrum M. Smith, *Conference Report,* 15.

16. Wayne J. Anderson, *Alone but Not Lonely* (Salt Lake City: Deseret Book Co., 1973), 54.

17. Christiansen, "Whom and Where," 646.

18. Young, *Journal of Discourses,* 12:262.

19. Richards, "The Duty of Marriage," 91-93.

20. Spencer W. Kimball, "Marriage," *Ensign* 6 (Feb. 1976): 4.

21. Spencer W. Kimball, as quoted in Gerry Avant, "Marriage Ordained of God" (report of speech), *Church News,* 4 Jan. 1975, 4.

22. McConkie, *Woman,* 108; Bruce L. Campbell and Eugene E. Campbell, "The Mormon Family," in *Ethnic Families in America: Patterns and Variations,* eds. Charles H. Mindel and Robert W. Habenstein (New York: Elseview North-Holland, Inc., 1977), 385; Ida Smith, "The Psychological Needs of Mormon Women," *Sunstone* 6 (Mar./Apr. 1981): 62.

23. Christiansen, "Whom and Where," 648. Others acknowledge that deprivation, social pressure, exclusion, and discouragement also afflict the single. See McConkie, *Woman,* 109; Orson Scott Card, "What They're Doing in Rochester, Orlando, Tempe . . . : A Report on Successful Programs for Single Adults," *Ensign* 8 (Feb. 1978); 10; Gerry Avant, "Single Adults: Activity in Ward Is Key to Success," *Church News,* 18 July 1981, 7.

24. Hyde, *Journal of Discourses,* 84.

25. Richards, "The Duty of Marriage," 92; David O. McKay, *Conference Reports,* 1953, 17.

26. Harold B. Lee "Understanding Who We Are Brings Self-Respect," October general conference address 1973, *Ensign* 4 (Jan. 1974): 100.

27. Donald L Wight, interviewed by authors Feb. 1982, Salt Lake City, notes in possession of Marybeth Raynes.

28. Neal A. Maxwell, "The Women of God," April 1978 general conference address, *Ensign* (9 May 1978): 11. Such assertions may emerge from a stereotyped view that women are "naturally" spiritual, kind, sweet, and nurturing while men are "naturally" rebellious and disobedient. Hence, they must bridle their urges and fight their basic natures to achieve spirituality.

29. Elizabeth Haven Barlow to Elizabeth Howe Bullard, 24 Feb. 1839, in Kenneth W. Godfrey, Audrey M. Godfrey, and Jill Mulvay Derr, *Women's Voices: An Untold Story of the Latter-day Saints* (Salt Lake City: Deseret Book Co., 1982), 115.

30. Susa Young Dunford (Gates) to Lucy Bigelow Young in ibid., 331, 334.

31. Susa Young Gates, "Editor's Notes," *Young Woman's Journal* 8 (Jan. 1897): 183.

32. Carol Clark, *A Singular Life: Perspectives for the Single Woman* (Salt Lake City: Deseret Book Co., 1974), 3.

33. Thompson, "Prepare for Life," 7.

34. Ida Smith, "Psychological Needs," 2.

35. Clark, *Singular Life,* 2.

36. Higginson, "Single Voices," 79.

37. Maryruth Bracy "Single Voices," *Dialogue: A Journal of Mormon Thought* 6 (Autumn-Winter 1971): 78; Anonymous, ibid., 77; Beth Vaughn, "Sisters Speak: The Single Woman in the Church," *Exponent II* 6 (Dec. 1971): 16; Thompson, "Prepare for Life" 7; Senzee, "Single Survival," 6; Louise Durham, "Profiles: Research Director Speaks Out," *Exponent II* 6 (Autumn-Winter 1971): 12.

38. Janeen Jacobs Aggen, "Does a J.D. Rule Out a Mrs.?" *Exponent II* 7 (Fall 1980): 4.

39. Bracy, "Single Voices," 78.

40. Clark, *Singular Life,* 3.

41. Bracy, "Single Voices," 78.

42. Anderson and Johnson, "Endangered Species," 2-3.

43. Anne Osbom, "The Ecstasy of the Agony: How to Be Single and Sane at the Same Time," *Ensign,* 7 (Mar. 1977): 8.

44. Card, "What They're Doing," 7.

45. Anderson and Johnson, "Endangered Species," 4.

46. Wright, interview.

47. William D. Payne and Merlin B. Brinkerhoff, "Negative Social Labelling: Some Consequences and Implications," *Dialogue: A Journal of Mormon Thought* 11 (1978): 44.

48. Lee, "Understanding Who We Are," 120.

49. Brigham Young, 9 Aug. 1868, *Journal of Discourses,* 12:262.

50. Christiansen "Whom and Where," 646; Joseph Fielding Smith, "Marriage in Eternity," *Improvement Era* 60 (Oct. 1917): 702; Campbell and Campbell, "Mormon Family," 385.

51. McConkie, *Woman,* 113.

52. Eleanor Knowles, "A Look at the Single Person," *Ensign* 1 (Aug. 1971): 40.

53. Kimball, "Marriage," 4.

54. Avant, "Single Adults," 4.

55. James E. Faust, "Reaching the One," April 1973 general conference address, *Ensign* 3 (July 993): 87.

56. Card "What They're Doing," 7.

57. Knowles "A Look at the Single Person," 40. Since we cannot recall similar recommendations for married people who are not suffering from obvious difficulties, this statement may reflect the assumption that singleness in and of itself constitutes a personality defect or problem.

58. Osbom, "Ecstasy of the Agony," 49.

59. McConkie, *Woman,* 113.

60. *Church News,* 2 Apr. 1982, 6.

# 11. A Lone Man in the Garden

*Delmont R. Oswald*

I AM A DIVORCED FATHER WITH TWO BEAUTIFUL CHILDREN. MARRIED for eleven years, I have been divorced for ten. I continue to experience the joys and responsibilities of fatherhood; I consider myself a member in good standing; and I remain sealed to my children. But because I have not remarried and because I have received a cancellation of sealing to my ex-wife, I am technically in the same category as the never-married. I am not eligible to obtain "a fullness of glory and exaltation in the celestial kingdom" unless and until I remarry. I am devoted to my religion, however, and I want to see the Mormon church lovingly include and encourage all members to become active participants.

In the 1988 April general conference priesthood session, President Ezra Taft Benson addressed the single adult brethren of the church concerning the need to take on the responsibilities of marriage. Although his speech focused on the never-married male, the implications apply equally to all unmarried adult male members, including the divorced and perhaps the widowed. (I qualify the category "widowed," because although widowed men are often encouraged to remarry and provide the means for another sister to enter "the fullness of celestial glory," they are viewed as having fulfilled their covenants honorably.)

When I heard President Benson's speech, I must admit my emotions were mixed. On one hand I was very pleased to hear President Benson address the issue of the single male in the church. For too long the singles issue has been seen only as a woman's problem. Also, the fact that the highest rate of inactivity in the church lies among divorced males and the second highest among never-married males marks this issue as urgent.

On the other hand, the speech was painful to me, not just because it was reminding me of obligations and calling me to change, but because of its tone and approach. This was disconcerting because I have been raised to accept unquestioningly the authority of church leaders.

I do not take issue with the doctrine expressed in the speech or with the right of the prophet to call members to change their ways. This is, after all, his right and calling. As for marriage, I believe that two people in a good relationship, loving and supporting one another equally through the trials of life and, if possible, creating children, is wonderful and good. And I believe that happily married couples can experience a higher level of joy than a single person. I believe this because the times I feel the most like "a lone man in the Garden of Eden" are those times when something especially positive or pleasurable happens and I have no one to share it with. Sharing happiness is truly a higher experience than feeling happy by yourself. We singles often repeat the adage, "There are a lot worse things than being single." And we are right, but we must likewise admit that there are also better things.

It was the tone of President Benson's speech that troubled me. I heard his words as those of an adult lecturing a child. Singles are perhaps overly sensitive to this approach because they often find themselves treated as eternal teenagers both in their congregations and in their immediate families. Too often adulthood comes to be defined by marital status rather than by age and maturity.

To be fair, I realize the limitations of any speech given in a conference setting. It must be directed at an audience with a wide and diverse spectrum of emotional, intellectual, and cultural backgrounds; it is restricted by time; it must quickly develop an ideal goal based on doctrine; it must be translated into teaching examples; and it must end with a call for behavioral change. This is not an easy achievement for any speaker. I also recognize that the prophet is viewed as a father figure representing our Father in Heaven and that he frequently speaks to the membership in that capacity. However, in a speech that called me at age forty-eight to radically change my lifestyle, I would have felt more comfortable being addressed as a brother and fellow adult.

But this father-to-errant-child approach by itself would not have evoked such a strong reaction to the speech. It was President Benson's concluding quote from 2 Nephi 1:21 that troubled me most: "Arise from the dust, my sons, and be men." Not only did I feel that this placed me in company with Laman and Lemuel, but that my very masculinity and adulthood were being questioned—simply because I was not married. My first highly emotional response to this quote preempted the logical and intellectual responses upon which I usually pride myself. I also felt that an issue I find complex was being treated simplistically. The message this quote sends to an often already sensitive audience is, "O.K. children, quit playing childish games and grow up. It's time to change your ways." To an adult male who has never married and who has spent a lifetime developing his particular personality and life patterns, this implies that profound change is simply a matter of saying, "I will." Yet very seldom is willpower alone successful. And to divorced males it implies that there are no complexities involved in their situations. It is the inevitable complexities involved in any divorce, however, that so frequently lead these men to inactivity.

One of the major complications that single males in the church must deal with is guilt. The assumption is often made that single males are sinning by choosing to remain in that state. According to this reasoning, they are not only keeping themselves from obtaining the celestial kingdom, but they are responsible for not helping some worthy sister to achieve her exaltation as well. In effect, then, they are not living up to their priesthood obligations. They often feel this guilt toward their parents and their church leaders, because they sense they have disappointed the very authority figures whose approval they most desire. It is also frequently difficult for them to seek counsel and aid from bishops or other church authorities, who are generally neither single, divorced, nor professional counselors, and who frequently have a difficult time relating to the pain and problems of their single brethren. We can assume, perhaps, that as the number of divorces in the church continues to increase, so will the number of divorced authorities; but if the sensitivity of our leaders is left to evolve through slow experience unaided by education, many good members will meanwhile be lost.

Guilt is further inculcated by priesthood lessons that define the husband/father as the steward responsible for the happiness and success of the family unit. These lessons facilely reassure the Mormon husband that as long as he is living the commandments and doing everything the Lord would have him do, his family will be blessed and problems alleviated. When divorce occurs, then, the implication is that it is primarily the husband's fault. The ensuing sense of guilt is often reinforced during interviews; not many men can look their bishop in the eye and say, "But, Bishop, I was living the gospel perfectly."

During a divorce the agency of all parties must be considered. One person cannot be held totally responsible for every idea and action of other family members. Traditional stories and generalized statistics aside, each divorce is a unique situation. Why should we not strive to salvage all the souls involved with the least amount of damage to self-esteem?

Frequently a man will seek a second marriage for all the wrong reasons: to repent, to grasp at a second chance, to avoid being alone, etc. Another divorce often follows, and his sense of guilt is multiplied; this second failure convinces him that he must be at fault. This guilt, if not relieved by wise counseling, can become so unbearable that the only solution he sees is to remove himself from the sources. So he separates himself from God, parents, family, and church—all the authority he respects but feels he has disappointed.

Even in the best of circumstances the obligations and commitments of marriage are difficult. But in a good marriage partners provide each other encouragement, support, security, and stability. For unmarried people the church itself is the partner from which we expect strength and support, even though it occasionally can unwittingly send negative messages to its single partners. I mentioned earlier that single women in the church are usually seen as victims of their situation and single men as perpetrators. We must recognize, though, that there are some women who, for whatever reason, do not intend to marry. Men are as threatened by fears of rejection as their female counterparts and can also be equally misled and treated poorly. Neither sex holds an exclusive claim to victimization or exploitation.

The message frequently received by single males is that they are second-class church members. The only single general authorities are widowers. Occasionally a single male is placed on a general board or in a bishopric, but certainly not to serve as a role model. Yet single women frequently serve on general boards and in Relief Society presidencies for that purpose. For years policy at Brigham Young University restricted the hiring of single males but not single females. I recognize the church's need to stress the ideal of the united family, but what about individual worth? Single males are not respected in the same way as married males.

It is not a surprise that the "marry at any cost" philosophy is so rampant in the church. People marry because their biological clocks, their worthiness clocks, and their guilt clocks are all sounding alarms. The attitude that life begins at temple marriage is constantly taught in fairy tale marriage stories related to young Latter-day Saints as they grow and develop into adults. Adult single members find themselves behind church-ordained fences. In an attempt to meet their "special" needs, they are shuttled into single ward ghettos or single ward activities that separate them from "regular" members. Friends try to introduce them to other singles rather than people with common interests, and more and more they find themselves pushed away from the mainstream membership of the church.

Even within the priesthood, where all men share the same calling, married men are insensitive to their single brethren. Priesthood holders are taught to revere women and motherhood, but little is done to create a bonded brotherhood or a support system.

Sex roles established by tradition reemphasize the marginalization of single males. Men are seen basically as bread-winning stewards, women as nurturers and comforters. If these traditions become locked into individual psyches, the believers become doomed to live even more incomplete lives. For females this can entail the lack and rewards of self-sufficiency and -assurance; for males the lack and rewards of sensitivity and compassion.

The single male must also face the constant specter of homophobia. Male friends from the age of twenty-five on view their unmarried associates with a jaundiced eye. Now that homosexuality is more open, church members are even more suspicious and judgmental. It is probably for this reason that single men in the church do not form support groups, do not show physical recognition or acceptance by hugging or placing an arm on the shoulder. They don't touch. This fragile public image affects fellowshipping and social activity. It also causes economic problems for the single heterosexual male because he is reticent about finding a roommate to share living costs.

There are additional problems specific to divorced males that put added stress on their church membership. In most divorce situations it is the husband who is cast out of the home, the family, the quorum, the ward, and the neighborhood. All immediate support systems are stripped away and new ones must be established at a time of great emotional upheaval. Moving to a new apartment and ward, adjusting to a new lifestyle, separation from loved ones, and building new relationships are difficult activities in the best of circumstances; added to the disruptions of divorce, the difficulty is multiplied a hundredfold. And on top of all this, the divorced father must now support two households. Sometimes he may find himself struggling to pay both tithing and child support. To renege on either, he forgoes a temple recommend, which curtails his activity and respectability in the church when he needs it the most.

Those who have divorced know there is no way of receiving absolute fairness under the law. Children cannot be equally shared, household goods and material property can never be divided to the complete satisfaction of both parties involved. Almost inevitably each divorced person sees his or her circumstances under divorce law as unfair. When the church stands behind the law, it is frequently seen as equally unfair. Of course the church upholds the law to maintain order in society; but it must carefully explain this position to divorced members, or it may be perceived as an adversary.

Another common problem among singles is health. Usually singles—especially men—have poorer health than their married counterparts because they don't have partners encouraging visits to doctors or good eating habits. They are often overtired and overworked. Busy married people sometimes joke that they wish they had the freedom and leisure of a single male, but generally the image of the free and easy lifestyle is a false one. Most singles have to do everything for and by themselves—work, care for children, shop, cook, clean, juggle church assignments, etc. There is no one with whom to share the work load. All these demands tax their stamina and their mental as well as physical health. Usually these people are too tired for dating and social engagements. The process of daily living becomes one of drudgery rather than one that is acceptable or even pleasurable as when shared with another adult partner. Further, to stay active in the church they also must suppress their natural sexuality. The resulting loss of self-esteem is often demonstrated by a lack of interest in personal appearance.

Church attendance is not easy for a divorced male. Every time he enters the ward he is reminded of everything he has been taught his whole life to strive for and doesn't have—the family unit, loving children, participation in scouting programs for his sons, daddy-daughter dates. If his former wife remarries or moves the family, the reminder of what he doesn't have becomes almost unbearable.

There is also a growing fear throughout society of child molesters, and singles are always more suspect than married men. Thus they are overlooked as potential scoutmasters or youth leaders, which further separates them from children. They themselves are sensitive to these images and often become afraid to even hold a friend's child.

Singles are also seen as threats to friends' marriages, which means that long-time friendships frequently are dissolved after a divorce. Many married couples become uncomfortable with single friends because the common ground has changed between them. To fill the gap they usually try to line the single up with another single acquaintance. They mean well, but this often places great pressures on a friendship just when friendship is needed most. Marrieds often do not recognize the single's fear of another failed marriage, nor do they understand that dating expectations are much different as people get older. Usually the single has learned from his experiences to see more clearly what characteristics he should look for in a mate. Not wanting to date just to date, he becomes much more selective. But he also recognizes he might get caught in the trap of defining an ideal that is impossible to find.

What then would I recommend to help alleviate the growing alienation and inactivity of the single male in the church? I would ask first that the church address the question: "Should all people be married?" What about those members who feel, for whatever reasons, that it would be unwise for them to marry? Some people do have personality abnormalities, low sex drives, are homosexual, or prefer a solitary life. Some simply suffer from an acute fear of marriage. Should these members be encouraged to marry and make two people unhappy? If they are wise enough to recognize characteristics that would be a problem in marriage, we should encourage them to seek help. But we should not encourage them to marry unless and until they are ready.

Church leaders at all levels should also be taught more sensitivity to singles issues and problems. Singles could be shown that they are loved equally in the eyes of God. Church-authorized support groups could be organized. There might be less judging by peers and more equal treatment in callings. Singles should not be segregated from other members, and most church activities should include both marrieds and singles. These things would best be accomplished if priesthood lessons were developed that made members aware of these issues.

To the single male in the church not anticipating marriage, I can only say, "Endure to the end." Make the commitment to take the difficult path of activity rather than the easy path of inactivity. You and your families and associates will all be better for such a decision. Pray for strength and the Holy Spirit to help you understand the insensitivity you meet and to get you through the difficult times. Remember that for all the difficulties you face as a single in this life, should you die in that state, all is forgiven. Your eulogies will undoubtedly mention your opportunities in the second life; and perhaps there we will have the wisdom of more perfected beings, and none of us will make the same mistakes we make here.

# 12.
# In Defense of a Mormon Erotica

*Levi S. Peterson*

DESPITE MY TITLE, I DO NOT INTEND TO DEFEND PORNOGRAPHY, Mormon or otherwise. I do intend to discuss Mormon attitudes toward erotica and suggest that a dearth of sexuality in Mormon literature may be a kind of obverse pornography—and also to suggest that expressions of sexuality and other human functions are not intrinsically offensive to God.

In defining pornography I would like to cite that apostle of the erotic, D. H. Lawrence, an English writer much respected for his realistic study of the Oedipus complex in one novel, *Sons and Lovers* (1913), and much deprecated for his graphic treatment of adultery in another, *Lady Chatterley's Lover* (1928). Although by today's standards it is not a sensational book, Lawrence was forced to publish *Lady Chatterley's Lover* privately in Florence, Italy. In 1932, two years after his death, his publisher put forth an expurgated version. As late as 1957, when Grove Press published the unexpurgated version in the United States, the U.S. Post Office banned the work from the mails. Following a successful suit by the publisher, the work was circulated without hindrance. Utterly sincere as a prophet of the liberated sexual instinct, Lawrence responded to critics who called *Lady Chatterley's Lover* pornographic by writing a pugnacious essay entitled "Pornography and Obscenity." I personally find his definition of pornography persuasive: "It isn't sex appeal or sex stimulus in art. It isn't even a deliberate intention on the part of the artist to arouse or excite sexual feelings. There's nothing wrong with sexual feelings in themselves, so long as they are straightforward and not sneaking or sly. . . . Pornography is the attempt to insult sex, to do dirt on it."[1]

I will apply Lawrence's definition to a hypothetical magazine which I will have to buy at a truck stop on the Interstate outside of Utah—say, in Idaho or Wyoming. The magazine has little text. It consists rather of numerous color photographs of human genitalia and of nude adults engaged in many sorts of benign sexual intercourse. Benign means that these participants appear to be mutually consenting—not necessarily in love with one another but at least not distressed by their activity. In my opinion, these photographs "do dirt" on sex, to repeat Lawrence's term. The unrelieved accumulation of genitalia, the incessant scenes of intercourse are distressing, inordinate, unseemly. But surely they constitute a mild rather than an egregious pornography. There is no reason to ban the magazine utterly from the universe. If travelers on the Interstate want to buy it, let them.

What is egregious pornography? I find, in another hypothetical magazine which I buy in an adult bookstore in Las Vegas, photographs of a terrified nude woman chained to a stake, of a man inflicting sodomy on an anguished girl, of a female torso with bloody, half-severed breasts. Sexual depictions associated with violence, brutality, and humiliation unquestionably do dirt on sex and worse. In fact, I consider the depiction of violence unrelated to sex far more pornographic than the nonviolent depiction of sexual parts and acts. Ironically, millions of readers and television watchers who pride themselves on their militancy against sexual display calmly ingest graphic shootings, stabbings, decapitations, and disembowelments. A movie replete with violence can easily be rated PG; a single scene of nudity makes it an R.

The Committee on Pornography established by the Attorney General of the United States issued in the mid-1980s a two-volume report showing a link between pornography and crimes of violence. I find myself strongly agreeing with a witness before the committee who testified, as reported in *Time* magazine, that the link is the violent content of pornography rather than the sexual: "If you take out the sex and leave the violence, you get the increased violent behavior. . . . If you take out the violence and leave the sex, nothing happens."[2]

I contemplate the morally self-satisfied ingesters of violence with alarm and irritation, finding their inconsistent behavior unworthy of the reasoning species to which they belong. I also respond irascibly to those fervent, punctilious Mormons who flee all mention of sex. Several years ago in my American novel class at Weber State University, I included John Updike's *Couples* among the assigned works. When it came time to read that novel, three Latter-day Saint students, a young man and two young women, demurred. Though I exhorted and cajoled, and though they were apologetic and distressed, they maintained their position: they preferred not to read a book about spouse swapping. I therefore negotiated a substitute novel for the three, and my class went forward in a dichotomous fashion. A year later, when I had replaced *Couples* with Erica Jong's *Fear of Flying*, four students demurred, all young Mormon women. Already defeated, I allowed them to make an exchange with scarcely a breath of expostulation.

I accepted their scruples, but I didn't admire them. I was ashamed of these young adults for their illiberal understanding of human nature and their cloistered virtue. In particular, I regretted their inability to test their character in the vicarious arena of literature. They will go on assuming that vice is unconquerable, that flight is the only weapon the righteous have against evil. Though they do not commit a sin of lust, they commit an obverse sin of prudery. Prudery forces the sexual impulse underground, banishes it to the territory of the abnormal and forbidden. Ironically, prudery reinforces pornography.

Perhaps I am attempting to corrupt model young Latter-day Saints. Perhaps I should admit that I am perverse, that I am one of those unvaliant spirits who does not fare well in the probation of mortality and is fated to spend eternity on the lower rungs of glory. I remember a winter night when, five or six years old, I knelt behind the glowing wood stove in obedience to my mother's orders to say my evening prayer. I was angry about something, perhaps simply about having to go to bed. Instead of whispering my usual prayer, I muttered a four-letter word over and over. Was that a sign of my innate depravity? Perhaps Joseph Smith should not have revised the venerable Puritan doctrine of infant damnation.

Truly, what might God think of my obscene prayer? Does he

despise me for defecating and urinating? Has he a lesser tolerance for these vital body functions than my gastroenterologist? Is he indignant over the angry, scornful four-letter words by which I sometimes name these functions and their products? I for one think obscenity is a human, not a divine, issue. I can't conceive of Almighty God, creator and sustainer of galaxies, occupying himself with my four-letter words. Obscenity is a matter of taste and discretion, not of morality and sin. Had she heard me, my mother would have thought the less of me for muttering obscenities instead of pieties behind the stove on that winter night, but I believe God only laughed. Surely he was not so petty as to be angry over my pettiness.

Although I am overawed in argument by those who have the Holy Ghost as their immediate second, I have some faith in my intuitions about God's attitude toward human sexuality. On the basis of those intuitions I accept that fidelity is better than infidelity, that committed sex is better than promiscuity, that marital sex is better than extramarital sex. I believe the church properly assumes the role of inculcating sexual mores and standards and of defining sexual sin. However, I believe that on the whole Mormons overreact to sexual sin, that they make far too much of it. I do not believe the church should excommunicate or even disfellowship for sexual sin. I believe it can achieve its purposes of teaching propriety and order without such punitive measures, which indeed seem startlingly contrary to the church's mission of saving rather than damning sinners.

I have difficulty believing that God has infused the human psyche with the powerful sexual impulse merely to sift the obedient from the disobedient, the self-controlled from the self-indulgent, the ascetic from the sensuous. I do not believe that God admires chastity for its own sake nor that he ordains celibacy and a denial of appetite. I do not believe that God frets over the lush practices and heights of passion between me and my wife, so long as they please both of us. Our manner of making love is our affair, not his. Nor will he be astonished if I sin. I do not blame God for my contrary personality, but neither do I believe that he blames me. It is our mutual problem. I will trust in his tolerance for my errant experimentations with life. He gave me a Savior because he knew I would need one.

I can hear the rustling of pages in the Bible and the Book of Mormon as knowing persons search for scriptural passages proving me wrong. Isn't it true that all the holy prophets have been sexually reticent and clean of speech and that they have declared God's pleasure with such qualities among his children? I remember that David and Solomon had concubines; that by God's command Hosea married a whore; that Joseph Smith and Brigham Young and my grandfather took plural wives; that even Jesus himself when he denounced the scribes and Pharisees with angry, insulting names, calling them hypocrites, fools, and vipers, came close to obscenity. I think it would not be at all impossible to develop a Mormon theology more tolerant of sexuality and bold speech. I hope some gifted scholar of the scriptures will step forward to do it.

If God's people are sexual creatures and if they are sometimes angry and scornful, and if their anger and scorn sometimes well up into obscenities, the literature which expresses God's people should reflect those facts. Literature should reflect life. Ultimately it should reflect all of life. Nothing that people feel, nothing that they do, should be denied a place in literature.

Then how shall I distinguish between an acceptable expression of sexuality and pornography? It is a matter of proportion. Proportion is fundamental in any theory of art. It suggests a variety of elements standing in harmonious relationship with one another, none without due representation, each fitted to each, each shaped by the shape of the whole.

Proportion applies to morality as well as to art. The Golden Mean, the point of balance between opposite excesses, is a matter of proportion. Body and spirit, obedience and initiative, action and contemplation, altruism and self-centeredness, appetite and conscience are to be reconciled and harmonized to be made proportionate to one another. If we respect proportion, we can dispense with foolish discussions in our Priesthood and Relief Society lessons about whether we would jump off a cliff if the prophet ordered us to. Obedience carried to excess is sin.

It is gross disproportion that creates pornography. Neither sexual images nor obscene words nor even depictions of violence in themselves make literature pornographic. If they are amassed, concentrated, enormously emphasized–if they become the single end and purpose of the writing–they are pornographic. But if they are intermittent in an action, if they mingle with other images and deeds, balancing proportionately, appearing as a part rather than the whole of life, then they are not pornographic.

Writers are not obliged to create sexual images or attribute obscenities to their characters if they have no instinct for that kind of writing. It is easy to name numerous great works of literature devoid of such qualities. Yet I for one find it sad and, yes, even eerie to contemplate the acres of shelf space occupied in local libraries by Mormon novels and to realize that there may not be a half dozen satisfying obscenities nor a single good orgasm among the lot. Writers who eschew entirely the sexual and the obscene fail to exploit an immense reservoir of energy, vigor, and sensory experience. It is as if they are piloting a twin-engined airplane but insist by reason of their scruples to operate only one engine. Timid authors fall into the error of incompleteness. Sexuality is a part of living. There is health in treating the broad range of experience in literature, in viewing clearly the full spectrum of human act and emotion, thereby helping to domesticate disorderly impulses and to disarm an unfounded fear of those that only seem disorderly.

I have said this in a different way in my short story, "Night Soil," about an aging man in a Utah village who yearns for redemption but compulsively resists righteousness. Named Pickett, he is, I suppose, a kind of grotesque. He has only one leg, the other having been amputated and, by his insistence, given a formal burial. As the story opens on a Sunday morning, he is lurching along with the assistance of an artificial leg to pay a visit to the grave of the amputated leg. Despite his vow to respect the Sabbath by staying out of the poolhall, he quickly finds himself there, where in the course of events he maligns the local bishop by telling his cronies the following tale:

> "I had me a dream about Delbert," Pickett said. "One night in vision I saw me and him in the Celestial Kingdom."
>
> "I imagine you did, all right," Jorley said.
>
> "No fooling. There I was in the Celestial Kingdom and it was time to go to the bathroom and all they had was an old-fashioned privy. I went in and peered down the hole and who did I see bogged down in that privy pit but Delbert himself? I backed out and looked up the Angel Moroni, and I says, Brother Moroni, I can't go to the bathroom in that privy because a feller I knew in mortality, Delbert Wheatley, is in there mired up to his neck; did you know that? Sure, I knew he was in there,

> Moroni says; now you just go ahead and relieve yourself according to custom. Oh, no, I couldn't do that, I says. You bet you could, Moroni says; all your life he done it on you and now it's your turn to give a little back."

It is an obscenity on Pickett's part to tell this story. But I testify that I came by the story, with different locale and characters and more forceful diction, directly from the mouth of a real Mormon villager. It would have been a crime of high order if, in the name of a timid morality, I had let this energetic tale, this Chaucerian fabliau from northern Arizona, sink into oblivion.

Pickett hobbles on toward the cemetery, carrying a burlap bag filled with bottles of beer he has won playing pool. He hopes to proceed safely past the house of a temptress named Pansy. Pansy, however, engages his sense of duty by telling him that her outdoor toilet has been demolished during a quarrel with her half-witted brother Wendell. After Pickett has helped reassemble the shattered privy, Pansy invites him into the house to eat a meal. Shortly she entices him to make love:

> "You haven't had a bath in a while," Pansy said, wrinkling her nose.
>
> "No'm, I haven't, that's true."
>
> She put a washpan of water on a burner. "Strip off and I'll wash you."
>
> She brought him a pillowcase to cradle his crotch like a diaper because he was too modest to have her see his privates. He dropped his coveralls, unstrapped his leg, and stood clutching the pillowcase with one hand and gripping a chairback with the other, his gullied face morose, his scarlet stump pulsing. She soaped his back and belly and armpits and wiped off the lather with a washcloth. "Time for your dainties," she said, laying the soap and cloth on the table within his reach. "My back is turned. I won't peek. I promise."
>
> When he was through she said, "Look at me, Pickett!" She had pudgy knees, dimpled thighs, billowing buttocks, narrow shoulders, bulbous breasts. "Am I pretty?"
>
> "Oh, lord, just like a sunrise," he said.
>
> Afterwards they lounged against the headboard of the bed, each with an arm around the other, drinking beer slowly, coughing and belching and gazing at the motes adrift in the afternoon sunlight. Pickett peered into his empty bottle. He saw foamy bubbles stretching like cobwebs between slick glass walls, he saw an amber glow like a moon

> about to rise over the horizon. "Don't begrudge the back side of things," he said.
>
> "Oh, I never do," she said hastily.
>
> "For example, take your privy pit which is foul with stink. I'm lying here thinking, Ain't Pansy and Wendell ate many a fine meal; ain't they been hungry to eat and they ate? You laughed many a time, had many a fine thing happen. And you left a bit of all that pleasure in that privy, didn't you? It ain't a pit full of mire and mess. It's a picture album, it's a museum, it's your grandmother's trunk full of wonderful old things out of the past."
>
> "Gosh, Pickett, are you crazy?"
>
> "No," he said, "don't begrudge poor things."[3]

That isn't the end of the story, for Pickett lurches on toward the cemetery; but he has expressed, perhaps with a clumsy directness, a minor theme. I tried to suggest that human taboos are not necessarily God's taboos, that the human repugnance for defecation and urination and scandalous words is not shared by God. Compared to God's perfection, perhaps every living ounce of the human body, the heart and brain as well as the emunctories, is no better than night soil. Yet in the light of his redemption, can any particle or shred of the human creature be less than eternal gold?

So I will close with a summary exhortation to Mormon writers—and to those Mormon readers who finally dictate the tone and tenor of what those authors write. Don't be paralyzed by prudery. Don't fall into the opposite excess of pornography. If you are bold enough to write and read about characters eating a meal, be bold enough to write and read about characters making love or going to the bathroom or uttering angry, scatological expressions. There is a vitality in sexual imagery and obscenities. Shaped proportionately, they do not corrupt and vitiate a work of literature. Like a tributary river, they add to the swelling current of ideas, images, and emotions that makes the reading of a good book a consummate experience.

*NOTES*

1. D. H. Lawrence, "Pornography and Obscenity," in *Selected Literary Criticism,* ed. Anthony Beal (New York: Viking Press, 1956), 37.

2. "SexBusters," *Time,* 1 July 1986, 15.

3. Levi S. Peterson, "Night Soil," in *Night Soil and Other Stories* (Salt Lake City: Signature Books, 1990), 182-83, 197-88.

# 13.
# The Demography of Utah Mormons

*Tim B. Heaton*

UTAH MAY BE THE MOST "CHURCHED" STATE IN THE NATION.[1] IN LARGE measure, the state's religious orientation can be attributed to the dominance of the Church of Jesus Christ of Latter-day Saints, or Mormon. In 1980 Mormons constituted 70 percent of Utah's population.[2] Although this represents a modest decline from the 73.4 percent of a decade earlier, it is still a substantial majority. In fact, the cultural traditions and organizational effectiveness of the Mormon church may yield an influence even greater than that suggested by population figures alone.

As a consequence, no other religious group has a sizable minority. Only Roman Catholics, with just over 4 percent, can claim more than 1 percent of the population. Clearly, one of the major religious distinctions in Utah is Mormon versus non-Mormon. The first question addressed in this essay concerns the similarity or dissimilarity between these two groups. The second derives from regional and national comparisons: Since Mormons dominate in the state, how do Utah Mormons compare demographically with Mormons who form a minority in other states?

Demographic information for Utah is taken from the U.S. census, which does not contain information on religious affiliation. Demographic data for the Mormon population has therefore been drawn from a survey sponsored by the Mormon church. Unfortunately, these data have the disadvantage of not being directly comparable to

TABLE 1. COMPARISON OF THE UTAH CENSUS WITH A UTAH MORMON SAMPLE–DEMOGRAPHIC CHARACTERISTICS (IN PERCENTAGES)

| | Utah Census | | Utah Mormon Sample | |
|---|---|---|---|---|
| **Characteristic** | **Males** | **Females** | **Males** | **Females** |
| *Age* | | | | |
| 16-19 | 11.7 | 11.1 | 8.1 | 6.9 |
| 20-24 | 15.8 | 16.1 | 15.6 | 17.8 |
| 25-29 | 14.7 | 13.6 | 16.1 | 13.5 |
| 30-34 | 11.6 | 10.7 | 12.9 | 11.4 |
| 35-44 | 14.7 | 14.2 | 15.0 | 14.0 |
| 45-54 | 11.6 | 11.4 | 11.0 | 11.8 |
| 55-64 | 10.3 | 10.1 | 10.2 | 10.5 |
| 65-74 | 6.4 | 7.7 | 7.3 | 8.1 |
| 75+ | 3.2 | 5.2 | 3.8 | 5.9 |
| Total | 100.0 | 100.0 | 100.0 | 100.0 |
| *Race* | | | | |
| White | 92.6 | 93.1 | 98.2 | 97.9 |
| Black | .9 | .5 | .1 | .0 |
| Hispanic | 3.9 | 3.6 | .5 | .6 |
| American Indian | 1.1 | 1.2 | .4 | .6 |
| Other | 1.6 | 1.6 | .8 | .8 |
| Total | 100.0 | 100.0 | 100.0 | 100.0 |
| *Marital Status* | | | | |
| Currently Married | 67.4 | 64.2 | 70.7 | 67.5 |
| Divorced/Separated | 5.6 | 8.1 | 3.1 | 6.2 |
| Widowed | 1.6 | 8.4 | 1.2 | 7.7 |
| Never Married | 25.4 | 19.3 | 25.0 | 18.7 |
| Total | 100.0 | 100.0 | 100.0 | 100.0 |
| *Ever Divorced (Ever Married Population)* | | | | |
| No | 78.9 | 78.0 | 86.0 | 83.8 |
| Yes | 21.1 | 22.0 | 14.0 | 16.2 |
| Total | 100.0 | 100.0 | 100.0 | 100.0 |

TABLE 1 (CONTINUED)

| Characteristic | Utah Census | | Utah Mormon Sample | |
|---|---|---|---|---|
| | Males | Females | Males | Females |
| *Age at First Marriage* | | | | |
| 14-17 | 3.9 | 16.2 | 11.3 | 11.0 |
| 18-19 | 14.9 | 29.8 | 11.1 | 25.7 |
| 20-21 | 22.8 | 24.9 | 20.4 | 27.6 |
| 22-24 | 32.5 | 17.3 | 38.9 | 21.9 |
| 25-29 | 18.7 | 8.0 | 10.4 | 8.4 |
| 30+ | 7.2 | 3.7 | 7.8 | 5.5 |
| Total | 100.0 | 100.0 | 100.0 | 100.0 |
| *Children Ever Born* | | | | |
| 0 | | 28.4 | | 16.9 |
| 1 | | 11.8 | | 11.7 |
| 2 | | 16.8 | | 17.8 |
| 3 | | 15.2 | | 17.6 |
| 4 | | 12.0 | | 13.6 |
| 5 | | 7.2 | | 11.0 |
| 6 | | 4.2 | | 5.1 |
| 7+ | | 4.5 | | 6.3 |
| Total | | 100.0 | | 100.0 |
| *Education* | | | | |
| 0-8 | 5.7 | 5.8 | 3.9 | 4.4 |
| 9-11 | 18.4 | 18.3 | 11.2 | 12.6 |
| 12 | 31.8 | 39.4 | 32.9 | 38.9 |
| 13-15 | 24.7 | 24.6 | 27.5 | 29.7 |
| 16 | 9.2 | 8.0 | 11.7 | 9.9 |
| 17+ | 10.2 | 3.9 | 12.8 | 4.4 |
| Total | 100.0 | 100.0 | 100.0 | 100.0 |
| *Employment Status* | | | | |
| Employed | 75.6 | 46.7 | 80.0 | 45.0 |
| Unemployed | 4.3 | 2.6 | 4.4 | 4.4 |
| Not in labor Force | 20.2 | 50.7 | 15.6 | 50.7 |
| Total | 100.0 | 100.0 | 100.0 | 100.0 |

TABLE 1 (CONTINUED)

| Characteristic | Utah Census Males | Utah Census Females | Utah Mormon Sample Males | Utah Mormon Sample Females |
|---|---|---|---|---|
| *Hours Worked* | | | | |
| 1-19 | 6.4 | 16.6 | 5.0 | 18.7 |
| 20-34 | 9.2 | 21.6 | 8.3 | 20.9 |
| 35-44 | 51.7 | 53.0 | 50.2 | 51.4 |
| 45+ | 32.7 | 8.7 | 36.5 | 9.0 |
| Total | 100.0 | 100.0 | 100.0 | 100.0 |
| *Occupation* | | | | |
| White Collar | 41.6 | 65.0 | 48.2 | 69.2 |
| Blue Collar | 54.4 | 34.0 | 50.8 | 30.5 |
| Farm | 3.9 | .9 | 1.0 | .3 |
| Total | 100.0 | 100.0 | 100.0 | 100.0 |
| *Income* | | | | |
| $ 0-1,999 | 7.5 | 24.6 | 5.7 | 20.9 |
| 2,000-4,999 | 12.5 | 28.9 | 9.1 | 26.9 |
| 5,000-9,999 | 18.3 | 27.0 | 14.4 | 26.5 |
| 10,000-14,999 | 17.4 | 12.6 | 16.1 | 14.9 |
| 15,000-19,999 | 16.8 | 4.4 | 16.0 | 6.6 |
| 20,000-29,999 | 18.8 | 1.8 | 23.9 | 3.1 |
| 30,000-49,999 | 6.8 | .5 | 11.7 | .3 |
| 50,000+ | 2.0 | .2 | 3.1 | .9 |
| Total | 100.0 | 100.0 | 100.0 | 100.0 |
| *Mobility (Residence Five Years Ago)* | | | | |
| Same House | 44.8 | 46.5 | 50.1 | 49.5 |
| Different House, same county | 27.9 | 27.3 | 22.6 | 25.6 |
| Differnet county, same state | 8.1 | 8.5 | 9.4 | 10.6 |
| Different State | 19.1 | 17.7 | 17.8 | 14.4 |
| Total | 100.0 | 100.0 | 100.0 | 100.0 |

Sample size may vary across variables because of missing values and differences in the relevant population base.

census data. Nonetheless, they are the best source of demographic information on Mormons available.

Data collection for the Mormon survey was initiated in spring 1981. In the first stage questionnaires were mailed to a random sample of 7,446 adults aged 19 and over from a computerized list of all Mormons in the United States and Canada. A reminder postcard was sent out two weeks later. These two mailings generated a response rate of 54 percent. Additional follow-up efforts, including telephone or personal interviews, yielded a total response rate of 81 percent. Only 4 percent of the original sample refused to respond. One percent had died or were no longer members of the church. The final 14 percent were unknown to local church leaders and unavailable to telephone or mailing approaches.

Each respondent was asked to fill out a questionnaire loosely resembling the 1980 U.S. census form in content. All responses were confidential. Information was gathered from all members of a respondent's household ages 16 and over. Weighting was used to correct sampling bias favoring households with more adults.

I suspect some bias in terms of religious participation of respondents since those who refused and those who were not located are probably less involved in the Mormon church. This makes it impossible to establish a one-to-one correspondence between survey results and characteristics of all Mormons. The variables analyzed, however, do not involve religious attitudes or opinions. Thus I believe that response bias due to the church's official sponsorship of the survey or to patterns of the religious involvement of the respondents is minimal.

Table 1 contains information on the Utah population from the U.S. census and the Church Membership Survey. With the exception of the 16-19 age group, both groups are similar with respect to age structure. Comparisons are made separately for males and females aged 16 and over. The computation of sex ratios at the end of the table indicates a predominance of females in both populations. There are 95 men for every 100 women in the state and 94 men for every 100 women in the Mormon population.

Utah is a racially homogeneous state with over 92 percent of the population identifying themselves as white non-Hispanic. The Mormon population is even more homogeneous with over 98 percent white non-Hispanic. Hispanics constitute nearly 4 percent of the population, while American Indians and others (mostly Asian) make up over 1 percent. No minority contains over 1 percent of the Mormon group. Blacks are a small minority in either case.

Mormons are more likely to be married than the state as a whole. For men, about 67 percent of Utahns compared to 71 percent of Mormons are currently married. For women the figures are 64 percent and 68 percent, respectively. Correspondingly, Mormons have smaller percentages in the divorced/separated, widowed, and never married categories. Differences in race are even more pronounced when one looks at the proportion of men and women who have ever been divorced.

Age and marriage distributions indicate that Mormons marry older than the population as a whole. Only 32.8 percent of Mormon men marry before age 22 compared to 41.6 percent of Utahns.

Mormons have higher fertility than the state as a whole. In part, this could be due to the higher percentage of Mormons who marry. Mormons are less likely to be childless and have noticeably higher percentages reporting 3-5 children, as well as a slightly lower percentage reporting families of seven or more children.[3]

Educational distributions suggest a slightly more educated Mormon population. For men, 52 percent report post-high school education compared to 44.1 percent for the state. For women the values are 43.2 percent compared to 36.5 percent.

Employment figures indicate that Mormon men are more likely to be employed compared to the Utah data. Mormon women are just as likely to be employed but more likely to be unemployed than is the case for Utahns generally. The distribution of hours worked indicates the amount of time devoted to the job for the employed population is approximately equal, except that Mormon men are more likely to work more than 45 hours per week.

In the Mormon sample, both men and women are more likely to be found in white collar occupations than is true in Utah census data. Most of the difference is made up in blue collar occupations since farming is rare as a principle occupation.

Consistent with occupational status and educational achievement, Mormon men also tend to do better financially. Nearly 40 percent of Mormon men report an income of over $20,000 per year compared to less than 30 percent of the Utah sample. For women the figures are much lower. Still, 25.8 percent of Mormon women compared to 19.5 percent of all Utah women make over $10,000.

Finally, we consider residential mobility. Utah Mormons are more likely to report living in the same residence as they did five years earlier by about 5 percentage points. They are more likely to have moved across county boundaries but less likely to have made local moves within county boundaries. Consistent with the state's declining percentage of Mormons, a larger percentage of Utahns reports living in a different state five years earlier than is true for Mormons.

In sum, these data suggest differences between Utah Mormons and the entire population of the state. These differences are consistent with the ideology of the Mormon church which stresses family and socio-economic achievement, as well as with the historical Mormon role in populating the state and establishing its economy. In comparison with state census data, Mormons are characterized by higher rates of marriage, lower divorce, larger families, and higher levels of educational, occupational, and financial success.

For comparative purposes, the U.S. sample of Mormons is divided into three groups. Utah, the core of Mormon culture, is the first. Characteristics for this group have already been reported but bear repeating for comparison. The second group includes Mormons in the western states where they constitute an important minority. Outside the West Mormons are a small minority, so all non-western states are included in the third category. Characteristics for these three groups are presented in Table 2.

The three groups are similar with respect to age structure, but regions outside Utah have a lower sex ratio. There are 89 males per 100 females in the West and 85 elsewhere.

Mormons outside Utah are less likely to be white non-Hispanic. Still, whites constitute over 90 percent of the Mormon population in each region.

In terms of marital status, the main difference is that Utah Mormons are less likely to be currently divorced or separated. The differences are even greater when one looks at the percentage of men and women who have ever divorced. For men, the values are 14.0 for Utah, 19.3 for the West, and 18.4 elsewhere. For women, they are 16.2, 22.5, and 24.2, respectively.

TABLE 2. COMPARISONS OF UTAH MORMONS WITH MORMONS IN THE WESTERN AND OTHER U.S.–DEMOGRAPHIC CHARACTERISTICS (IN PERCENTAGES)

| | Region | | | | | |
|---|---|---|---|---|---|---|
| | Utah | | West | | Other | |
| Characteristic | Male | Female | Male | Female | Male | Female |
| *Age* | | | | | | |
| 16-19 | 8.1 | 6.9 | 7.0 | 7.1 | 7.76 | 5.5 |
| 20-24 | 15.6 | 17.8 | 14.0 | 15.1 | 14.4 | 14.5 |
| 25-29 | 16.1 | 13.5 | 15.1 | 13.9 | 19.0 | 17.1 |
| 30-34 | 12.9 | 11.4 | 13.5 | 12.8 | 14.5 | 14.7 |
| 35-44 | 15.0 | 14.0 | 18.0 | 15.8 | 19.7 | 18.9 |
| 45-54 | 11.0 | 11.8 | 12.1 | 13.4 | 10.7 | 12.5 |
| 55-64 | 10.2 | 10.5 | 10.2 | 9.9 | 8.2 | 9.2 |
| 75+ | 3.8 | 5.9 | 4.1 | 4.7 | 1.7 | 3.1 |
| Total | 100.0 | 100.0 | 100.0 | 100.0 | 100.0 | 100.0 |
| *Race* | | | | | | |
| White | 98.2 | 97.9 | 96.4 | 94.3 | 93.4 | 92.4 |
| Black | .1 | .0 | .1 | .1 | .5 | .3 |
| Hispanic | .5 | .6 | 1.4 | 3.0 | 2.0 | 2.6 |
| American Indian | .4 | .5 | 1.2 | 1.2 | .7 | 1.2 |
| Other | .8 | .8 | 1.0 | 1.4 | 3.4 | 3.4 |
| Total | 100.0 | 100.0 | 100.0 | 100.0 | 100.0 | 100.0 |

TABLE 2. (CONTINUED)

| Characteristic | Region | | | | | |
|---|---|---|---|---|---|---|
| | Utah | | West | | Other | |
| | Male | Female | Male | Female | Male | Female |
| *Marital Status* | | | | | | |
| Currently Married | 70.7 | 67.5 | 66.8 | 66.8 | 64.5 | 64.9 |
| Divorced/Separated | 3.1 | 6.2 | 5.3 | 8.2 | 5.4 | 10.8 |
| Widowed | 1.2 | 7.7 | 1.4 | 6.5 | .2 | 4.8 |
| Never Married | 25.0 | 18.7 | 26.5 | 18.6 | 30.0 | 19.6 |
| Total | 100.0 | 100.0 | 100.0 | 100.0 | 100.0 | 100.0 |
| *Ever Divorce (Ever Married Population)* | | | | | | |
| No | 86.0 | 83.8 | 80.7 | 77.5 | 81.6 | 75.8 |
| Yes | 14.0 | 16.2 | 19.3 | 22.5 | 18.4 | 24.2 |
| Total | 100.0 | 100.0 | 100.0 | 100.0 | 100.0 | 100.0 |
| *Age at First Marriage* | | | | | | |
| 14-17 | 1.3 | 11.0 | 1.3 | 12.6 | 2.0 | 15.4 |
| 15-19 | 11.1 | 25.7 | 11.6 | 28.6 | 11.9 | 30.6 |
| 20-21 | 20.4 | 27.6 | 21.9 | 25.3 | 22.3 | 24.0 |
| 22-24 | 38.9 | 21.9 | 35.0 | 18.2 | 34.3 | 15.4 |
| 25-29 | 20.4 | 8.4 | 20.3 | 9.0 | 19.4 | 9.6 |
| 30+ | 7.8 | 5.5 | 10.0 | 6.2 | 10.3 | 5.1 |
| Total | 100.0 | 100.0 | 100.0 | 100.0 | 100.0 | 100.0 |

TABLE 2. (CONTINUED)

| | Region | | | | | |
|---|---|---|---|---|---|---|
| | Utah | | West | | Other | |
| **Characteristic** | **Male** | **Female** | **Male** | **Female** | **Male** | **Female** |
| *Children Ever Born* | | | | | | |
| 0 | | 16.9 | | 24.4 | | 23.6 |
| 1 | | 11.7 | | 12.1 | | 13.5 |
| 2 | | 17.8 | | 18.5 | | 18.5 |
| 3 | | 17.6 | | 16.7 | | 18.5 |
| 4 | | 13/6 | | 12.0 | | 11.6 |
| 5 | | 11.0 | | 7.2 | | 7.0 |
| 6 | | 5.1 | | 4.7 | | 3.6 |
| 7+ | | 6.3 | | 4.4 | | 3.7 |
| Total | | 100.0 | | 100.0 | | 100.0 |
| *Education* | | | | | | |
| 0-8 | 3.9 | 4.4 | 5.7 | 4.4 | 5.9 | 6.4 |
| 9-11 | 11.2 | 12.6 | 11.2 | 13.4 | 13.3 | 14.1 |
| 12 | 32.9 | 38.9 | 32.8 | 38.3 | 34.5 | 37.2 |
| 13-15 | 27.5 | 29.7 | 27.5 | 32.5 | 19.0 | 28.6 |
| 16 | 11.7 | 9.9 | 9.6 | 6.8 | 11.0 | 8.0 |
| 17+ | 100.0 | 100.0 | 100.0 | 100.0 | 100.0 | 100.0 |

TABLE 2. (CONTINUED)

| | Region | | | | | |
|---|---|---|---|---|---|---|
| | Utah | | West | | Other | |
| Characteristic | Male | Female | Male | Female | Male | Female |
| *Employment Status* | | | | | | |
| Employed | 80.0 | 45.0 | 79.8 | 45.0 | 79.8 | 45.6 |
| Unemployed | 4.4 | 4.4 | 4.7 | 6.3 | 6.2 | 6.4 |
| Not in Labor Force | 15.6 | 50.7 | 15.6 | 48.7 | 13.9 | 47.9 |
| Total | 100.0 | 100.0 | 100.0 | 100.0 | 100.0 | 100.0 |
| *Hours Worked* | | | | | | |
| 1-19 | 5.0 | 18.7 | 4.6 | 16.1 | 3.5 | 13.8 |
| 20-34 | 8.3 | 20.9 | 5.9 | 20.2 | 4.9 | 19.0 |
| 35-44 | 50.2 | 51.4 | 49.2 | 52.0 | 48.9 | 54.8 |
| 45+ | 36.5 | 9.0 | 40.4 | 11.8 | 42.7 | 12.3 |
| Total | 100.0 | 100.0 | 100.0 | 100.0 | 100.0 | 100.0 |
| *Occupation* | | | | | | |
| White Collar | 48.2 | 69.2 | 47.6 | 66.5 | 48.4 | 62.3 |
| Blue Collar | 50.8 | 30.5 | 51.1 | 33.0 | 50.9 | 37.3 |
| Farm | 1.0 | .3 | 1.3 | .5 | .7 | .4 |
| Total | 100.0 | 100.0 | 100.0 | 100.0 | 100.0 | 100.0 |

TABLE 2. (CONTINUED)

| | Region | | | | | |
|---|---|---|---|---|---|---|
| | Utah | | West | | Other | |
| **Characteristic** | **Male** | **Female** | **Male** | **Female** | **Male** | **Female** |
| *Income* | | | | | | |
| $ 0-1,999 | 5.7 | 20.9 | 5.5 | 21.1 | 3.7 | 17.7 |
| 2,000-4,999 | 9.1 | 26.9 | 8.0 | 26.5 | 6.3 | 20.8 |
| 5,000-9,999 | 14.4 | 26.5 | 13.3 | 23.8 | 13.1 | 31.6 |
| 10,000-14,999 | 16.1 | 14.9 | 14.6 | 15.5 | 16.5 | 16.2 |
| 15,000-19,999 | 16.0 | 6.6 | 15.7 | 7.6 | 14.3 | 8.8 |
| 20,000-29,999 | 23.9 | 3.1 | 25.5 | 4.5 | 24.9 | 3.8 |
| 30,000-49,999 | 11.7 | .3 | 13.6 | .5 | 15.2 | .9 |
| 50,000+ | 3.1 | .9 | 3.8 | .4 | 6.1 | .2 |
| Total | 100.0 | 100.0 | 100.0 | 100.0 | 100.0 | 100.0 |
| *Mobility (Residence Five Years Ago)* | | | | | | |
| Same House | 50.1 | 49.5 | 44.1 | 44.8 | 40.2 | 42.3 |
| Different House, same county | 22.6 | 25.6 | 25.4 | 25.2 | 18.7 | 21.4 |
| Different County, same state | 9.4 | 10.6 | 10.7 | 11.7 | 9.6 | 9.9 |
| Different State | 17.8 | 14.4 | 19.7 | 18.3 | 31.5 | 26.4 |
| Total | 100.0 | 100.0 | 100.0 | 100.0 | 100.0 | 100.0 |
| Na | 2091 | 2229 | 2554 | 2867 | 1182 | 1392 |

Sample size may vary across variables because of missing values and differences in the relevant population base.

Early marriage does not appear to be any more common among Utahns than among other Mormons. In comparison with other regions, fewer Utah men marry after age 30, but marriage before age 20 is most common among Mormon women who live outside the West—46 percent compared to 36.7 percent in Utah and 31.2 in the West. Utah Mormons also have larger families than other Mormons. They are less likely to be childless and more likely to have four or more children.

In terms of education, Utah and the West are roughly equal; about the same percentages report some college experience. Mormons outside the West are less likely to enter college, but the percentage with post-graduate education is just as high or higher than in Utah or the West.

Employment status is comparable in the three regions, but part-time employment may be more common in Utah. Also, there is a slight tendency for more white collar work among women in Utah compared to the other regions.

Income appears to be slightly lower in Utah. Of men in the Utah group, 36.7 percent report incomes greater than $20,000 compared to 42.9 in the West and elsewhere. Likewise, 25.8 percent of Utah women report incomes above $10,000 compared to 28.5 in the West and 29.9 elsewhere.

Finally, Utah Mormons are less mobile than other Mormons. A higher percentage report having lived in the same house for at least five years and are less likely to have moved across state lines.

Most of the differences we find between Utah Mormons and Mormons elsewhere in the U.S. are probably not significant. There does appear to be more of an emphasis on traditional family values in Utah with less divorce and larger families. Since Utah is at the core of Mormon culture these results are not surprising. In terms of socio-economic achievement, Utah Mormons do better in schooling and occupation but not when it comes to actual income. Simply put, Utah Mormons are not distinctive compared to Mormons elsewhere.

*NOTES*

1. See *The 1983 Church Almanac* (Salt Lake City: Deseret News Press, 1982).

2. See Wayne L. Wahlquist, ed., *Atlas of Utah* (Provo, UT: Brigham Young University Press, 1981).

3. It bears repeating that differences in the two data sets belie strict comparisons between the two groups. For example, a childless rate of 16.9 percent for Mormons and 28.4 percent for Utahns generally would require a rate of 55 percent for non-Mormons (assuming that the state is 70 percent LDS). The magnitude of this figure indicates that comparisons between rates can only suggest possible differences, not indicate the magnitude of those differences.

# Epilogue: Mormon Ideas of Home

## *Stephen L Richards*

MY FRIENDS, I PROPOSE FOR DISCUSSION THIS MORNING A VERY HUMBLE theme—one that is commonplace but I hope not cheap or unimportant. I speak of the home. What is the evolution of this noteworthy institution?

It would not be possible to trace even the outline of its history in the time allotted. May I, however, merely call attention to a few well recognized and outstanding facts concerning it. The government initiated in and growing out of the home was the first known form of human government. The head of the family came to be the chieftain of the tribe or clan. The patriarchs were not only prophets they were law-givers.

Then too throughout the history of civilization, blood ties and race have been the strongest cohesive factors in the grouping of society. Many of the greatest nations have been but enlarged families with blood strains of remarkable purity. I do not mention this in argument against a rather pronounced tendency in modern times for cosmopolitan composition of our social and governmental groups, but merely to indicate the large part which the institution of home has played in sociology.

The home has ever been the center of economic interest. It has undoubtedly produced a greater part of the wealth of the world and it has also spent it.

It is the primary educational institution. Important as schools have been they have never occupied a position more than complementary to the home which is the nursery not only of all human beings but of all virtue.

Governments which have attained high places in the world's history and affairs have, I think without exception, been those which have given due recognition to the home as a fundamental institution of society. They have enacted laws for its protection and advancement, and crimes against the home and its sanctity have been regarded as among the most heinous offenses.

In this connection I recall the statement of an eminent man who at one time, speaking in the British House of Parliament against the imposition of a tax on the homes of the poor, said, in substance, "My home may be a poor and rude one; the roof may leak; the wind may enter; the rain may enter, but the King of England with all his army cannot enter. My home is my castle, sacred and inviolate to me and my family." Such a conception of home has lain at the very foundation of English and American law and government and that conception is in no small way responsible for the rights and liberties which we now enjoy.

What is its prospect in this dramatic evolution of persons, things and institutions which is now in process? I would not venture a sure prediction but I do agree with Dr. Henry Van Dyke who said that "If old-fashioned American family life vanishes nothing can take its place."

What was an old-fashioned American home, or rather I should say, what is it, because I am thankful to note that there are still some such homes left in the land. You know what it is. You know that it is not just a house, however grand and imposing the house may be and however embellished it may be with costly furniture, rich hangings and floor coverings woven of the toil of far-off Persia. You know that it is not a mansion wherein reside a man and a woman, fretting under the bonds of a marriage contract, a poodle dog and a retinue of servants whose chief function it is to see that the three chief occupants of the house, the man, the wife, and the dog, enjoy equality of right and privilege. And you know that such an old-fashioned home is not ordinarily located among the costly residences of the rich. You know that it is usually to be found among the modest and humble, but not among the poor of the land for they are not truly poor who maintain a real home. You know that in an old-fashioned American home you will find a large family of happy boys and girls, for whom father and mother willingly, patiently and lovingly devote lives of toil and service; not for ostentation and pride and the gratification of selfish desires but to fulfill high conceptions of duty and the laws of God. Are such homes happy?

I used to live in the heart of a city. My nearest neighbor lived in a real home. He had a yard in which his children might play. They had flowers and gardens, trees and welcome shade from the summer sun. His girls, educated, cultured, and refined, helped their mother with house work. His boys assisted in keeping up the place outside. They loved their home. It belonged to them all. The feeling of ownership and proprietorship was with them. It begat thrift, economy and industry. Their common interest stimulated mutual confidence and affection that cement and enrich the natural ties of family. They were happy and content and they were splendid citizens.

Most of the other people who resided in my neighborhood lived in large apartment houses, not in homes. Some few had children. These boys and girls had no yards, no gardens, no flowers, no places to play, no property to care for, and no responsibility. They came to my lot and my neighbor's. I did not blame them. They had no place to go. They injured and destroyed the shrubs and lawns and other property. I forgave them. They had had nothing of their own of similar kind consequently they had never learned how to care for property.

The girls that lived in these apartments did not do house work. There was not much to be done and besides they had not time for it because it takes all the time of these girls to take care of themselves. It is a big job. Their first task of the day is to prepare themselves for public presentation. I have not time to describe the perplexities of that operation. Suffice it to say that it requires a very great deal of labor and material to produce the finished product. There are the daily movies, the teas, the auto rides, the dances and the cabarets all requiring constant re-arrangement of toilet and appearance and involving an immense expenditure of energy. These girls of the apartments are really hard-working girls. They have my sympathy but like the boys they do not have good homes and I fear they are not learning to be real women.

Yet this life of the apartment is the new home life; perhaps here depicted in the extreme. Its advocates say that it is more desirable than the old home life; that it has more conveniences, ease and luxury and less of work and responsibility. They clinch the argument by declaring that it costs less. It does and it is worth less. The old-fashioned American family life costs more but it is worth more. It costs more in work, self-sacrifice, patience, sleepless nights, heart-aches, and loving service, but the smile of a babe, the kiss of a beautiful daughter, and the handclasp of a manly boy are worth more than all the cost.

The cry of the world is for men and women. I know of no place where they can be found except in the homes of the people. The homes which produce real men and women must be presided over and maintained by men of strength and courage, of virtue and of vision. and by women of tenderness, unselfishness and infinite patience and love endowments of God for the motherhood of the race. Good living is the first requirement of every parent. God pity the unfortunate parent who comes to the realization, as some day all must surely do, that the sins of the child are chiefly attributable to his or her own bad example or neglect.

Criminologists tell us that most of our delinquencies originate in bad or neglected homes. Economists say that the training of the home is largely responsible for the thrift, industry, and prosperity of the nation. Doctors advise us that the health of the people depends on its care and teachings, and the eugenist assures us that the whole trend of human happiness, intelligence, goodness, and endurance depends on it.

Do you know that statisticians have scientifically calculated that the United States will support a population of not to exceed two hundred million people, and that we are very rapidly approaching "this point of saturation"? The character of the nation and its destiny depend almost entirely on the families who shall make up the two hundred million. Will they be families descended from the old stocks of America who set up her great institutions and who have fought for and fostered her liberty, her equity and her justice, or will they be families in the stream of whose blood does not course the great impulse, the indomitable will, and idealism which have been and are the genius of our Democracy? Such questions must give pause and concern to every lover of America.

To the members of our church the home has an enlarged significance that is subordinate to nothing else in life, for it constitutes not only the source of our greatest happiness here in this life, but also the foundation of our exaltation and glory in the life to come. After all, it is essentially a religious institution. It has its origin in religious ceremony. It is the fulfillment of divine command. Its government is of a religious nature, and the finest of its products are spiritual.

So it is here in the humble and yet exalted institution of the home that I find the greatest opportunity and mission for men and women. I am sorry to say, however, that the record does not in all cases disclose a very creditable response to this big opportunity and obligation. Modern education has not always produced good home-makers. Recently published data informs us that the average number of children in the families of the bootblacks of America is slightly over four, while the average number of children in the families of school teachers is slightly under two. Now it may be that two school teachers exercise more and better influence than four bootblacks, but how long will it take on the present respective rates of increase for the bootblacks to crowd out the school teachers? I present this illustration from a popular scientist, not in derogation of people who follow humble vocations, but to emphasize the fact that the world supply of intelligence, goodness, and beauty is largely a matter of propagation.

There is in this respect a traditional and rather well advertised distinction which our people enjoy. They have been noted for their large families and had they been better understood they would be famous for their good families. Children have been our best crop and in the good old homes there has been an abundance of them. Eight, ten, and a dozen in a family were common numbers.

What families they have been! In days of privation and striving how they have stood together! The sacrifices which they have made, one for another; the love, the service, and nobility which have come from these great homes will probably never be known to many, but those who know of it and speak of the accomplishments of our church in the first century of its existence mention first the noble fathers and mothers who in log cabins of the frontier or mansions of luxury have served faithfully as priests and priestesses in the temple of the home.

Our church calls to its members and to all people to maintain the integrity, the purity, and the high purposes of this sacred institution. I trust that no one will ever so yield to the insidious appeals of selfishness, vanity, and the world, as to be swerved from so doing.

To warn of a great danger I must speak of it more specifically. I do so most reverently. If it shall please the Lord to send to your home a goodly number of children, I hope, I pray, you will not deny them entrance. If you should, it would cause you infinite sorrow and remorse. One has said that he could wish his worst enemy no more hell than this, that in the life to come someone might approach him and say, "I might have come down into the land of America and done good beyond computation, but if I came at all I had to come through your home and you were not man enough or woman enough to receive me. You broke down the frail footway on which I must cross and then you thought you had done a clever thing."

I said that for the Church of Jesus Christ of Latter-day Saints the home had a great religious significance. We believe that the marriage compact is not for life only or until death doth part, but for all eternity; that when the covenant is entered into in the proper manner and place and sealed by the power of the Holy Priesthood, which is the delegated authority of God to man, it becomes an everlasting union, an eternal institution into which there shall enter all children born in such wedlock, and that the ties of kinship so created are eternal ties recognized in heaven as on earth. Our heaven is little more than a projection of the sacred institutions of our homes into eternity. The spirits of men, which are the literal children of the Father, are by him permitted to take on mortality through a home, it being the chief purpose of the administrators of the home to guide the spirits so entrusted to their keeping back to the eternal presence whence they came. So it is that we strive so diligently to maintain our children in the bond of this eternal covenant and union. We do not fear death because death does not break this bond. We must all go by way of it to find place in the eternal family circle. But we do fear sin that may deprive us of the presence of a loved one when we meet in our future homes.

We deplore divorce. It strikes at the very foundation of the home. The number of divorces among our people is very low.

Perhaps this mere glimpse into our philosophy of life and heaven and exaltation will serve to justify our undying interest in the homes of the people. We rely on these institutions to produce the manhood and the womanhood for the church and the nation. Respect for law, order and established institutions must come from good family life if it comes at all. Boys and girls who grow up to call father "the old man" and mother "the old woman" are not likely to be easily amenable to the necessary restrictions which society imposes. If they cannot respect and love home and parents, their affection and regard for any worthy cause and institution are doubtful.

# CONTRIBUTORS

LESTER E. BUSH, M.D., is author of *Health and Medicine among the Latter-day Saints: Science, Sense, and Scripture,* part of a multi-volume series on "Health/Medicine and the Faith Traditions," sponsored by the Park Ridge Center, Chicago, Illinois. "Ethical Issues in Reproductive Medicine: A Mormon Perspective" first appeared in *Dialogue: A Journal of Mormon Thought* 18 (Summer 1985): 42-66.

HAROLD T. CHRISTENSEN is professor emeritus of sociology at Purdue University. "The Persistence of Chastity: Built-in Resistance in Mormon Culture to Secular Trends" was first published in *Sunstone* 7 (Mar.-Apr.): 7-14.

EUGENE ENGLAND is a professor of English at Brigham Young University, Provo, Utah, author of *The Quality of Mercy: Personal Essays on Mormon Experience*, and co-editor of *An Open World: Essays on Leslie Norris*. "Fidelity, Polygamy, and Celestial Marriage" first appeared in *Dialogue: A Journal of Mormon Thought* 20 (Winter 1987): 138-54.

LAWRENCE FOSTER is a professor of history at the Georgia Institute of Technology, Altanta, and author of *Women, Family, and Utopia: Communal Experiments of the Shakers, the Oneida Community, and the Mormons*. "Between Heaven and Earth: Mormon Theology of the Family in Comparative Perspective" was first published in *Sunstone* 7 (July-Aug. 1982): 6-13.

KLAUS J. HANSEN is a professor of history at Queen's University,

Kingston, Ontario, Canada, and author of *Quest for Empire: The Political Kingdom of God and the Council of Fifty in Mormon History* and *Mormonism and the American Experience*, as well as numerous articles on Mormonism and American social and cultural history. "Changing Perspectives on Sexuality and Marriage" first appeared as chapter five in Hansen's *Mormonism and the American Experience* (Chicago: University of Chicago Press, 1981), 147-78.

TIM B. HEATON is a professor of sociology at Brigham Young University, Provo, Utah, and co-editor of *Utah in Demographic Perspective*. "The Demography of Utah Mormons" was first published as chapter thirteen of *Utah in Demographic Perspective* (Salt Lake City: Signature Books, 1986), 181-93.

JEFFREY E. KELLER, M.D., is an emergency physician in Idaho Falls, Idaho. "Gender and Spirit" first appeared as "Question: Is Sexual Gender Eternal?" and "When Does the Spirit Enter the Body?" in *Sunstone* 10 (Nov. 1985) 38-39, and 10 (Mar. 1985): 42-44.

ROMEL W. MACKELPRANG, D.S.W., is an associate professor of social work, Eastern Washington University, and editor of *Sexuality and Disabilities: A Guide for Human Service Professionsals*. "'They Shall Be One Flesh': Sexuality and Contemporary Mormonism" was first published in *Dialogue: A Journal of Mormon Thought* 25 (Spring 1992): 49-67.

ROCKY O'DONOVAN, founding director of the Lesbian and Gay Historical Society of Utah, is a writer living in southern Utah. "'The Abominable and Detestable Crime Against Nature': A Brief History of Homosexuality and Mormonism, 1840-1980," is published here for the first time.

DELMONT R. OSWALD is executive director of the Utah Humanities Council and past president of the Utah Academy of Sciences, Arts, and Letters. "A Lone Man in the Garden" first appeared in *Dialogue: A Journal of Mormon Thought* 23 (Spring 1990): 139-46.

ERIN PARSONS is news director for WMXN radio station in Norfolk,

Virginia. "Single Cursedness: An Overview of LDS Authorities' Statements about Unmarried People" was first published in *Dialogue: A Journal of Mormon Thought* 16 (Fall 1983): 35-45.

LEVI S. PETERSON is a professor of English at Weber State University, Ogden, Utah, and author of *The Canyons of Grace, Night Soil, The Backslider,* and *Juanita Brooks: Mormon Woman Historian.* "In Defense of a Mormon Erotica" first appeared in *Dialogue: A Journal of Mormon Thought* 20 (Winter 1987): 122-27.

MARYBETH RAYNES is a clinical social worker and marriage and family therapist in private practice in Salt Lake City, Utah, and co-editor of *Peculiar People: Mormons and Same-Sex Orientation.* "Single Cursedness: An Overview of LDS Authorities' Statements about Unmarried People" was first published in *Dialogue: A Journal of Mormon Thought* 16 (Fall 1983): 35-45.

STEPHEN L RICHARDS (1879-1959) was a member of Qurorum of Twelve Apostle of the Church of Jesus Christ of Latter-day Saints and head of the its missionary program. "Mormon Ideas of Home" was first delivered as a CBS radio address on 16 June 1935 and was later published in pamphlet form.

MARVIN RYTTING is a social psychologist with a keen interest in intimacy, sexuality, and family issues. He is currently publishing *Market Psychology* while on leave from his professiorial duties. "Exhortations for Chastity: A Content Analysis of Church Literature" was first published in *Sunstone* 7 (Mar.-Apr.): 15-21.